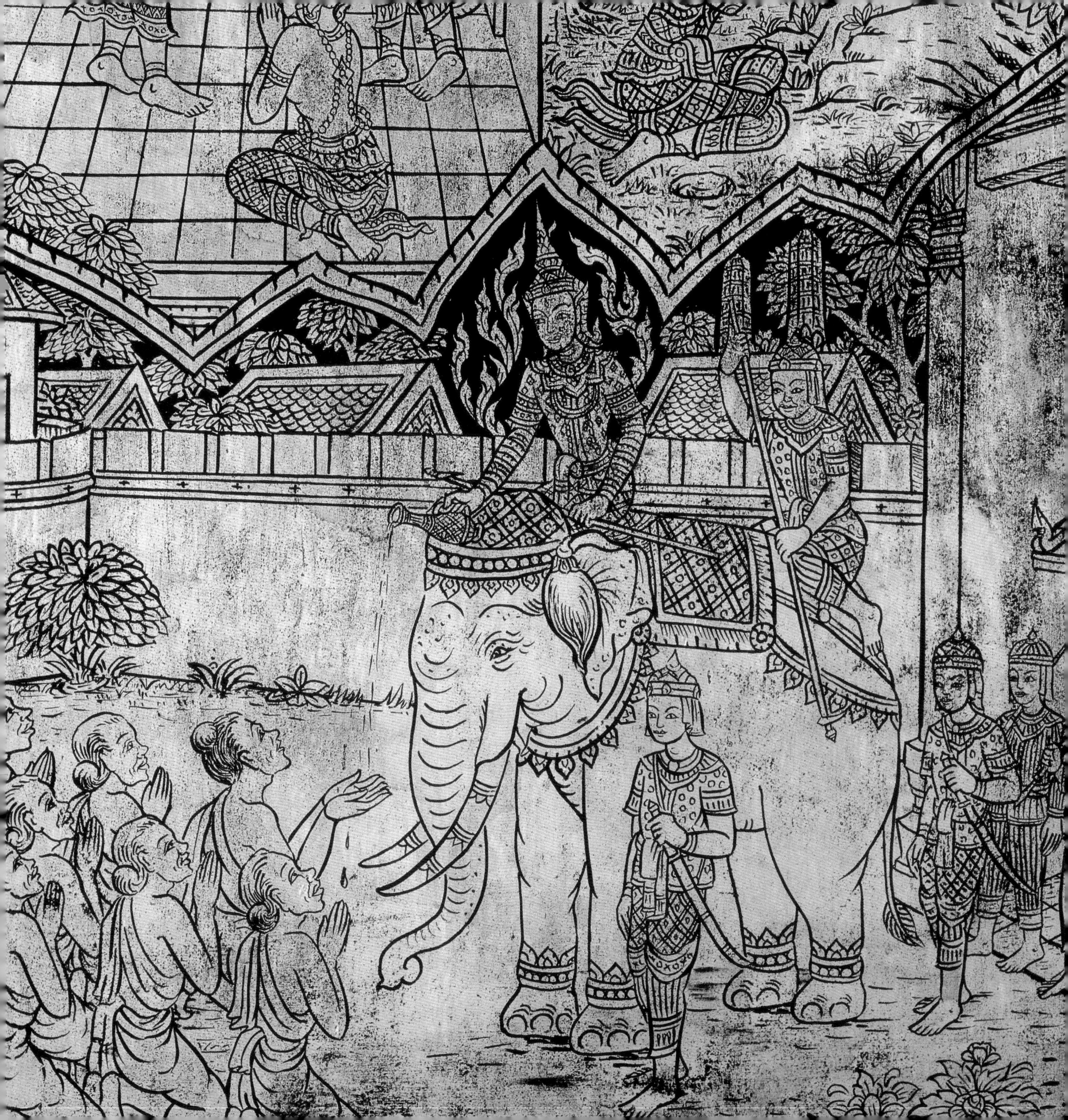

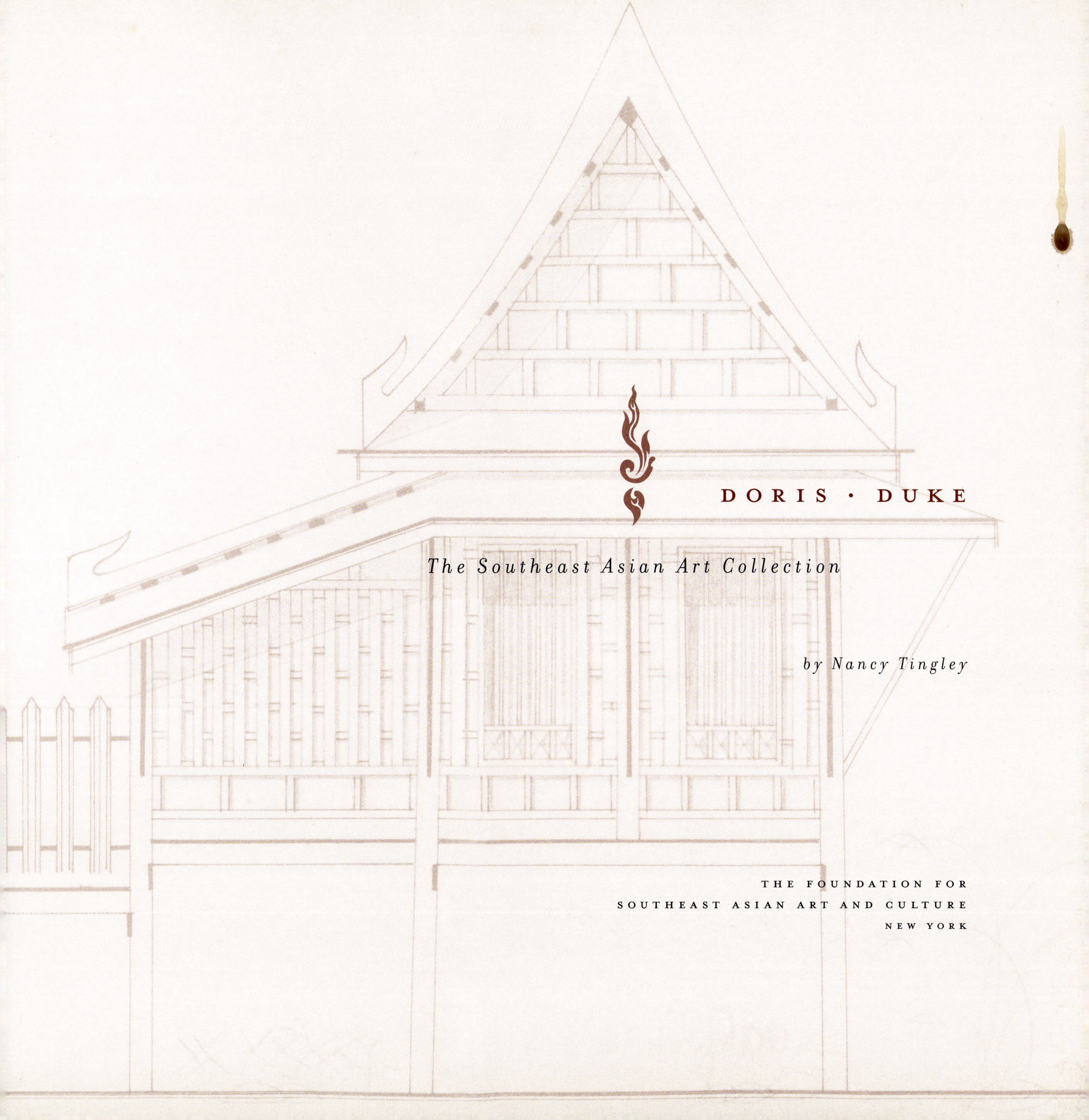

DORIS · DUKE

The Southeast Asian Art Collection

by Nancy Tingley

THE FOUNDATION FOR
SOUTHEAST ASIAN ART AND CULTURE
NEW YORK

Library of Congress Cataloging-in-Publication Data
Tingley, Nancy
Doris Duke : the Southeast Asian art collection / by Nancy Tingley.
p. cm.
Includes bibliographical references and index.
ISBN 0-8248-2773-2 (hardcover : alk. paper)
1. Art, Southeast Asian. 2. Duke, Doris, 1912—Art collections. 3. Art—Private collections—United States. I. Foundation for Southeast Asian Art and Culture. II. Title.
N7311.T55 2003
709'.59'074—dc21

∞ The paper used in this publication meets the minimum requirements of the American National Standard for Information Sciences—Permanence of Paper for Printed Library Materials, ANSI Z39.48-1984.

DISTRIBUTED BY:
University of Hawai'i Press
2840 Kolowalu Street
Honolulu, Hawai'i 96822
www.uhpress.hawaii.edu

Jacket: Devotee from a Burmese altar (see Plate 28, p. 50) WAM; background: Aphonphimok Pavilion at the Royal Palace, Bangkok (see Figure 7, p. 17)

Frontispiece: Vessantara giving away the white elephant (detail of Plate 49, p. 72) WAM

Pages 4–5: Dragon-shaped *pattala*, tuned percussion instrument from Burma (see Plate 76, p. 94)

Photography by Richard Walker, except DDCF Photo Archive, Figures 1, 3–7, 10, 16, Plate 3; Camera Associates Inc., NYC: Figures 2, 17; Leedom Lefferts, Figures 18–19; Forrest McGill, Figure 8; Nancy Tingley, Figure 11, detail of Plate 36, Plate 45; Kaz Tsuruta, Asian Art Museum of San Francisco, Plates 9, 17, 43, 51; Walters Art Museum: Figure 14.

Edited by Lorna Price
Proofread by Laura Iwasaki
Designed by Susan E. Kelly
Typeset by Marie Weiler
Color separations by iocolor, Seattle
Produced by Marquand Books, Inc., Seattle
www.marquand.com
Printed and bound by CS Graphics Pte., Ltd., Singapore

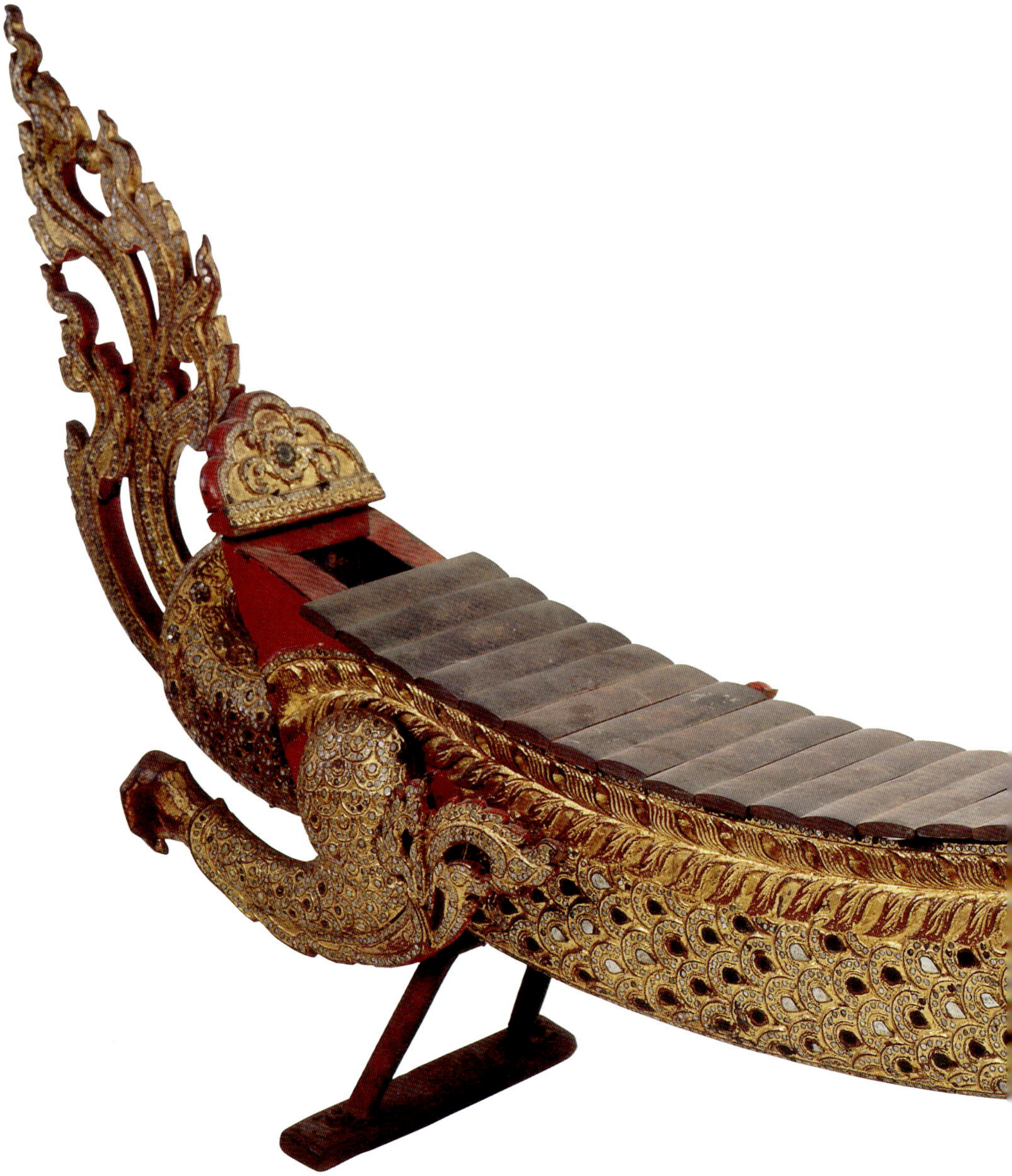

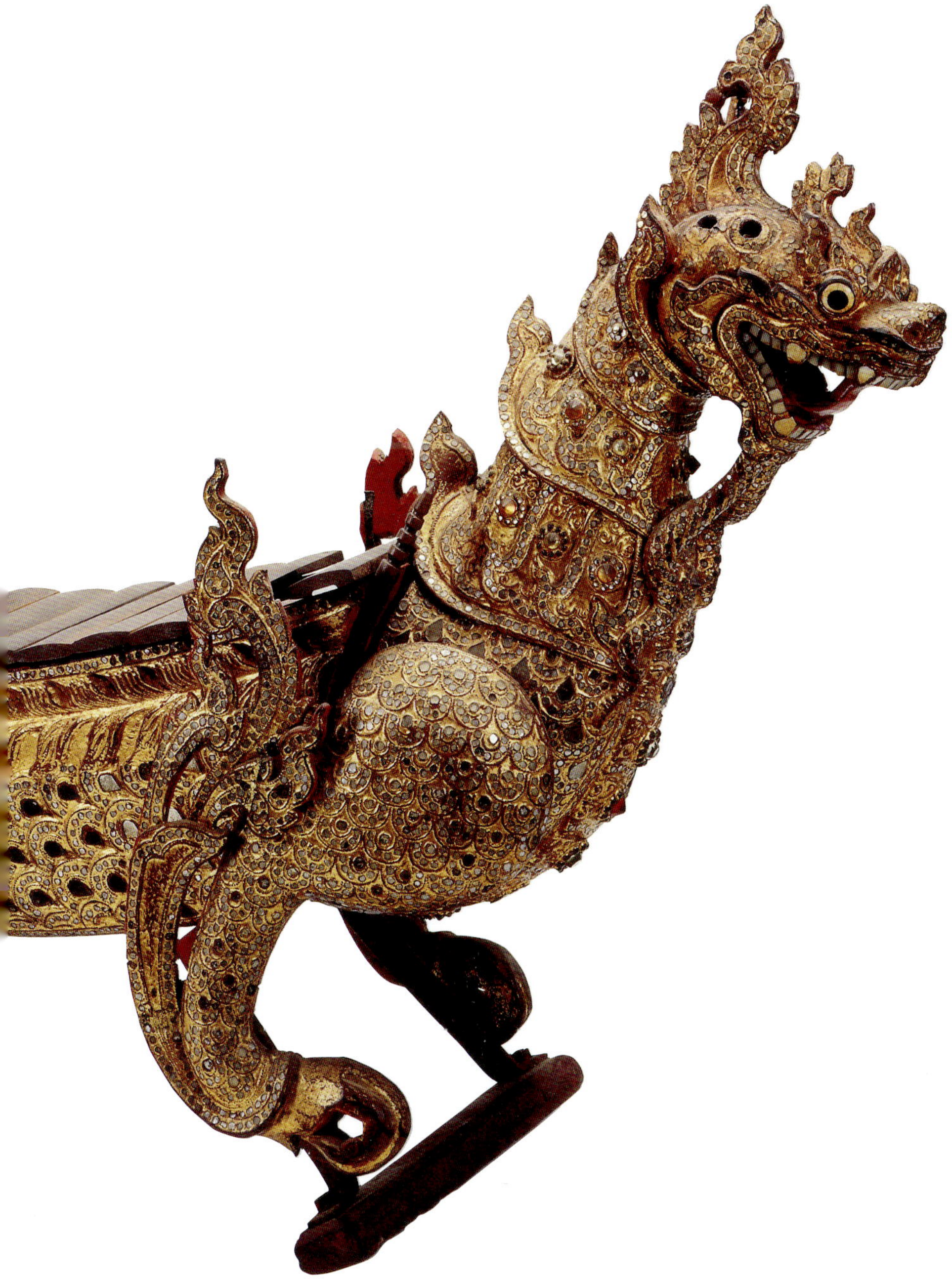

Contents

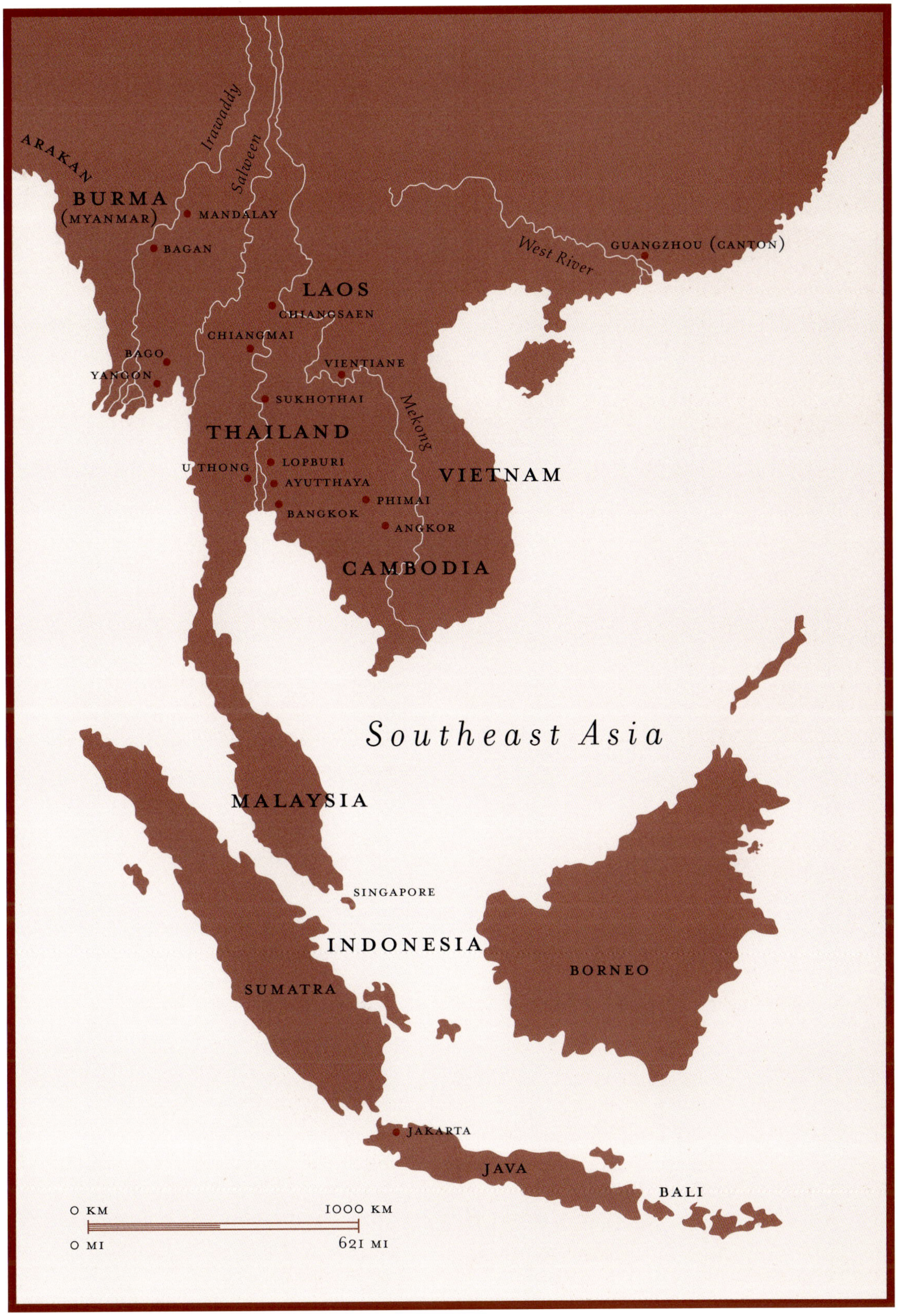
ARAKAN
BURMA
(MYANMAR)
Irawaddy
Salween
MANDALAY
BAGAN
LAOS
CHIANGSAEN
CHIANGMAI
BAGO
YANGON
VIENTIANE
SUKHOTHAI
Mekong
THAILAND
U THONG
LOPBURI
AYUTTHAYA
BANGKOK
PHIMAI
ANGKOR
VIETNAM
CAMBODIA
West River
GUANGZHOU (CANTON)
Southeast Asia
MALAYSIA
SINGAPORE
INDONESIA
SUMATRA
BORNEO
JAKARTA
JAVA
BALI
0 KM
1000 KM
0 MI
621 MI

Preface

ALTHOUGH DORIS DUKE WAS WIDELY KNOWN AS A WEALTHY heiress, we at the Doris Duke Charitable Foundation have come to understand that she was an imaginative, independent, and disciplined woman with an adventurous spirit and a lifelong fascination with other cultures. A devoted and innovative collector of Islamic and Southeast Asian art, she had a passion for both fine and vernacular objects. One accomplishment of Miss Duke's avid collecting and distinctive aesthetic is Shangri La, her home in Honolulu, which houses a vast and unique collection of Islamic art and architecture. Another is her collection of Southeast Asian art, the subject of this book, which comprises the vibrant decorative arts of Thailand, Burma, Cambodia, and Laos.

When Doris Duke died in 1993 at the age of eighty, she left the major portion of her estate to the Doris Duke Charitable Foundation. She had expressed her desire that the public should be able to visit her various estates and collections and learn from them something of the lives and cultures of those who created the artifacts. Since the inception of the Foundation, we have been working to create the opportunities that she envisioned. After commissioning a scholarly appraisal of the Southeast Asian art collection, we learned of its artistic and historical value and decided that it should be shared with the broader public. To that end, we have donated a significant portion of the collection to two museums distinguished for their collections of Southeast Asian art: the Asian Art Museum of San Francisco, and the Walters Art Museum, in Baltimore (respectively, AAM and WAM, as noted in the illustration captions).

This study by Dr. Nancy Tingley documents Doris Duke's Southeast Asian art collection as a whole; we hope it will make an important contribution to the scholarly literature on Southeast Asian art and culture and to a better understanding of Doris Duke herself. We are pleased and honored to be able to offer this publication to the public and the scholarly community.

James F. Gill, Chairman, and the Trustees of the Doris Duke Charitable Foundation (DDCF) and the Foundation for Southeast Asian Art and Culture (SEAAC) provided encouragement and guidance as we explored, documented, and donated the SEAAC collection. Our discovery of the historical and artistic value of the collection would not have been possible without the help of many individuals, including board and staff members of the Asian Art Museum of San Francisco, among whom are Johnson S. Bogart, Dr. Emily Sano, Dr. Forrest McGill, Dr. Pat Chirapravati, and Donna Strahan. We also acknowledge the help of Dr. Gary Vikan, Director of the Walters Art Museum, and his team, consisting of Dr. Hiram W. Woodward, Jr., Meg Craft, and Eric Gordon. Others who lent their advice include Dr. Henry Ginsburg and Dr. Susan Conway. Dr. Vishakha Desai, Senior Vice President of The Asia Society, was very helpful throughout the process.

Dr. Nancy Tingley, the author of this book, was indispensable: she researched and documented the collection in all its varied facets; determined the objects of "museum quality"; and helped identify the institutions that received the objects. Nancy carefully pieced together the history of Doris Duke's SEAAC collection and helped us to better understand the life of this public yet very private person. To this end, she received support from François Duhau de Bérenx and from several current and former Foundation staff members including Olga Garay and Patrick Lerch, who led the effort, Cupie Singh, Digi Singh, Violet Mimaki, Marianne Bowles, Elizabeth Steinberg, Antonio Canseco, Dr. Sharon Littlefield, Deborah Pope, Chris Carden, and the entire Duke Farms staff. Finally, we would like to thank our photographers, Richard and Zibby Walker, as well as editor Lorna Price, book designer Susan Kelly, and the firm of Marquand Books, Inc., of Seattle, Washington. We hope all readers will enjoy learning about this collection and the lovely work produced by Southeast Asian artists as much as we have.

Joan E. Spero
President, Doris Duke Charitable Foundation

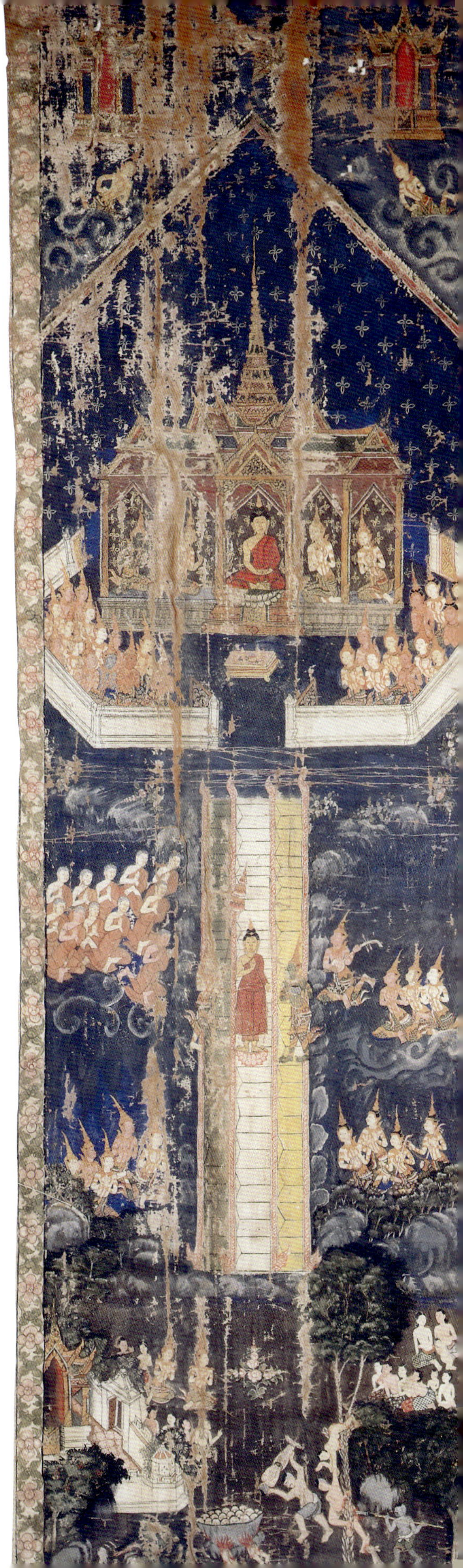

Cloth banner paintings *(phra bot)* up to 4 meters long hung from the ceiling around the main image of the Buddha in a Thai temple (h. 302 cm). See discussion, pp. 54–55. WAM

Introduction

UPON THE DEATH OF HER FATHER, JAMES BUCHANAN DUKE, Doris Duke inherited a fortune built on the Duke Power Company and the American Tobacco Company. The press styled her "the richest girl in the world," but shy and intensely private, she never embraced the role of celebrity. In 1935, at age twenty-two, she embarked on a round-the-world honeymoon with her husband, James Cromwell. On that journey, they visited Egypt, the Near East, India, Singapore, Bangkok, Indonesia, the Philippines, Hong Kong, China, and Japan (Figure 1). Thus began her lifelong love affair with the Orient.

This journey influenced and also set the stage for Doris Duke's life. Travel seemed to suit her nature, and from that trip until her death, she traveled extensively. Always fully engaged, she sought to understand the cultures and customs of the places she visited. In all her endeavors, she was a thorough student, researching and seeking information and counsel from knowledgeable people while resolutely pursuing her many projects. That first trip in 1935 also included Gibraltar, Cannes, Monte Carlo, Genoa, and Naples; she returned many times to Europe, living in both Paris and Italy for long periods of time.[1]

But it was in Asia that Miss Duke found inspiration for many of the projects she subsequently undertook, including her collections of Asian art, her Islamic-inspired home in Hawai'i, and the gardens at her home in New Jersey. The most immediate evidence of her infatuation lies in her residence, Shangri La, built in Honolulu, Hawai'i, during 1937 and 1938 and elaborated and refined throughout her life. The architect Marion Sims Wyeth, working closely with Miss Duke, incorporated Islamic architectural elements and art into her fantasy of Shangri La as an Oriental abode.[2] Initially she had considered including Asian art and furnishings from different countries and in varying styles (Figure 3) but finally settled on an Islamic theme. She had loved the Taj Mahal but had no interest in slavishly copying that or any other building she had seen, and in Shangri La, she incorporated sections of buildings in whatever manner served her aesthetic sense. The building defies simple categorization, as the architecture represents no single region. Over her lifetime, she also amassed an extensive collection of Islamic art from countries throughout the Islamic world.[3]

Except for the war years of 1942–1945, Miss Duke returned yearly to spend part of the winter at Shangri La, where she said she felt most comfortable. It wasn't until the late 1950s that she embarked on more frequent trips to South and Southeast Asia and the Middle East. In March 1957, on a trip to India and China, Doris Duke and her friends Joe Castro and the Iranian poet Parviz stopped in Thailand. During their exploration of Bangkok, they met François Duhau

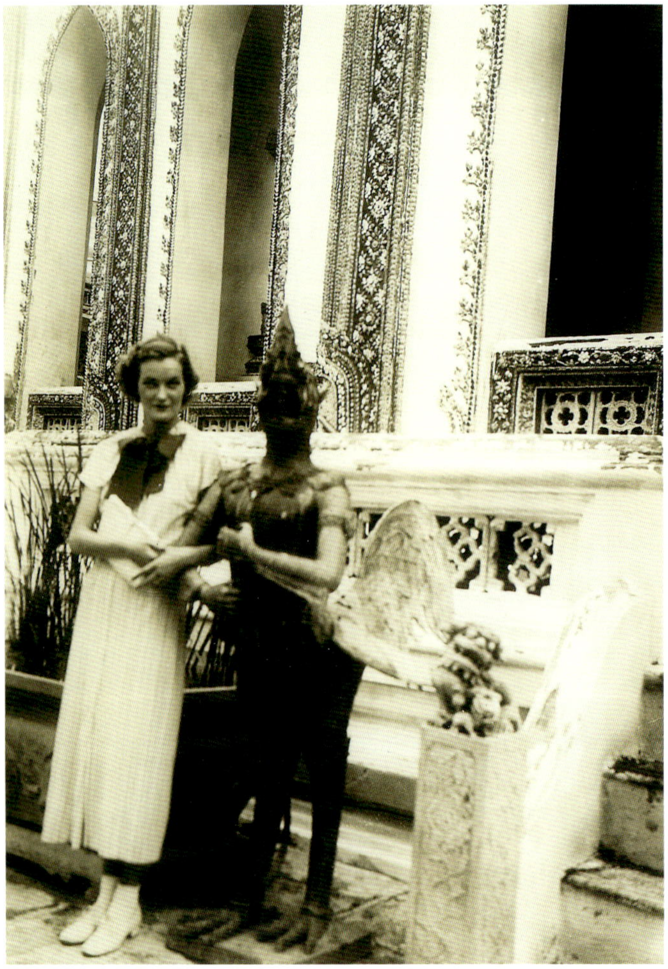

above **Figure 1** Doris Duke in Bangkok on her honeymoon, 1935.

opposite **Figure 2** A 1972 photograph of the interior of the larger of two rooms in the Coach Barn, Duke Farms, Hillsborough, New Jersey.

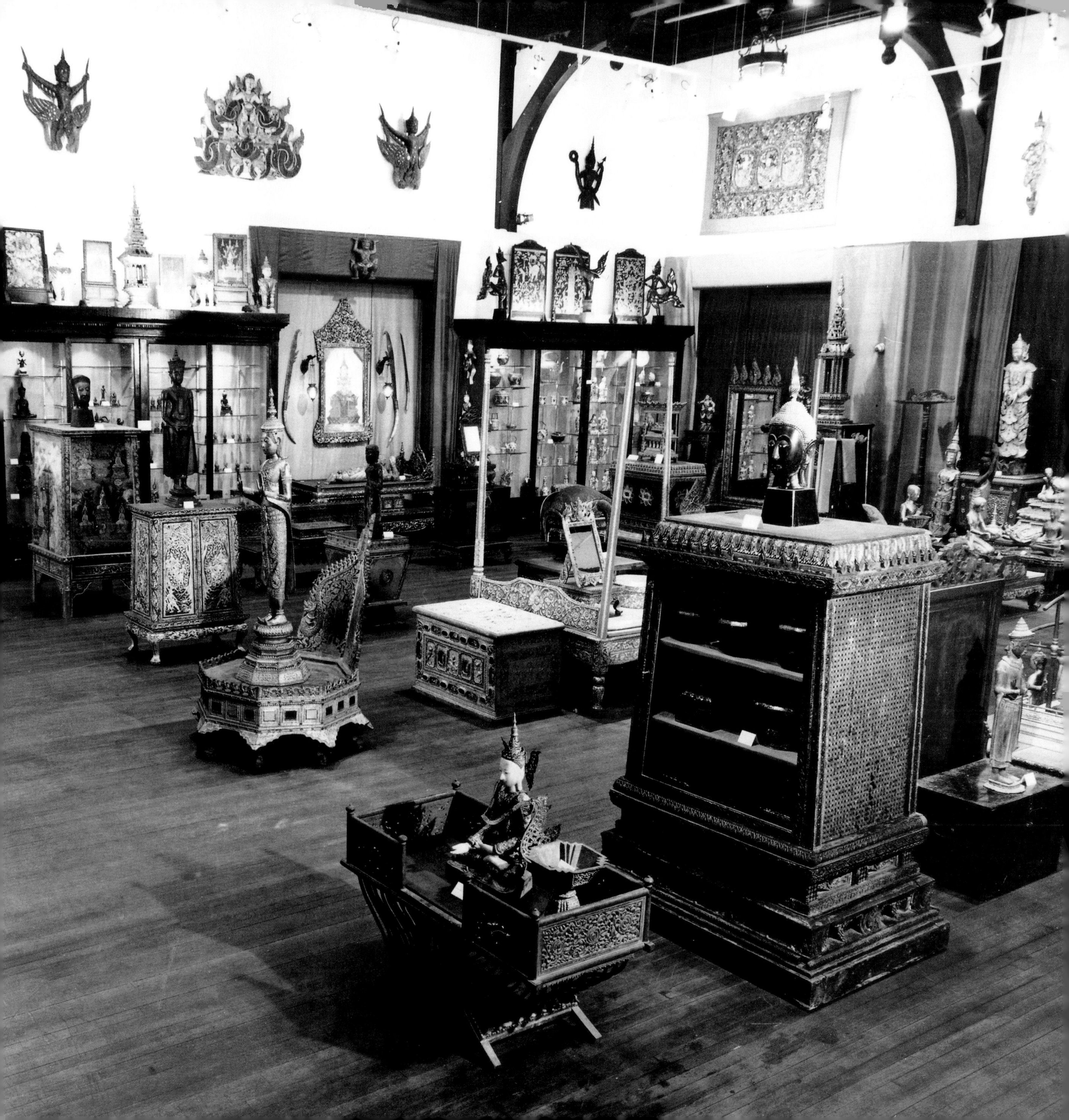

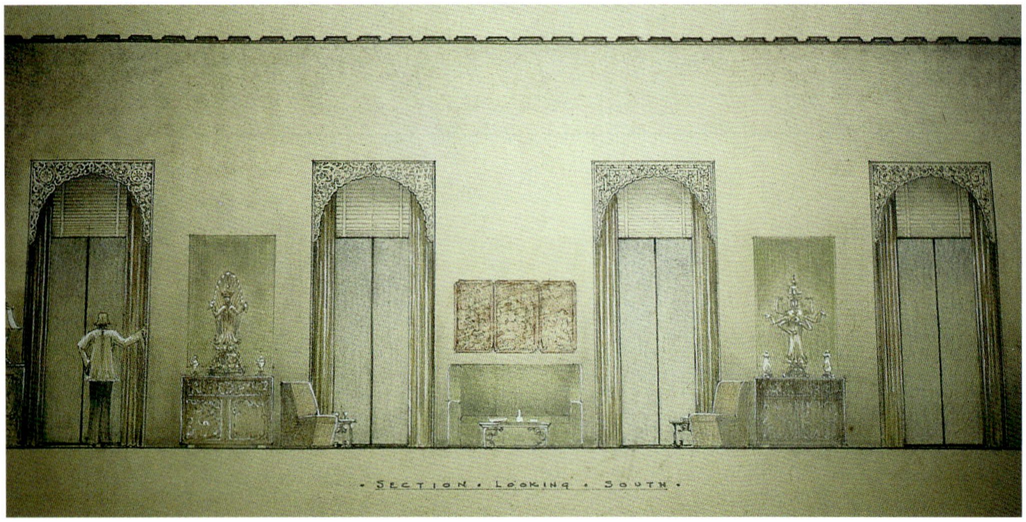

Figure 3 A 1937 watercolor proposal for the living room at Shangri La (drawn by Drew Baker) depicting Oriental art of various styles, which suggests that following her honeymoon, Doris Duke's interests were not confined to Islamic material.

de Bérenx, a young decorator and art dealer, who was working at the Star of Siam,[4] a silk shop, and who accompanied them around town. They went by boat through the *khlong* (canals) and admired the houses on stilts that crowded the banks. At that time, Bangkok retained much of its traditional charm; the *khlong*, many of which today have been filled and converted to roads, still connected many parts of the city, allowing leisurely travel by boat.

They met and dined with Prince and Princess Chumbhot, whose home (Suan Pakkad Palace) consisted of a group of five small, old Thai houses that had been brought from the countryside and reconstructed in the city.[5] Their fine collection of Thai and Cambodian art, arrayed alongside European furnishings, charmed Miss Duke. She had a good eye, and her subsequent embrace of Thai art suggests that the art and architecture she saw on that visit must have enchanted her, as had Islamic art twenty years earlier. During the visit, she established a congenial relationship with Bérenx, which continued when, in February 1959, Miss Duke brought him to Hawai'i for a visit. It was during his stay that she discussed her dream of creating a Thai village with houses similar to those she had seen when she dined with Prince and Princess Chumbhot. She had loved Thailand's *khlong* and houses on stilts and thought it would be possible to create the same serene ambience in Hawai'i. She wandered the island with Bérenx, casually pointing out possible sites, but when he left, he dismissed their fantasies as merely talk. Still, she had told him to keep an eye out for decorative art of high quality, and according to Bérenx, she opened an account in Bangkok in order to expedite purchases.[6]

More than a year passed before Doris Duke's idea of constructing the village was formalized, and in December of 1960, Bérenx was formally hired to help bring it to pass.[7] The Thai House Foundation was established on January 30, 1961; the name was changed to the Foundation for Southeast Asian Art and Culture (SEAAC) in June of that year. The Foundation's mission was to "advance and display Siamese art, both ancient and modern, and the art of Indo-China and other Far Eastern countries, with particular reference to painting, architecture, interior decoration and allied subjects, for the purpose of public inspection, instruction, education, and enjoyment."[8] The establishment of the Foundation resulted in a project that Miss Duke saw as a gift to Hawai'i, and one that occupied her for many years to come. Although our knowledge of Doris Duke's desires and dreams regarding the Thai Village Project is sparse, we do know that her stated intention was to acquire a collection of decorative arts.[9] The very idea of furnishing a village dictated that she collect certain types of objects, religious for the replicas of the Emerald Buddha temple *(ubosot)* and the Royal Pantheon of Wat Phra Kaeo, and the *sala* (a large, open-air meeting hall) and secular for the houses.

Southeast Asia is renowned for the variety and quality of its artistic productions, including wood carving, bronze casting, painting, mother-of-pearl inlay, textiles, ivory carving, ceramics, and metalwork. When visiting private homes in Thailand, Miss Duke would have seen objects similar to those she ultimately purchased—inlaid boxes and trays, carved ivory implements, weapons, *bencharong* ceramics (enameled porcelains and stoneware made in China specifically for the Thai market)—an eclectic selection, to say the least. One is struck by a similar diversity in the Islamic collection at Shangri La, where myriad objects of varying importance are displayed on the basis of their visual appearance rather than being organized in a chronological or regional presentation, and without regard to limitations of their significance or meaning. At Shangri La, she created a "unified whole,"[10] not unlike what one might imagine for the Thai Village Project, where simple teak buildings would hold lush interiors, and where the verdant landscape would create an environment that recalled Thailand. It is a great loss that she was never able to purchase a property appropriate to complete the project.

The creation of the Foundation for Southeast Asian Art and Culture in early 1961 and the visionary plan of constructing a Thai village fell in line with a series of projects, both public and private, that Miss Duke undertook in the course of her life.[11] The Shangri La project (1937–1938) had been the first, and it was followed by the design of Duke Gardens (est. 1958) at the Duke Farms in Hillsborough, New Jersey. Situated inside a grand greenhouse, the eleven gardens, the design of which Miss Duke oversaw, represent diverse cultures and regions of the world; they have been open to the public since 1964. The Thai Village Project was to be next; the establishment of the Newport Restoration Foundation in 1968 was the last.[12] One of her major contributions to the Newport Restoration Foundation involved the Samuel Whitehorne house, a Federal-style abode built in 1811. She oversaw its renovation, then furnished it with the finest representative examples of Newport furniture that she could collect; the house is now a public museum. Miss Duke was intensely involved in all of her projects. It is noteworthy that the intent of each was the creation or preservation of something of beauty and tranquility.

The stated mission of the Foundation for Southeast Asian Art and Culture (hereafter, the Foundation) could only be realized by first purchasing the houses and furnishings and then locating a property in Hawai'i where the Thai Village could be constructed. Extant records reveal a frenzied few years of acquisition. Bérenx sought works of all types—manuscript cabinets and manuscripts; temple banner paintings, modern paintings, and series of paintings hung in temples during the recitation of the Vessantara *jataka;* Thai ceramics, Chinese porcelains, and *bencharong;* wood, stone, bronze, and ivory sculpture; decorative arts of all media; weapons; textiles; jewelry; complete Thai houses; and musical instruments. The Foundation's records read like an inventory of later Thai and Burmese art, for the objects purchased were not only of Thai origin; a large number of them were Burmese, with a smaller selection of Cambodian, Laotian, and Chinese.

Most pieces came from dealers in Bangkok, though Bérenx and his assistant, Somchai Roumsamuk, traveled to Ayutthaya and its surroundings in search of manuscript cabinets and Thai houses. Somchai both translated and helped to negotiate purchases.[13] Bérenx wrote Miss Duke weekly to tell her of purchases and to seek her advice; unfortunately it does not appear those letters were preserved.

Miss Duke, accompanied by her dear friend Hannah Veary,[14] returned to Bangkok in 1961, 1964, and 1965.[15] One person she visited while in Bangkok was Jim Thompson, whom she had met in New York in the 1930s.[16] He had recently completed construction of a residence compound in Bangkok that consisted of six original Thai houses, which he had filled with Thai and Cambodian art. Thompson's home, created along the lines of the Thai Village Project she envisioned—simple houses sheltering a fine collection—must have further inspired her. Jim Thompson's passion for Thailand and his entrepreneurial spirit led to the revival of the Thai silk industry and, in 1958 and 1959, the construction of his residence. William Warren, a writer living in Bangkok who knew Thompson well, and who has written books about his home and his life, feels certain that Miss Duke's interest in creating a Thai village was influenced by meetings with Thompson. As well as being an avid reader, she also sought knowledgeable people with whom she could discuss her interests.

The Thompson compound (now a common destination for tourists), with its teak buildings situated on a *khlong,* its luxurious landscaping, and finely appointed rooms, remains an enchanting respite in a busy city. The Thompson home was, in a sense, a counterpart to her Shangri La, reflecting a taste for things 'Oriental' that have been adapted to and accommodate Western taste. One difference between the two homes is Thompson's close adherence to a single culture; Thai objects dominate his decor. This focused view of Thailand, which is also apparent in the Suan Pakkad Palace, would not have escaped Miss Duke's discerning eye. According to Warren, Miss Duke always dined with Thompson when she was in town in the 1950s and 1960s. She also accompanied him shopping in Nakhon Kasem, the "Thieves' Market," as the expatriates called the antique shops in Chinatown.[17]

During her visit in 1961, Miss Duke expanded her Southeast Asian horizons, going from Bangkok to Burma with Veary and Bérenx, stopping first in Rangoon (now Yangon), then Mandalay.[18] In Burma they purchased gilt and lacquered manuscript boxes, but the difficulties of exporting Buddha images or other large objects was daunting, and they did not attempt to buy anything else. Sarah Bekker, who worked on her dissertation while living with her husband, a diplomat in Burma at that time, spoke with Miss Duke on that visit and says that the project clearly engaged and excited her.

While her next stay in Hawai'i was not until June of 1962, the process of finding land for the Thai Village began at the end of 1961, with consideration of the Kualoa Ranch property.[19] The choice of an appropriate location ultimately proved the stumbling block to completion of the project. At least five sites were considered, and two smaller pieces were purchased,[20] though neither suited Miss Duke's conception, for the two properties did not have water, and so the *khlong*, which she considered part of the essence of such a village, could not be created. She also wanted to situate it on Oahu, feeling that the Big Island was not the right place for the Thai Village. She wrote the only known surviving letter that discusses the Thai Village Project to Bérenx during this period; it addresses the issue of land:

> I am in the process of buying another property in Hawaii. From Takata. I don't know if you saw where she lived; it's smaller than the other one we have but much better situated. It's on the edge of the Ala Wai canal which divides Waikiki from Honolulu, and I believe it will be ideal for us, because houses will naturally be at the edge of the canal so that they are visible from the road which runs along the other side of the canal. And we won't have to go through all the trouble of doing the construction on undeveloped land. There is already water, electricity, etc. I think it's a good deal. In any case, we won't lose anything even if we find something else because land prices are rising all the time. We can already sell the other one for double what we paid! It's impossible to say exactly when we can begin to build. It really depends on us; if we agree on the ground etc.; I am like you, I want to begin as soon as possible, but in these things there are always delays, which is actually not bad because it takes time to organize things well and not to make mistakes.[21]

The lengthy and complex history of the site search and village planning continued in the summer of 1962, when Miss Duke returned to Hawai'i and met with Louis Pursel of Louis Pursel and Associates, Architects and Engineers, to discuss their possible involvement in the project. They considered various sites; at that time Miss Duke preferred the Haiku Road property near Kaneohe.

The Highway Department's proposed plans for the area, which would have eliminated part of the property under consideration, were of concern, however, and she asked Pursel to contact the department regarding this matter. He and Hannah Veary tried to negotiate for the purchase of the Haiku Road property, but ultimately it was not consummated. As an architect, Pursel's role in the project included the siting of the Thai buildings, the possible design of additional buildings, grading, drainage, and plans for utilities. The reassembly of the imported houses, while under the direct supervision of a Thai architect, also required the involvement of a registered architect who knew local regulations.

In 1962, the Foundation, unable to come to an agreement with Pursel regarding the terms of payment, settled on the architectural firm of Wong and Wong, and in 1963 engaged the engineering firm of Towill Corporation. During these two years, the Foundation also exchanged correspondence with the Association of American Museums, investigating possible accreditation of the village as a museum.

A memo written by Bérenx in 1962 or 1963 provides us with our lengthiest description of the conception of the village:

> As Curator of the Museum for the Foundation of Southeast Asian Art and Culture, I am submitting a report of the proposed plans and purposes of this Foundation. I will attempt to give you in detail, a general description of the Museum after its completion.
>
> We intend to make this Museum a Center of the Traditional Life and Culture of Southeast Asia. In view of this, the Foundation will be stressing the Decorative and Minor Art Works rather than Archeology and the Major Arts. We have started with a collection of Thai and Burmese Art and hope to enlarge this collection by including other Southeast Asian countries in the future.
>
> From Thailand we have acquired 10 wooden classical antique Thai houses which are composed of 1 room (29½ × 16½ feet) and a large wooden pavilion (75½ × 46 feet). There will also be a reproduction of a classical Thai temple and a copy of a famous miniature pavilion which is situated on the grounds of the Royal Palace in Bangkok.
>
> The 10 small Thai houses will be supported by teak columns and built partially on land and in the water. The buildings are composed of specially designed wooden panels which will be joined together by wooden pegs. The roofs of the houses are high and have slanting sides which are covered with natural glazed tiles.
>
> We plan to use these houses to show how the people from the country lived in ancient times. To create the true atmosphere of a home of this type, we have acquired beautiful authentic furniture, all types of traditional textiles of silk and cotton, jewelry, silver and lacquer works.
>
> The large wooden pavilion with its high slanting roof is what the Siamese call a "sala." The roof will be covered with glazed tile of green, red and yellow and will be supported by teak columns. Ordinarily this building would be completely open on all four sides but because we will be using this building to display objects of art, we are enclosing it with antique carved wooden panels to protect the articles from any kind of weather. The ceiling and teak columns will be decorated with red and black lacquer.
>
> The display in this building will consist of a variety of art pieces, e.g., antique woodcarvings, cabinets, traditional costumes, antique materials, paintings, weapons, theatrical masks, books, musical instruments, porcelains and statues.
>
> The larger archeological pieces, e.g., statuary (religious and mythological images of wood, bronze and stone), a large collection of antique tapestries, paintings, and rare manuscripts will be displayed in the temple. This building will be supported by stone columns, and the roof will be carved gilded wood. The ornately carved ceiling and doors will be a typical example of religious architecture. Glazed tiles of red, green and yellow gold used on all religious structures will complete the decor.
>
> We will rebuild the miniature pavilion with its gilded spire and colorful tiles on a small lake in the Museum gardens. This pavilion will be the most typical example of Royal Thai art.
>
> We are planning to create the true atmosphere of Southeast Asia not only by the buildings and objects of art that we have acquired but also through the landscaping of the area. There will be lakes, canals, bridges, small gates, and all sorts of outdoor decorations.
>
> The entire property of the Foundation will be enclosed by a 9- to 12-foot wall with battlements etc., similar to the walls surrounding the Royal Palaces of Bangkok and Mandalay, Burma. Inside the gates are two towers, one on either side, which will house the concierge and other personnel. The Curator's private office and other offices of the Foundation will also be in one of these towers.
>
> There will be an open stone pavilion just beyond the towers which will be used as a waiting room for visitors waiting for their guides.
>
> There will be a large parking area just outside the main entrance of the Museum.[22]

Even though this memo indicates that Doris Duke intended the Thai Village to accurately interpret the way the Thai peoples live, in reality the household furnishings that were collected were of a quality indicative of use in the finest homes, rather than in

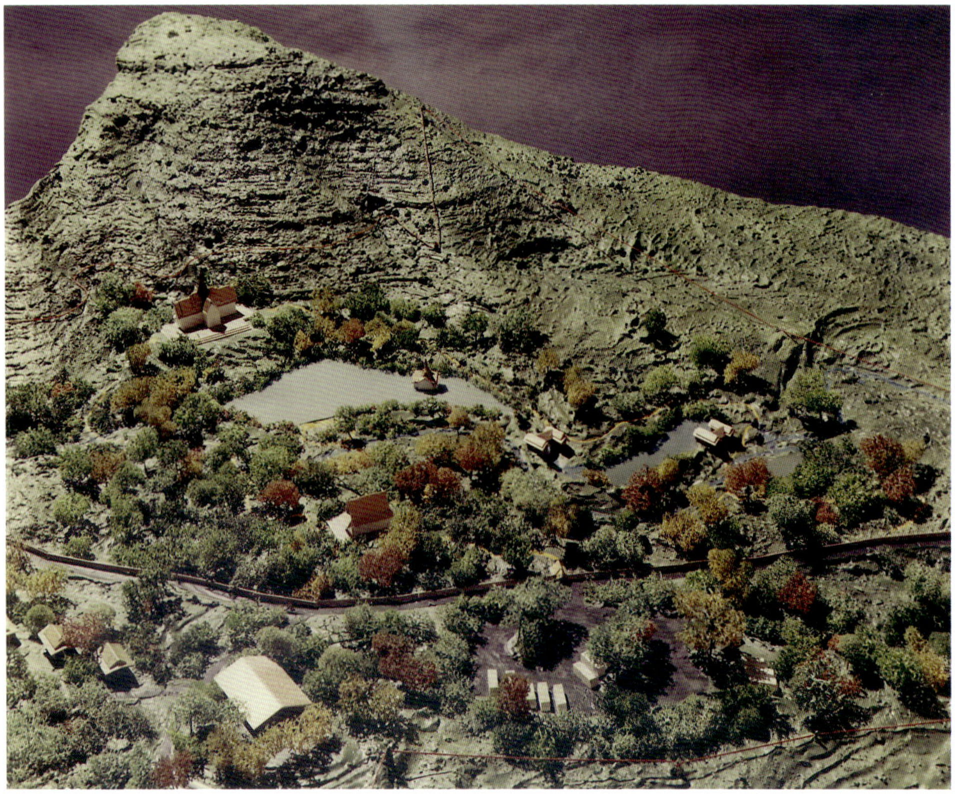

Figure 4 Maquette of the Thai Village Project from the mid-1960s.

the average country house. Many utilitarian objects—coconut scrapers (often engagingly carved), agricultural tools, everyday metal water bowls—are absent from the collection. In fact, its emphasis is artistic rather than mundane, religious rather than secular; a large proportion of the Duke Collection is in some way related to the worship of the Buddha. The high quality of many of the objects chosen, though considered by Bérenx to be "decorative and minor arts," would today place them in the category of fine art. The Doris Duke Collection thus gives us a comprehensive picture of eighteenth- and nineteenth-century Thai art, and to a lesser degree, Burmese art. In the 1950s and 1960s, she was the only active Western collector outside of Thailand with the foresight to gather materials of these categories and caliber.

In a letter dated June 30, 1963, Bérenx proclaimed the collection complete; he left the Foundation in July of 1963.[23] In October of that same year, the Foundation purchased Bérenx's private collection for $11,180.00.[24] After his departure, the Foundation hired a Thai architect, Somchai Panyangairm, and a decorator, Somnuk Phemthongkum. Somnuk Phemthongkum's duties included not only decorating the buildings once complete but also restoring artworks that had arrived in need of repair.[25] At the end of 1963, Miss Duke also hired Mung Yee as Vice President of the Foundation. At the same time, employees of the Foundation discussed seeking scholarly advice regarding the collection, as a memo to Mr. Pete E. Cooley attests;[26] the memo contains Alexander B. Griswold's name and address.[27] Mr. Griswold, an expert in the field of Thai art, lived in Thailand and Maryland. He, too, had an important collection of Thai and Cambodian art, the greater part of which is now housed in the Walters Art Museum in Baltimore, Maryland. (No correspondence with Mr. Griswold has survived, so it is unclear whether he visited the collection in Hawai'i, or later, after it was moved to New Jersey.)

The search for a suitable site continued: "During 1963 it appears Hanalei Valley on Kauai, Kahana Valley on Oahu, and Green Valley in Punaluu on Oahu were seriously considered for acquisition."[28] Miss Duke particularly liked Green Valley, and renderings and a scale model were done (Figure 4), but the unexploded ordnance left by the Army, which had trained at the site during World War II, discouraged the Foundation from purchasing it. By 1964, Miss Duke was considering the Waimea and Haiku valleys on Oahu. In the fall of 1964, Mung Yee drew up papers for the purchase of 38.5 acres and the long-term lease of 77 acres in Haiku Valley. But Miss Duke was unhappy with the idea of a long-term lease, and the deal was not consummated. Violet Mimaki was hired as Office Manager of SEAAC in 1964, and she recalls the final bid to buy property in 1965, this time in Kahana Valley, but the property was instead purchased by the state of Hawai'i for a state park.[29]

By June of 1964, the collection, begun in 1960, included 2,000 pieces of art, a *sala* (a building here intended as a museum), 14 Thai teak houses (Figure 5), 400,000 pieces of unglazed roof tiles, and 100,000 pieces of glazed roof tiles, all in storage on the docks of Honolulu.[30] Miss Duke's collection of Islamic art

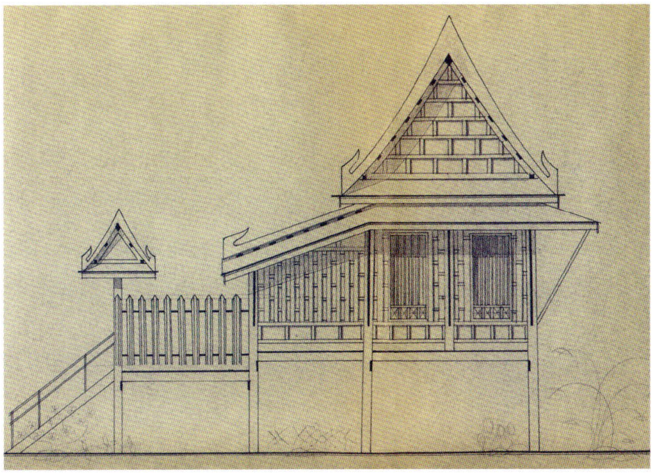

Figure 5 Elevation of one of the Thai houses purchased in Sangchan for the proposed Thai Village Project.

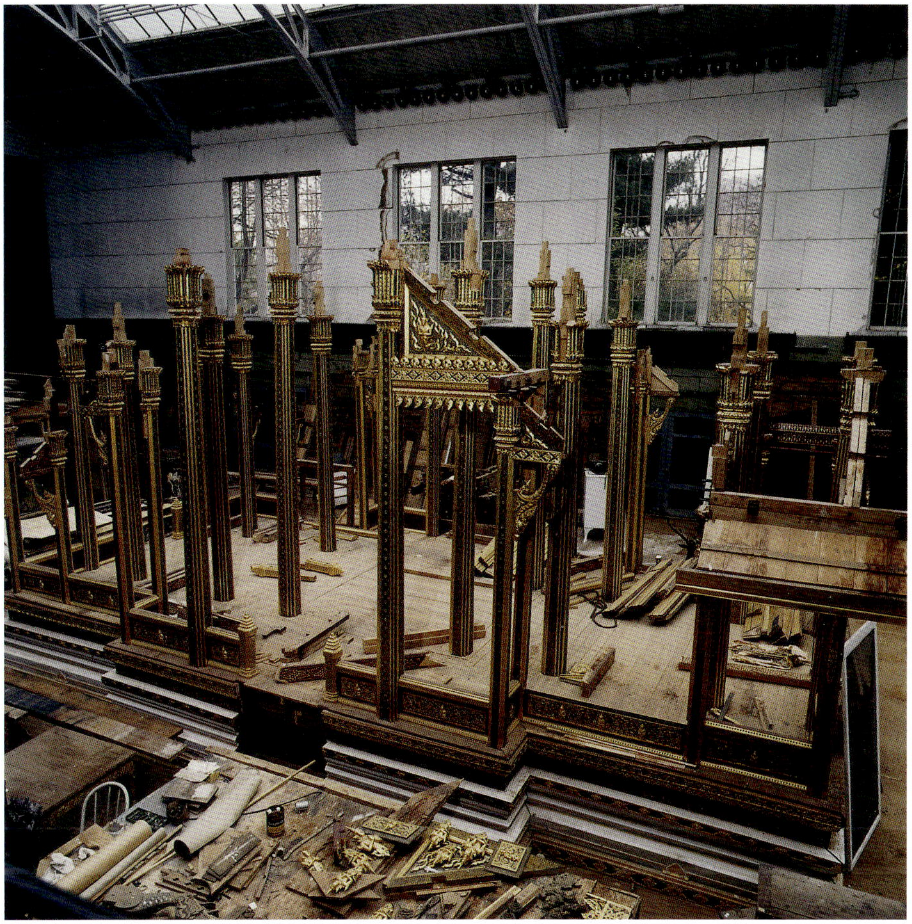

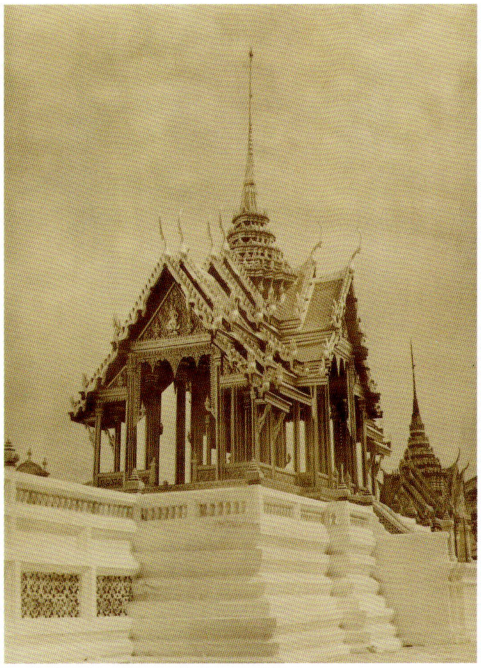

above Figure 6 The 'Golden Pavilion,' replica of Aphonphimok Pavilion, Royal Palace, Bangkok, partially installed in the indoor tennis court at Duke Farms, Hillsborough, New Jersey.

left Figure 7 Aphonphimok Pavilion at the Royal Palace, Bangkok (1960s photograph stamped "Chareon Sengthai Limited Partnerships").

for Shangri La, accumulated from 1935 to 1993, was larger (3,500 pieces).[31] By this time, the Foundation had also commissioned a replica (Figure 6) of the Aphonphimok Pavilion, a small pavilion located on the Royal Palace grounds in Bangkok (Figure 7), with completion of the building planned for November of 1964.

The original pavilion had been built during the reign of King Rama IV (1851–1868) for use in various ceremonies, such as the tonsure ceremony (haircutting ceremony for a novice monk) of his son, the future Rama V (1868–1910). Rama V constructed a copy of the pavilion at Bang Pa In, a palace built during the reign of King Prasat Thong (1629–1656), just outside the ancient capital of Ayutthaya. An undated photo in the Duke Archives of the Bang Pa In pavilion, which is situated in a lake, indicates Miss Duke knew of this site. The original building's charm, apart from Miss Duke's interest, has continued to captivate, and a replica of it was built for the Brussels World Fair in 1958; more recently, a copy was placed in the Olbrich Botanical Gardens in Madison, Wisconsin.[32] The pavilion has open sides, four porches, and a five-tiered spire. The Thai architect Somchai Panyangairm supervised the construction of this replica, for which Chareon Sengthai Limited Partnerships was the contractor. This same contractor may have built the Brussels replica.[33]

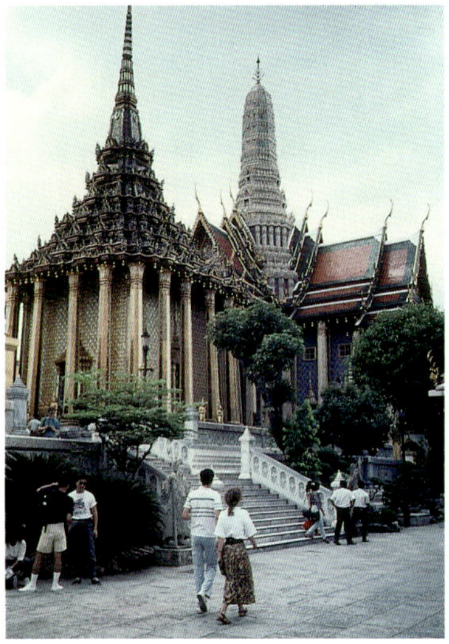

Figure 8 The Royal Pantheon in the foreground and the Temple of the Emerald Buddha *(ubosot)*, Wat Phra Kaeo, Bangkok.

The construction specifications for the pavilion required that it be built in "olden-Thai" style with a concrete base supporting a lotus-frieze secondary foundation of concrete beneath the wood foundation. This wood foundation was to be decorated with quartz and goldwork with vermilion stripes; it measured 120 cm (4 feet). From foundation to roof, the wood was carved teak decorated with gold, quartz, and vermilion paint. The intention from the beginning was to construct the pavilion in such a manner that it could be easily dismantled and also placed in the middle of a lake or pond, like the Bang Pa In pavilion.[34] The contract specified that the pavilion be completed by the end of November of 1964, and it was shipped to Hawai'i in February, 1965.[35]

Although the Golden Pavilion, as it was called by people connected with the Foundation, originally had been planned as the major building at the site, plans had recently been commissioned for replicas of the *ubosot* (ordination hall)[36] and the Royal Pantheon (Prasat Phra Thep Bidon), both located in the temple complex of Wat Phra Kaeo in Bangkok. During the late 1960s, SEAAC activities focused on these buildings and on finding a site for the Thai Village. A memo of July 1964 refers to research into purchasing tiles for the buildings. The *ubosot* of Wat Phra Kaeo (Figure 8) contains the central image of the complex, the Emerald Buddha, which is the most revered Buddha image in Thailand. The building itself, built in 1783 and renovated over the next 200 years, is elaborately decorated inside and out and houses an enormous altar bearing many images. Its replication would be an ambitious project.

In both Thailand and Burma, the *wat* (Thai) or *kyaungtaik* (Burmese) is the center of Buddhist life. The *wat* is not merely a temple, but rather a complex of buildings that serves the needs of both the monastic and lay communities and includes (in Thailand) a *wihan* (assembly hall), *ubosot*, *chedi* (reliquary mound), library, and monks' quarters. (Similar buildings are found in a Burmese monastery.) It does not seem that Miss Duke intended to reconstruct a complete monastery, but following her trips to Bangkok in 1964 and 1965, during which she continued to purchase art, she became very interested in re-creating important buildings in Thailand.[37]

The Foundation commissioned Professor Plue Chankao, Professor of Architecture in the Fine Arts University, Bangkok, to draw up the plans for both buildings.[38] The plans were eventually completed, though the structures were not built in Thailand because, unlike the pavilion and houses, both the Wat Phra Kaeo *ubosot* and the Royal Pantheon are brick and stucco buildings. The search for tiles appropriate for these two buildings ended with a purchase from a Taiwanese manufacturer.[39] While the temple's importance lies in the Emerald Buddha (which is probably carved of jade), the Royal Pantheon contains statues of the first five kings of the Chakri dynasty, which had founded the city of Bangkok at the end of the eighteenth century. Thus, Doris Duke had chosen two of the most important royal buildings in Thailand to replicate in her village. This was a deliberate decision, for she had assiduously studied and read all that she could about Thailand, its art, and Buddhism.[40]

Although there was discussion in 1965 of discontinuing plans for the Thai Village, letters and memos of 1966 suggest the search for a site continued. J. Harold Hughes, the lawyer representing the Foundation in Hawai'i, suggested the University of Texas.[41] In June of that year, Miss Duke once again requested the assistance of Pursel in plans to develop the center, to which she continued to be dedicated.[42] In 1965, a fire at Shangri La destroyed five of the Thai houses.[43] Up to this time, not only had they been stored at Shangri La, but artworks filled every available corner of the house itself—the Buddhas in the Damascus Room, the large Burmese altar in the foyer (Figure 9), and the furniture and other large items in the basement. When Miss Duke arrived at Shangri La during this period, the Damascus Room, with its Buddhas crowded together, was her first stop.

Miss Duke purchased little between 1966 and 1972, but still she continued to try to find a site for the village. Neither of the two small pieces of land that she had previously purchased offered the water source that she felt was necessary to re-create the ambience of Thailand. As Hibbard has pointed out, three of Miss Duke's close friends had passed away in the fifteen months at the beginning of this period, and these losses seem to have diverted her interest from her projects.[44] Then, in January of 1972, Miss Duke appointed Leon Amar to be Artistic Director of the Newport Restoration Foundation and Executive Vice President and Curator of SEAAC, and seemingly revived her interest in her many projects. The search for a site in Hawai'i finally came to an end, but since SEAAC had been established as a nonprofit organization with the stated mission of public education, she needed to develop another plan for the artwork.

In the late 1960s, they had moved all the art, the Golden Pavilion replica, and the houses with their thousands of roofing tiles, to a warehouse on Pier 26 in Honolulu because the neighbors had complained that the many crates of wood stored outside had attracted rats. Miss Duke then considered the Duke Farms, her 2,700-acre estate in Hillsborough, New Jersey, which had been assembled and built by her father in the early 1900s, as a possible site for the Thai Village, and plans were begun to ship the collection to New Jersey; the shipments arrived in August and September of 1972.[45]

She considered assembling the pavilion outdoors and inquired of Benjamin Moore Paint Company whether there was a preservative that would protect the lacquer and gold paint from the harsher New Jersey climate. The firm responded that it did not have a product to adequately protect it.[46] The pavilion, along with the houses, still broken down into piles of teak beams and walls, were stored in the indoor tennis court of the Duke Farms residence, and a carpenter was brought from Thailand to assemble the pavilion in the middle of the court (see Figure 6). The carpenter passed away during the construction, and it was never completed; it stands today as it was, partially assembled.

With 2,000 objects, no space in the main residence at Duke Farms would accommodate an installation, and since the intention was to provide a display for the public, a place was needed that would also assure Miss Duke her privacy when it finally opened. At the end of 1972, Miss Duke and Leon Amar began

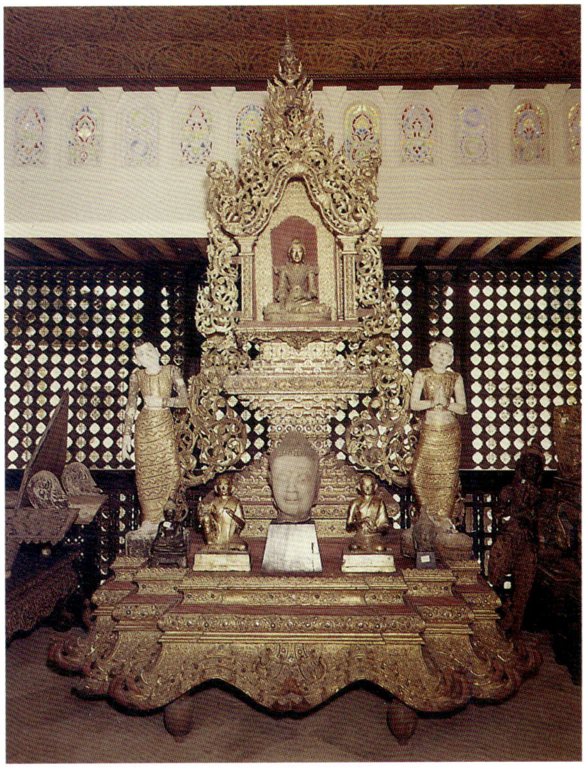

Figure 9 A large Burmese altar installed in the foyer of Shangri La in the 1960s. (Also see Plate 27, p. 49).

installing SEAAC in the Coach Barn (Figure 2, p. 11). This attractive, 19,000-square-foot building, designed in 1900 by Kendall Taylor and Stevens of Boston, Massachusetts,[47] has two large rooms where the art was installed, and where even the *thammat,* tall pulpits that required ceilings at least 20 feet high, fit in a pleasing manner. In December 1972, after a private preview for a number of Miss Duke's friends and acquaintances, the Coach Barn was opened to the public Wednesday through Sunday for an admission fee of $2.50, but little effort was made to draw people specifically to see the collection; it was offered as an additional tour for visitors of the gardens.

Having the art at the Farm revived her interest, and Miss Duke and Leon Amar traveled to Southeast Asia on buying trips in 1973 and 1974. Invoices of this period list many objects, including the purchase of an Ayutthaya Buddha, Bangkok-period Buddhas, a bronze Khmer-style Buddha, Burmese instruments, furniture, and a reclining Burmese Buddha.[48] These are among the last of the Southeast Asian art objects that she purchased. But a will drawn up in July of

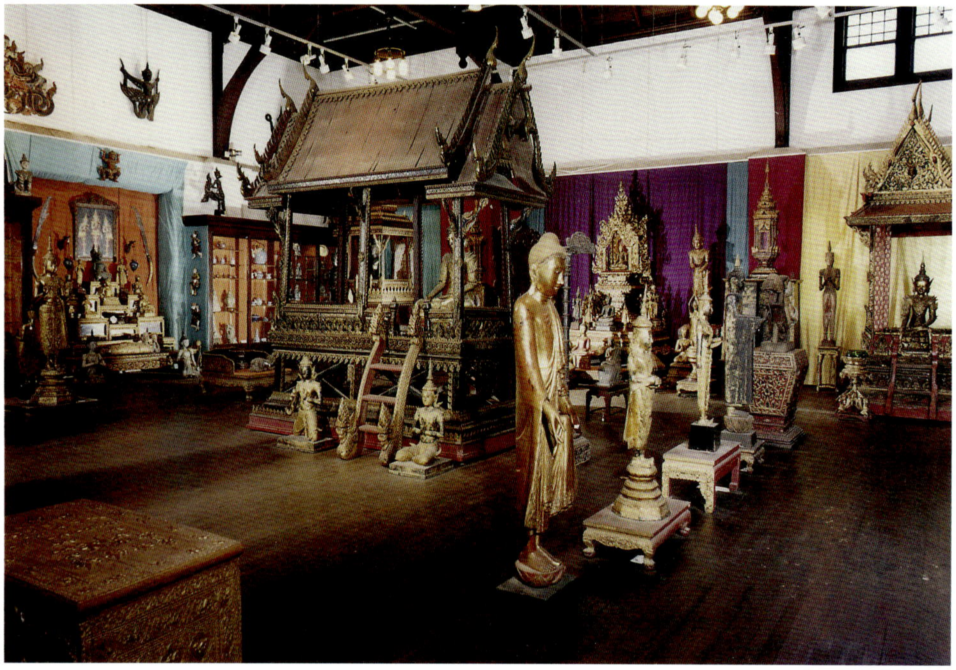

Figure 10 Interior of the larger of two rooms in the Coach Barn, Duke Farms, Hillsborough, New Jersey (2002 photograph).

1987 shows that she continued to hope the Thai Village would be constructed:

> My Executors are directed to investigate geographical areas of the United States that have approximately the same climatic conditions as exist in Thailand for the purpose of acquiring land upon which the Far Eastern Art Foundation [i.e., SEAAC] can reconstruct the Dismantled Thai Houses. In my judgement, the most appropriate areas for investigation are Florida, Louisiana, Texas, California and Hawaii. If they can do so within two (2) years of my death, my Executors are authorized to purchase such land for not more than Three Million Dollars ($3,000,000), and I give any land so purchased to the Far Eastern Art Foundation. . . .The Dismantled Thai Houses shall be erected as near and contiguous to running water as possible to approximate the circumstances that exist in Thailand.[49]

The will goes on to say that the premises would be open to the public. Her final will, drawn April 5, 1993, does not include this section. Yet her interest in Asia continued, as her collection of Chinese ceramics, bronzes, and jades attests, and she continued purchasing objects right up until her death in 1993.

Photographs of the Coach Barn today (Figure 10) illustrate changes that were made since the original installation, though there is no record of when those changes were made or who helped Miss Duke; Leon Amar left her employ in May of 1976. Cupie Singh, the Residence Manager at Duke Farms, remembers that Miss Duke always liked to take visitors to view the art that has remained on display. In 2002, the Doris Duke Charitable Foundation decided to donate museum-quality pieces to institutions with established collections of Southeast Asian art. The Asian Art Museum, San Francisco, and the Walters Art Museum, Baltimore, received the first of these gifts.

Although Doris Duke's dream of the Thai Village was never fulfilled, in the dispersal of its works of art to museums across the country, the collection will advance the display of Thai and Burmese art, just as she had hoped. The period when she most actively collected in Thailand, from 1960 to 1974, coincided with the Vietnam War, and she felt strongly that she could serve the best interests of Southeast Asia by preserving the material culture of the region.[50]

NOTES

1. Don J. Hibbard, "Shangri-La: Doris Duke's Home in Hawai'i" (unpublished manuscript, Nov. 2001; not fully paginated), first page of Appendix B, "Chronological Reference: Doris Duke Abroad."

2. Sharon Littlefield and Carol Bier, *Doris Duke: Shangri La* (Honolulu: Doris Duke Foundation for Islamic Art, 2002), and Hibbard, "Shangri-La," not fully paginated.

3. Littlefield and Bier, *Doris Duke: Shangri La.*

4. In the Erawan Hotel, and owned by Vera Cykman.

5. Suan Pakkad Palace is now a museum open to the public.

6. François Duhau de Bérenx, personal communication, 8/28/02. The first invoices in the records date to December 1960.

7. Doris Duke Charitable Foundation (DDCF) Archives, SEAAC.8: Land General file, 8/20/62.

8. DDCF Archives, SEAAC.8: SEAAC 1961–65 file, certificate of incorporation of Thai House Foundation, 1/30/61. Amended to Foundation for Southeast Asian Art and Culture; DDCF Archives, SEAAC.8: SEAAC 1961–65 file, Amendation 6/6/61.

9. François Duhau de Bérenx, personal communication, 8/28/02.

10. Littlefield and Bier, *Doris Duke: Shangri La,* xvii.

11. Hibbard, "Shangri-La," 35.

12. Doris Duke's home in Newport, Rough Point, was opened to the public in 2000.

13. In 1959, Bérenx hired Somchai Roumsamuk, who continued to work for the Foundation until November of 1964. Bérenx departed in July of 1963.

14. Veary was a friend of Miss Duke's and Executive Vice President of SEAAC beginning in 1964 (DDCF Archives, SEAAC.8: General file 1964).

15. Violet Mimaki, personal communication, 9/5/02. In March 1957, she traveled to China and India, and though the records do not include a stop in Bangkok, Bérenx (personal communication, 8/28/02) confirms that she was there. She again traveled to Bangkok as well as Yangon and Mandalay in March of 1961, then again in January of 1964, and February of 1965. DDCF Archives, SEAAC.8: SEAAC Trip file, 1961, invoices; SEAAC Summary Statements 1963–66, invoices; and Hibbard, "Shangri-La," Appendix B.

16. William Warren, personal communication, 10/02.

17. William Warren, personal communication, 8/22/02.

18. DDCF Archives, SEAAC.8: Travel Thai 1961 file, invoice of 5/9/61.

19. DDCF Archives, SEAAC.8: Land General 1961–64 file, memo of 10/10/61.

20. DDCF Archives, SEAAC.8: Real Property owned by Foundation in Hawai'i. A Haiku Road property was purchased 11/9/62 and a property in Kaneohe in March of 1973.

21. Written to François Duhau de Bérenx, February 23, 1961 (the year is not given: Bérenx suggests 1961). Translated from the original French by Jessie Hock.

22. DDCF Archives, SEAAC.8: François Duhau de Bérenx file, 1962–63. Typographical errors have been silently corrected.

23. Ibid., 6/30/63 and 7/8/63.

24. Ibid., 1962–63 file, 10/25/63.

25. DDCF Archives, SEAAC.8: General file 1963, 8/23/63 and 10/25/63. Somchai Panyangairm's name was also spelled Panya-Ngarm in the archive records (for example, General file 1963–64, 7/64).

26. Pete Cooley was the Business Manager at the Duke Farms in Hillsborough, New Jersey, and was appointed a Director of SEAAC in January 1964. The other directors were Doris Duke, John Munroe, Mung Yee, and David B. Rimmer (DDCF Archives, SEAAC.8: Directors' Information 1963–64 file; list of Officers, Directors, bank accounts).

27. DDCF Archives, SEAAC.8: General file 1963, letter of 8/27/63.

28. Hibbard, "Shangri-La," 37–39 (as in note 1). Mr. Hibbard has lucidly reconstructed the events of those years from the scant remaining correspondence.

29. Ibid., 38.

30. DDCF Archives, SEAAC.8: Land, Haiku Valley—Bishop Estate, 1963–65 file, memo of 6/23/64. This same memo also describes the various employees of the Foundation at that time.

31. Littlefield and Bier, *Doris Duke: Shangri La*, 35 (as in note 2).

32. Website: http://www.olbrich.org.

33. DDCF Archives, SEAAC.8: General file 1963–64. In a letter dated 2/14/64, Mung Yee says that the builders for the Duke pavilion were the same as those for the palace pavilion. It is more likely that they are the same builders who constructed the Brussels pavilion.

34. DDCF Archives, SEAAC.8: Construction Pavilion 1 file, 1964 drawings and specs.

35. DDCF Archives, SEAAC.8: General file, 1965–68, letter of 2/20/65.

36. DDCF Archives, SEAAC.8: General file 1964, letter of 2/14/64. Mung Yee mentions that the temple replica would be at one-half the size of the original structure and that the architect has recently left the employ of the "National Palace" (he may have meant the Royal Palace).

37. Violet Mimaki, personal communication, 9/6/02. Ms. Mimaki said that it was very important to Miss Duke that she recreate Thai buildings in the village.

38. DDCF Archives, SEAAC.8: General file, 1965–68 file, 1/16/65.

39. DDCF Archives, SEAAC.8: Construction of Pavilion file, 1963–64.

40. Violet Mimaki, personal communication, 9/6/02.

41. DDCF Archives, SEAAC.8: General file, 1965–68, letter from J. Howard Hughes, 10/26/66.

42. DDCF Archives, SEAAC.8: General file, 1965–68, letter from Pursel, 6/22/66.

43. DDCF Archives, SEAAC.8: General file, 1965–68, memo of 8/65.

44. Hibbard, "Shangri-La," 39 (as in note 1).

45. DDCF Archives, SEAAC.8: SEAAC Transportation 1972 file, bill of lading of 8/31/72.

46. DDCF Archives, SEAAC.8: SEAAC 8.1, letter from Benjamin Moore & Co., 1/14/77.

47. Betty Bird and Associates, "Coach Barn (Building 12), Duke Farms, Hillsborough, New Jersey," July 2002 (unpublished manuscript).

48. DDCF Archives, SEAAC.8: Transport Thailand shipments file, 1973–74; invoices of 1/15/73, 2/16/73, 2/21/73, 3/8/73, 4/1/73, 4/11/73, and 7/23/73.

49. DDCF Archives: Will executed 7/28/87.

50. Violet Mimaki, personal communication, 9/6/02.

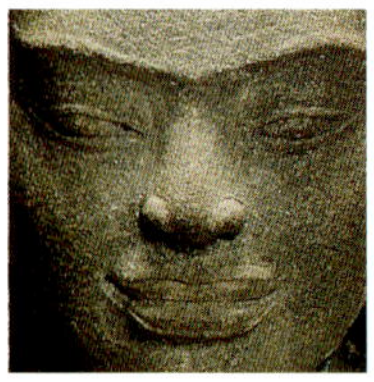

Sculpture

SCULPTURE COMPRISES THE LARGEST GROUP OF HOLDINGS IN the Doris Duke Southeast Asian Art Collection. The majority of these sculptures served a religious purpose, either as decoration for temples or as images to which one paid obeisance. Most are Thai of the eighteenth and nineteenth centuries, with the second largest group Burmese of the same period. A small number of works was produced by the Mon people, who dominated south-central Thailand during the sixth through eleventh centuries, while an additional few represent Khmer (Cambodian) artistic expression of the eleventh through thirteenth centuries.

Eighteenth- and nineteenth-century Thai and Burmese sculpture is generally gilded and sometimes lacquered and inlaid with glass—a flamboyant aesthetic at odds with twentieth-century Western taste, which has valued the subtlety of the Orient. Scholars and collectors of Southeast Asian art have focused on earlier, so-called classical sculpture and architecture, a fact made abundantly clear when one visits museum collections in Europe and the United States. Doris Duke's astute appreciation of eighteenth- and nineteenth-century Thai and Burmese material—more or less ignored by other Westerners in the 1960s, and which more recently has been acquired by Southeast Asian collectors or Western decorators—led to her compiling the finest collection of this material in the West. Today it would be impossible for a collector to amass a comparable group of objects, for the marketplaces of Thailand and Burma have been drained of most authentic works of that period.

If the Thai Village Project that Miss Duke imagined had been completed, each house would have held fine furniture, decorative arts, the highest-quality imported ceramics, and religious sculptures, for Buddhist altars are maintained in Thai homes. In the early stages of planning, the *sala* was intended to hold the bulk of religious paintings and sculptures, but by 1964, with the plan now including replicas of the *ubosot* and the Royal Pantheon of Wat Phra Kaeo, a portion of the sculpture would certainly have been placed in those buildings. The display would have comprised not only freestanding sculpture but also decorative elements, as the exterior and interior of a Buddhist temple are adorned with wood carving and, in some instances, stucco decoration. (In the period represented in this collection, many of the religious buildings in central and southern Burma and Thailand were constructed of stuccoed brick, while those in the north of Burma and Thailand were of wood.)

above **detail, Plate 6, page 29**
opposite **Dry-lacquer Burmese Buddha; see p. 49 and Figure 14.**

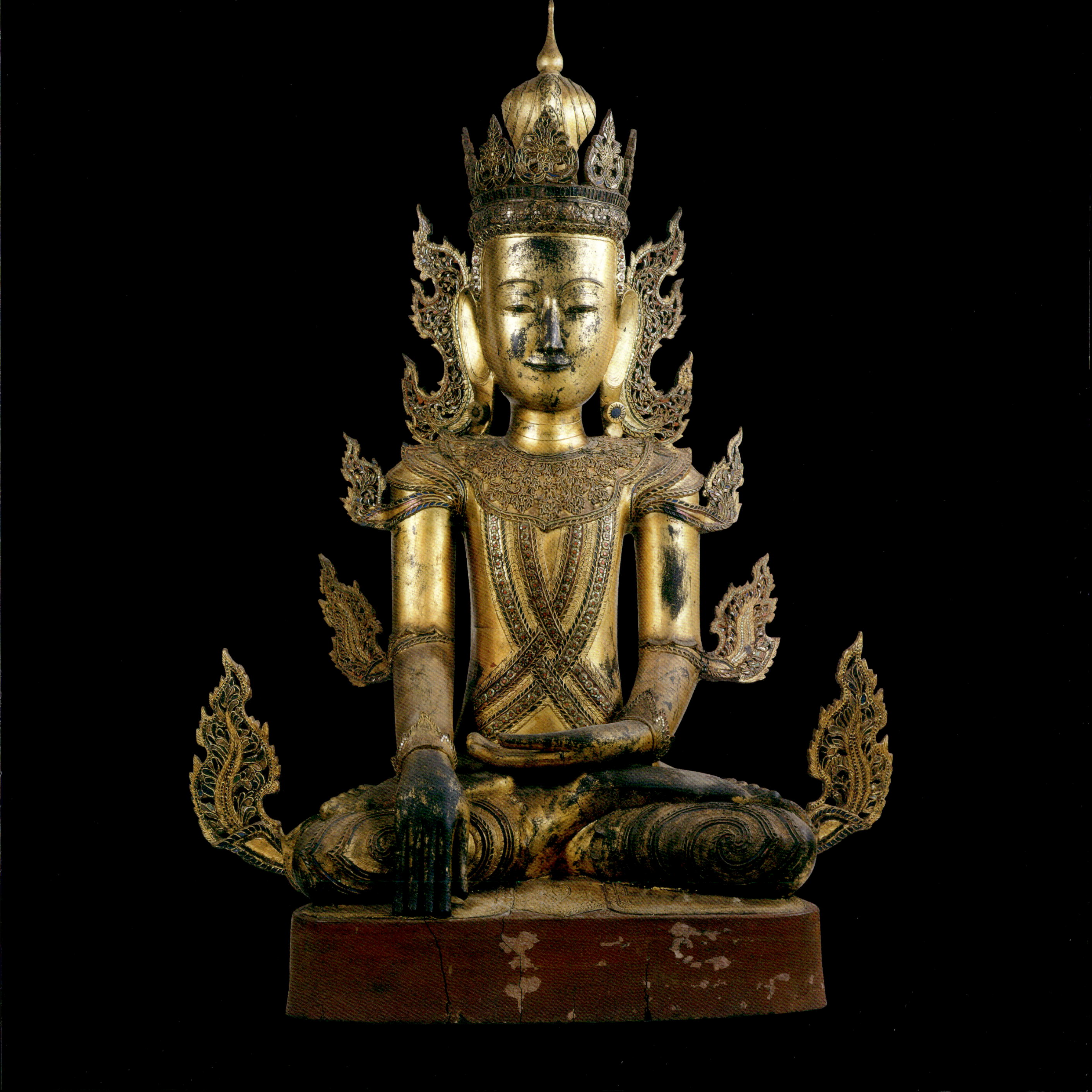

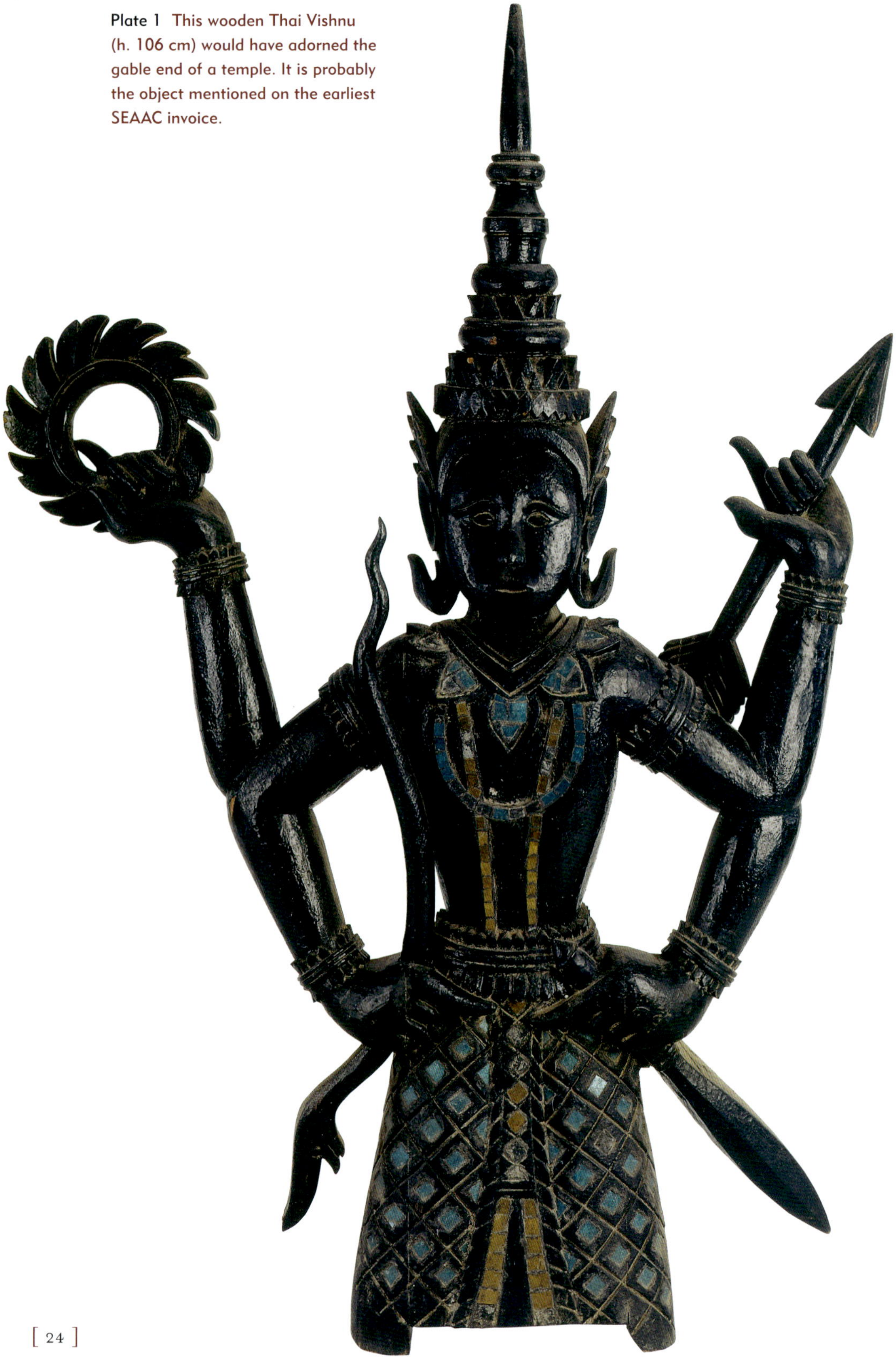

Plate 1 This wooden Thai Vishnu (h. 106 cm) would have adorned the gable end of a temple. It is probably the object mentioned on the earliest SEAAC invoice.

One of the first pieces purchased for the collection, a Vishnu (Plate 1), may well have adorned the gable end of a temple.[1] Vishnu is a Hindu god, but as the deity who protects and preserves humankind, he has been associated with Thai royalty, and temples adorned with images such as this were royal dedications known as *wat luang*. Other figures of an auspicious nature, such as lions (Plate 2) and the *kinnara* (Plate 3), a figure that is half man and half bird, helped to establish the supramundane aspect of the temple.

To place the collection in a larger cultural context, one must understand how Buddhism, originating in India, came to Southeast Asia and became the religion of the majority of the mainland's population. For millennia, traders plying the seas between China, India, and the West have found shelter from the shifting trade winds along the coasts of mainland Southeast Asia (see map, p. 7). They also sought the natural products of the area—hardwoods, spices, and other luxury items—and brought with them tales of their own countries, culture, arts, and religions. By the early centuries CE, entrepôts were located along the coastline, and Indian theories of statecraft and religious beliefs—Hinduism and Buddhism—had begun to profoundly affect the local peoples.

By the sixth century, Hinduism, a social and religious system based on Brahmanism and which incorporates a multitude of deities, had become the state religion in Cambodia and southern Vietnam (where it was practiced by the Cham people). During the same era, the peoples of Thailand and Burma adopted Buddhism, a religion that had arisen from the teachings of one man, Siddhartha Gautama of the Shakya clan, a prince born, by tradition, circa 563 BCE. Following his enlightenment, Shakyamuni (a title that means seer of the Shakya clan, an enlightened being) taught that the universe is a cycle of eternal flux, that life is an endless chain of events, and that *samsara* is an endless cycle of rebirth—all assumptions shared with Hinduism. Buddhism offered a promise of escape from that cycle—an escape possible through meritorious deeds.

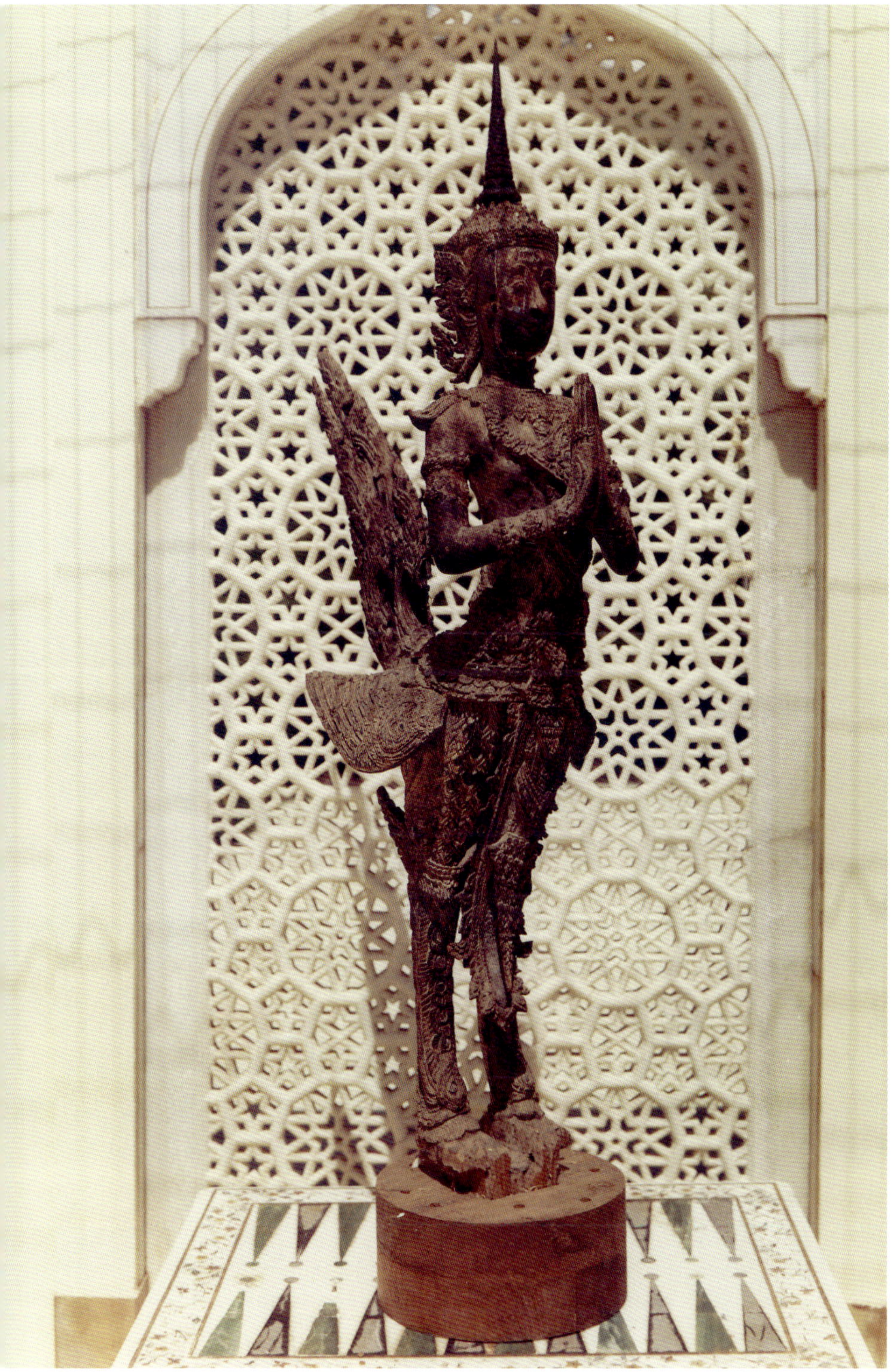

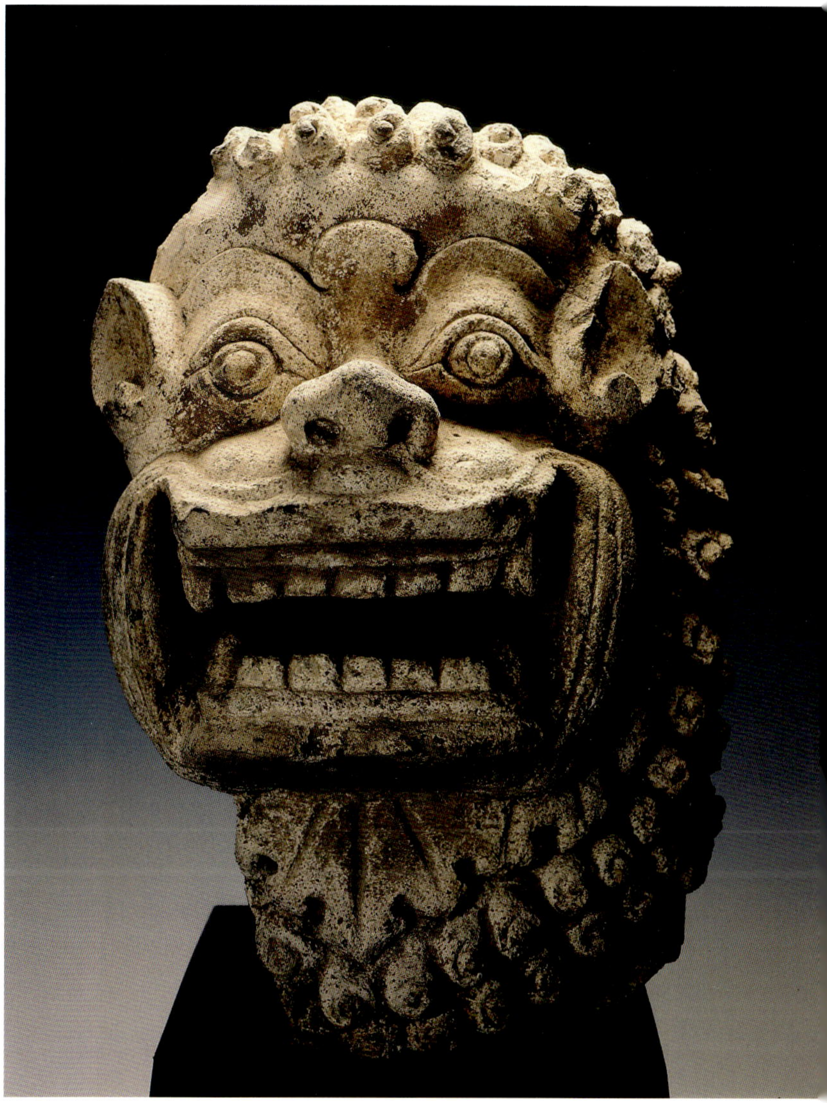

above **Plate 2** Stucco lion (h. 46 cm) from a building of the Dvaravati period (6th–11th centuries in Thailand). Lions, as important symbols of royalty, often protected temples. WAM

left **Plate 3** *Kinnara,* half human and half bird, reside in Himaphan forest at the base of Mount Meru, the cosmic mountain. This Thai *kinnara* (h. 128.5 cm) was photographed in the 1960s at Shangri La, Miss Duke's home in Hawai'i. AAM

Furthermore, Buddhism's rejection of the caste system made it more appealing to foreigners, and its adaptability allowed indigenous belief systems to coexist with it. As one Buddhist scholar wrote: "Southeast Asian Buddhism locates human beings within a complex cosmology of various divine, human and subhuman powers and provides a system for coping with them."[2] This cosmology involves the great stories of Buddhism as well as reverence for local spirits and ancestors. The life story of the Buddha and the *jatakas* (tales of his previous incarnations) are the most commonly depicted stories in the art.

At his birth, Siddhartha's father was told that his son would be a great man, a *cakkavattin* (one who turns the wheel of the law), either in the religious or the secular world. Disturbed to think of his son as a religious mendicant, the king confined him to the palace in hope of diverting him from any but a secular path. As a young man, having married and had a child, Siddhartha left the palace one day to see more of the world. In this and subsequent trips he saw a dead man, a sick man, an old man, and a holy man, and he realized that suffering was the fate of all men. He determined to follow the path of the holy man in order to put an end to such suffering.

Knowing that his father would never willingly allow him to leave, he silently slipped away in the middle of the night, the gods muffling his horse's footsteps. Once away, he turned back his groom and horse and cut off his hair; in subsequent years, he attempted various austerities as he sought enlightenment. Only when he followed the Middle Path, one

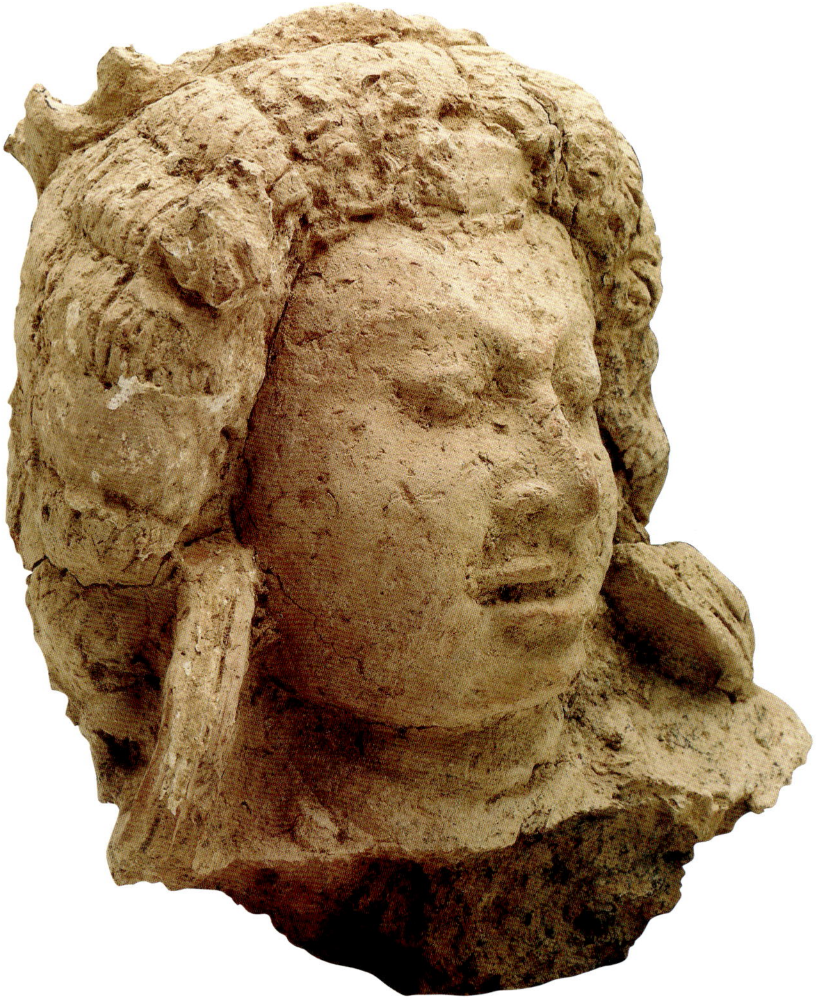

Plate 4 Stucco head (h. 17 cm) of an attendant figure from a Dvaravati-period relief (6th–11th centuries, Thailand). WAM

of moderation, did he achieve his goals. In Southeast Asian art, he is most often depicted seated, his fingers pointing downward, at the moment he calls the earth to witness his accumulation of merit and announces his enlightenment.

Various sects of Buddhism exist throughout the world, but Theravada Buddhism has been the form practiced in the Southeast Asian countries of Burma, Thailand, Laos, and Cambodia since the thirteenth century, and it is the form represented in the art of the Duke Collection. Pali is the language of the Theravada Buddhists, whose practice is closely linked, both historically and in practice, with the Buddhism of Sri Lanka. A multitude of Buddhas preceded Siddhartha Gautama; hence we refer to Gautama Buddha as historical, someone who has lived in our present memory. The Theravada Buddhists adhere to what they believe was the life and word of the historical Buddha. Theravada Buddhism teaches ideals of wisdom, compassion, and selflessness; the last is epitomized in the story of Vessantara, the prince *bodhisatta* (which literally translates 'enlightened being') of the penultimate life of the historical Buddha Shakyamuni. (See below, p. 60, for story.)

CENTRAL THAILAND

Like most art in Thailand and Burma, a majority of the works in the Doris Duke Collection are related to Buddhism and were created to pay homage to the great teacher. Most date to the eighteenth to twentieth centuries, though a few are from an earlier time, with the earliest dated to the Dvaravati period (sixth–eleventh centuries). The Mon people of the Austroasiatic linguistic group, who lived in Burma and central Thailand, had adopted Buddhism by the sixth century. In Thailand, they built *chedi* (reliquary mounds) and other religious buildings decorated with stucco ornament, and they carved stone figures of the Buddha that recall, though do not imitate, contemporary Indian-style sculpture. They predominantly followed a Theravada Buddhism similar to that of later centuries, and the imagery uses the same iconographic types seen in more recent centuries—images of the historical Buddha, attendant figures, and the characters in the *jataka* tales.

During the Dvaravati period in Thailand, the Buddha is represented in monastic robes, devoid of jewelry, and standing or sitting in an iconographically prescribed manner that identifies what moment in his life is being depicted. His attendants, on the other hand, are elaborately garbed to show their princely status (Plate 4), in poses of obeisance, and often quite relaxed compared to the more iconic portrayal of the Buddha. This deeply modeled head represents an attendant or a character from a *jataka* tale and would have been part of a relief on a large *chedi.* He wears hoop earplugs and an elaborate hairdo, and though detached from the body, we sense the motion of his head as it turns to one side. Stucco lends itself to fine and expressive modeling, and the stucco sculpture of the Dvaravati period shows great variety and liveliness. A large lion (Plate 2), which would have stood sentry at a Dvaravati temple, exemplifies this duality as it opens its mouth to roar.

To explain Southeast Asian periods of rule and the extent of power in Western terms of states and political boundaries requires many adjustments, as Southeast Asians did not think of land ownership in the manner of peoples of the West; rather they considered land that lay fallow for three years as reverting to state control.[3] Their model for hegemony consisted of an area some scholars describe as a *mandala,* a periphery with commercial ties to a powerful center that offered protection. When discussing Southeast Asia, it is also important to recognize that today's political borders do not necessarily relate to historical boundaries (see map, p. 7).

For instance, the Khmer, who spoke an Austroasiatic language related to that of the Mon, lived in the area known today as Cambodia and ruled a region that shrank and grew, depending on the power of the king. The period of Khmer hegemony, centralized in Angkor (near modern-day Siem Reap) from the early ninth to fifteenth centuries, on occasion extended as far as the Burmese border, embracing present-day Thailand. Thus artistic styles within the

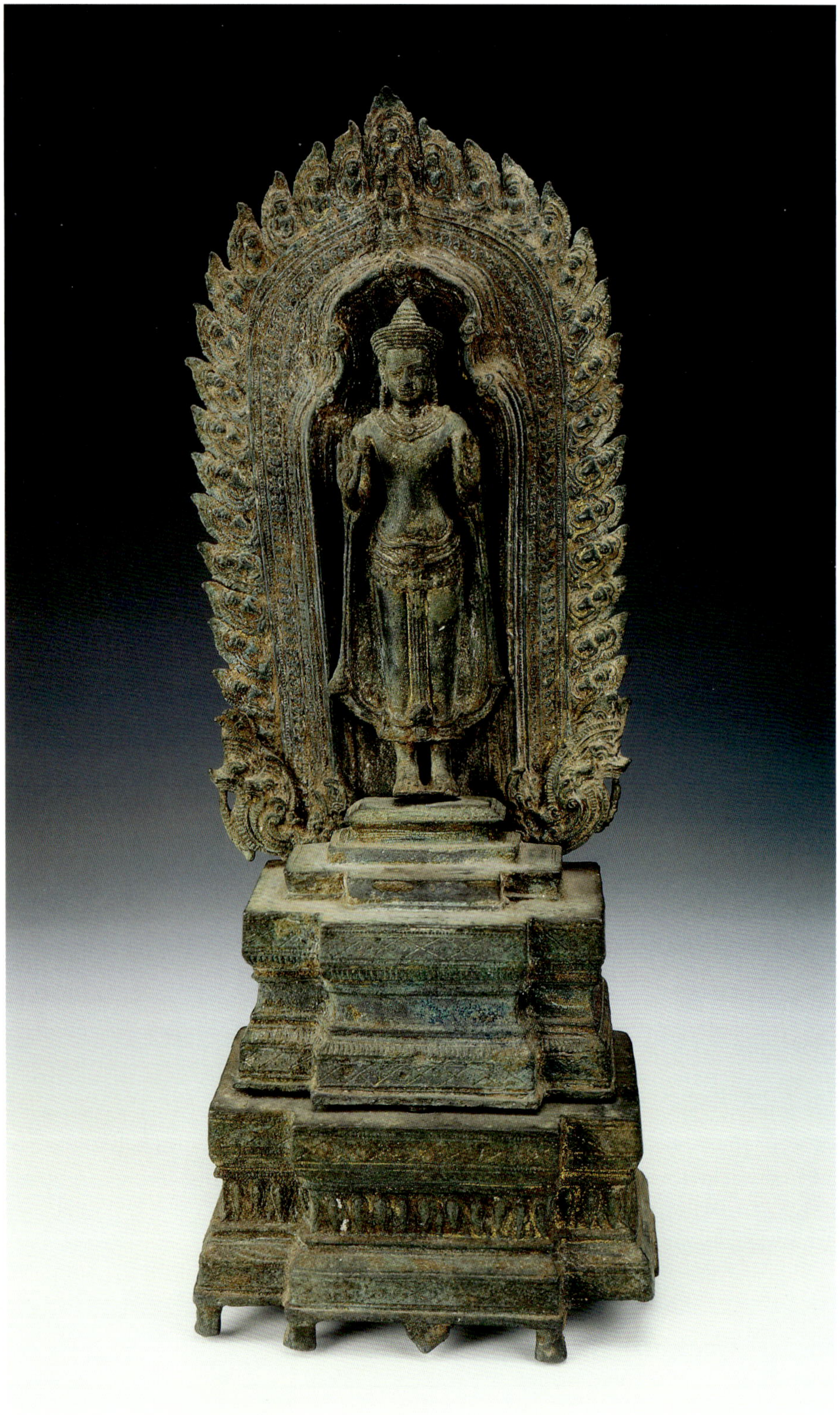

Plate 5 This 12th-century standing Khmer-style Buddha (h. 44.5 cm) holds his hands in the teaching gesture. WAM

area we now call Thailand were at times not merely Khmer-influenced, but Khmer in actuality. Most of the Khmer kings were Hindu, with a few notable exceptions, but Buddhism was always practiced by some of their followers. The same artisans produced stylistically related Buddhist and Hindu art.

By the eleventh century, the Khmer dominated central Thailand, their influence extending to religion and the arts. Dvaravati-style art was subsumed into Khmer, with specific iconographical types, such as the standing Buddha with two hands raised in teaching gesture *(vitarka mudra)*, being adopted by the eleventh century. Stone sculpture, stucco relief, and small bronzes, like this mid twelfth-century Buddha with raised hands (Plate 5), were created throughout the region at the important production centers of Lopburi, in central Thailand, and Phimai, in the northeast on the Khorat Plateau.[4] Portable bronzes, created for personal altars or as gifts to temples, had existed in Southeast Asia from the sixth century.

Many of these portable bronzes incorporate a throne and an aureole. Aureoles with a treatment similar to that of this Buddha image are rare, but not unknown, and aid our interpretation of the moment in the Buddha's life that is being depicted. In looking closely at the individual flames, one sees in each a tiny crowned Buddha seated in a posture of meditation. One interpretation of depictions of multiple Buddhas is that they represent the Buddhas of the past, usually numbering twenty-eight;[5] this interpretation may not be applicable to this example, which includes thirty Buddhas, unless we assume the artist miscalculated.[6] If we view the flames as emanating from the Buddha, the most likely explanation for this multiplication of Buddhas is the canonical story of the Miracle of Sravasti, which took place when the Buddha emitted fire and water from his body and multiplied his form in response to a challenge by six rival teachers. This example differs from most Indian and Southeast Asian illustrations of the subject in the crowns worn by each of the Buddhas.

The crown became popular in Southeast Asian art in contradiction to Pali texts that stipulate the Buddha be dressed as a monk without jewels or headdress and with identifying characteristics such as a cranial protuberance *(ushnisha)* and the distended earlobes that refer to his once having worn princely jewels.[7] An apocryphal story that seems to have originated in about the eleventh century appears as the most common explanation of the crown on the Buddha in Southeast Asian art. In this second story, the Buddha converts a heretic king (Jambupati) by donning royal attire and magically appearing as the Universal Monarch, expanding himself to enormous size. In both the Sravasti and the Jambupati stories, magic plays a role in the Buddha's display and may explain why multiple Buddhas symbolizing the Sravasti tale wear crowns.[8] In Southeast Asia, the crown may be a sign of sovereignty, symbolizing the common identity of all Buddhas and hence appropriate garb for any image.

A seated stone Buddha in the collection (Plate 6) also dates to the latter half of the twelfth century. The figure is in the meditation gesture *(dhyana mudra)* under the protective hood of Mucalinda, the serpent *(naga)* who protected the Buddha from a fierce storm during the first week of his enlightenment, when he continued meditating. Snakes are commonplace in Southeast Asia, and the frequency with which this theme is depicted in sculpture may result from a desire to placate them by honoring their positive qualities. While the standing bronze discussed above (Plate 5) and this stone piece represent different moments in the life of the Buddha, stylistic similarities, such as the crown and the high arc of the waistband, place their production under the period of Khmer domination. The proportions of this seated stone figure, especially the treatment of the *naga* hoods that branch out from below the Buddha's shoulders, and the manner in which two hoods join at the top, may suggest the sculpture was created in central Thailand.[9]

The sculptural reliefs of the Khmer temples of Angkor, evoking the chaos of battle and the bustle of commerce (Figure 11), confirm thirteenth-century Chinese descriptions of the frequent state of war in Southeast Asia and the luxurious life of the wealthy citizens of Angkor, the great Khmer city of the tenth

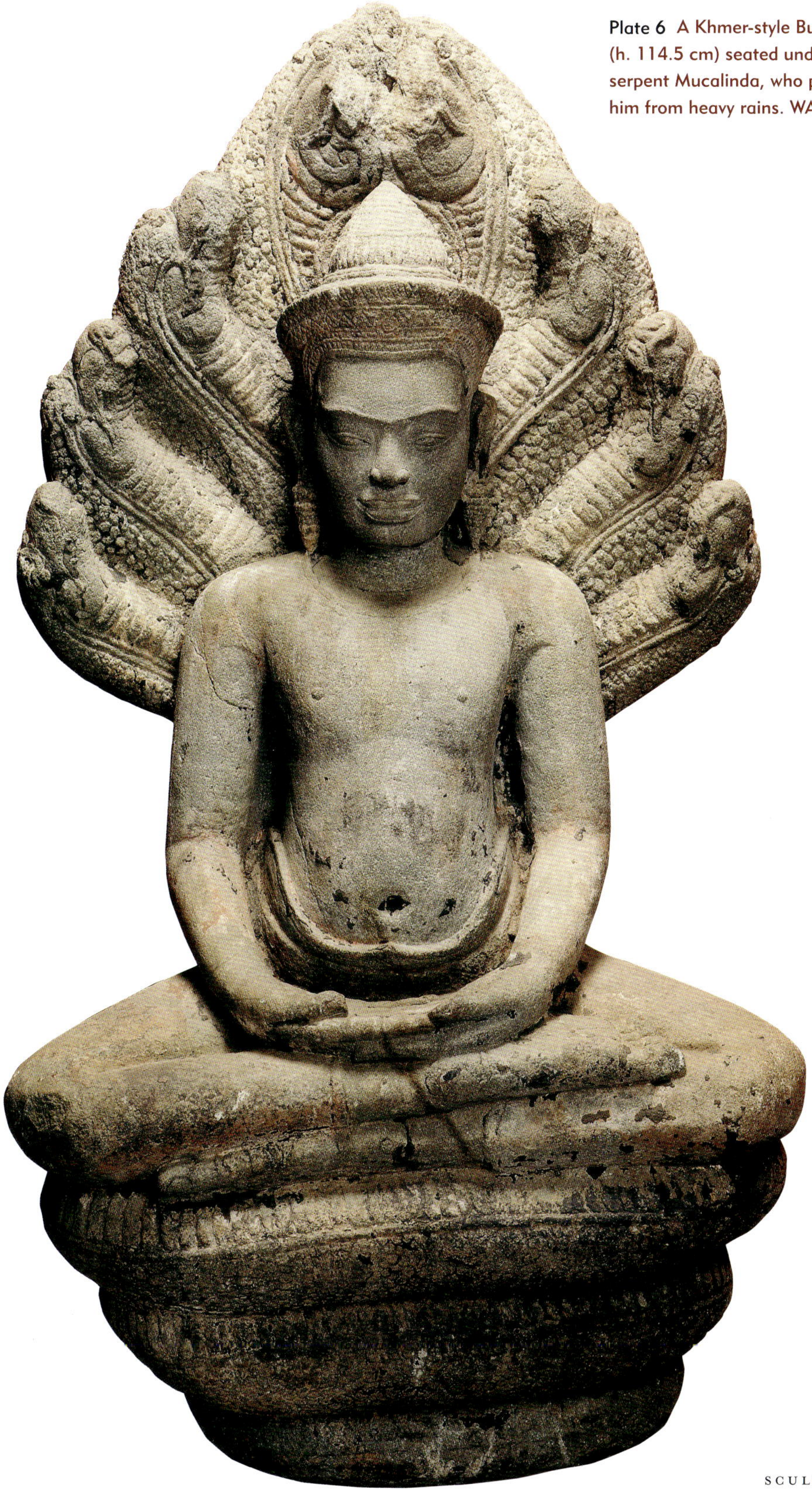

Plate 6 A Khmer-style Buddha (h. 114.5 cm) seated under the serpent Mucalinda, who protected him from heavy rains. WAM

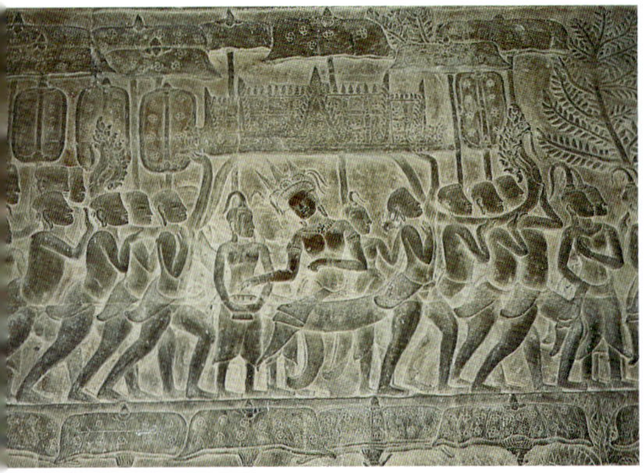

above **Figure 11** Relief of a woman in a palanquin, from the southern gallery of Angkor Wat, Cambodia (late 12th century).

right **Plate 7** Pair of *naga* (serpents: average h. 20.6 cm). Both religious images and decorative elements, such as these fittings for either a howdah or palanquin poles, were cast in bronze. WAM

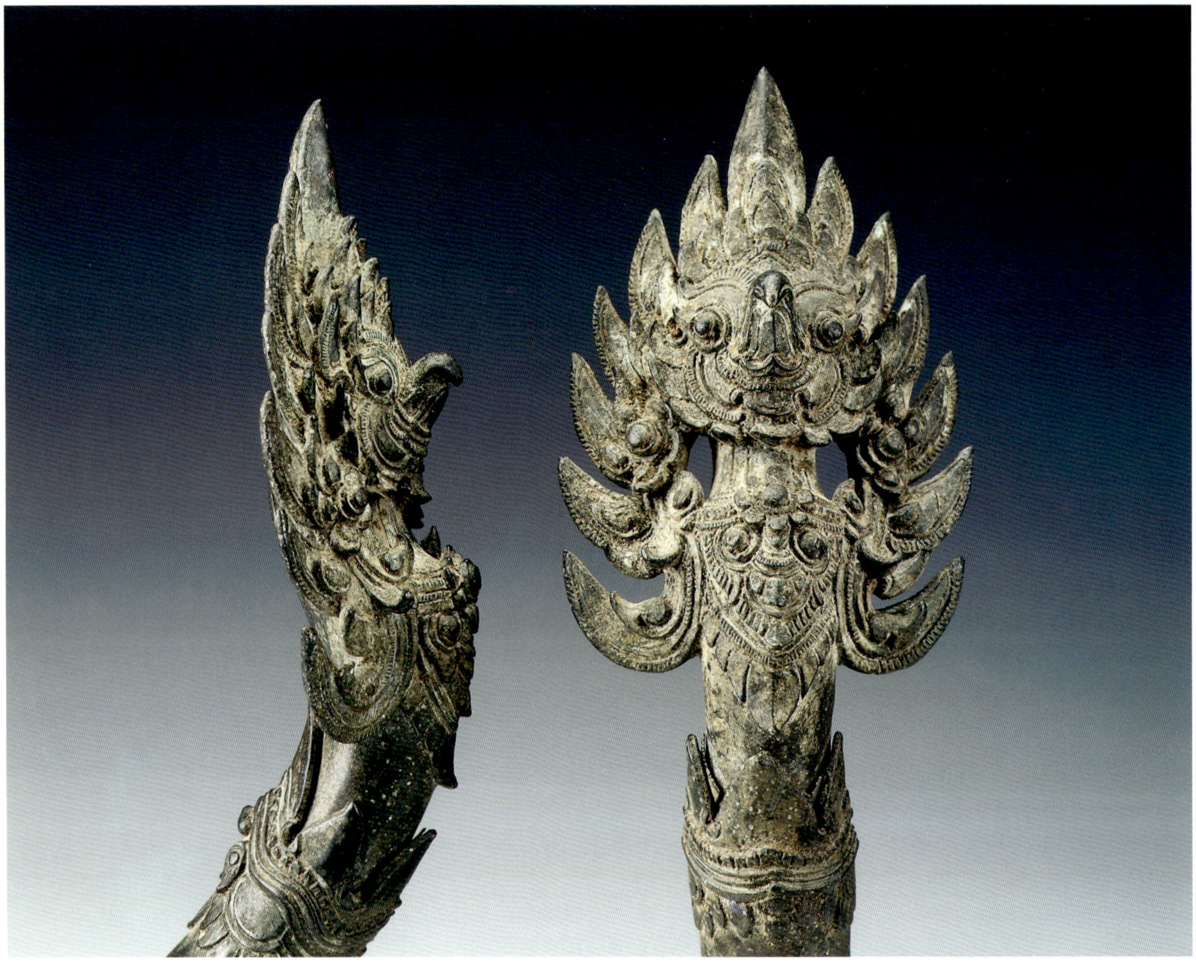

to fifteenth centuries. Rulers and generals rode horses or elephants, while wealthy women were carried in palanquins adorned with a variety of bronze fittings. *Naga* and *garuda* (birds) were the most common motifs for these decorative elements, and this pair (Plate 7), which would have fit on the ends of wooden poles from which the palanquin was suspended or embellished the howdah carried by the elephants, are typical of the multiheaded *naga*. They could have been produced either in Cambodia or in present-day Thailand.

Bronze, cast by the lost-wax technique, proved a marvelous medium for the fashioning of all types of accoutrements for the regalia of battle, everyday life, and the rituals of Hindu and Buddhist religion. One such item is the conch (Plate 8) used both to call troops to battle and as a ritual implement in Hindu or Buddhist temples. Few of these conchs have survived, and this one is unusual, as a conch shell has been inset in the bronze bracket.

Khmer domination of Thailand came to an end in the thirteenth century with the rise of Tai-speaking[10] principalities, in the far north, Lan Na, and in north-central Thailand, Sukhothai. In central Thailand, the city of Lopburi, a locus of power during the period of Khmer rule and a center for the arts, retained its regional importance. The founding of the state of Sukhothai in north-central Thailand around 1279, by Ram Khamhaeng, signaled the beginning of a Thai state distinct from earlier Mon Dvaravati cultures. The establishment of Sukhothai also signaled the beginning of a new style of art distinct from Khmer or Mon influence and considered by many to be the high point of Thai sculpture. Then, in 1351, in lower Thailand, the Thai principality of Ayutthaya was established on the Chao Praya River, and in 1438 Sukhothai was brought under its rule. Two artistic traditions developed in this new center of Thai culture, one growing out of Khmer styles and the other related to the Thai idiom of Sukhothai; each had its own unique characteristics.[11]

Ayutthaya became an important trading center in Southeast Asia, and it is this Thai city that early Western visitors describe in some detail: "The emperor or king of Siam is surrounded by as much magnificence and such splendid ceremonial as any other king in all the Indies. His foot never touches earth: wherever he wishes to go, he is carried on a golden throne, and he shows himself once a day to the lords and nobles of his court with a display of ostentation which exceeds that of any Christian king."[12] But in 1767 the Burmese sacked Ayutthaya, and in 1782 Bangkok was established downriver in a more desirable location for trade and defense from the Burmese. While some sculptures in the Duke Collection come from the Ayutthaya period, many more were made during the Bangkok period, which in its early years (Rama I, 1782–1809, and Rama II, 1809–1824) retained close ties to the artistic traditions of Ayutthaya.

The fantastic *kinnara*, half human and half bird, resides in Himaphan forest at the base of Mount Meru, the cosmic mountain (Plate 3, p. 25). The special place of *kinnara* in Thailand is demonstrated by the popularity of the Indian story of a *kinnari* (a female *kinnara*), Manora. A hunter captures her and takes her to the human world, where she falls in love with Prince Suthon but then is separated from him. Unable to live without her, he finds his way to her heavenly forest and wins her back by performing seven feats. Thai sculpture of the Ayutthaya period is characterized by elegance of line and, by the seventeenth century, an attention to detailed ornamentation. This *kinnara* exemplifies these traits, with the elegant balance of long legs and thin neck and the weighty body, with its layering of feathers.

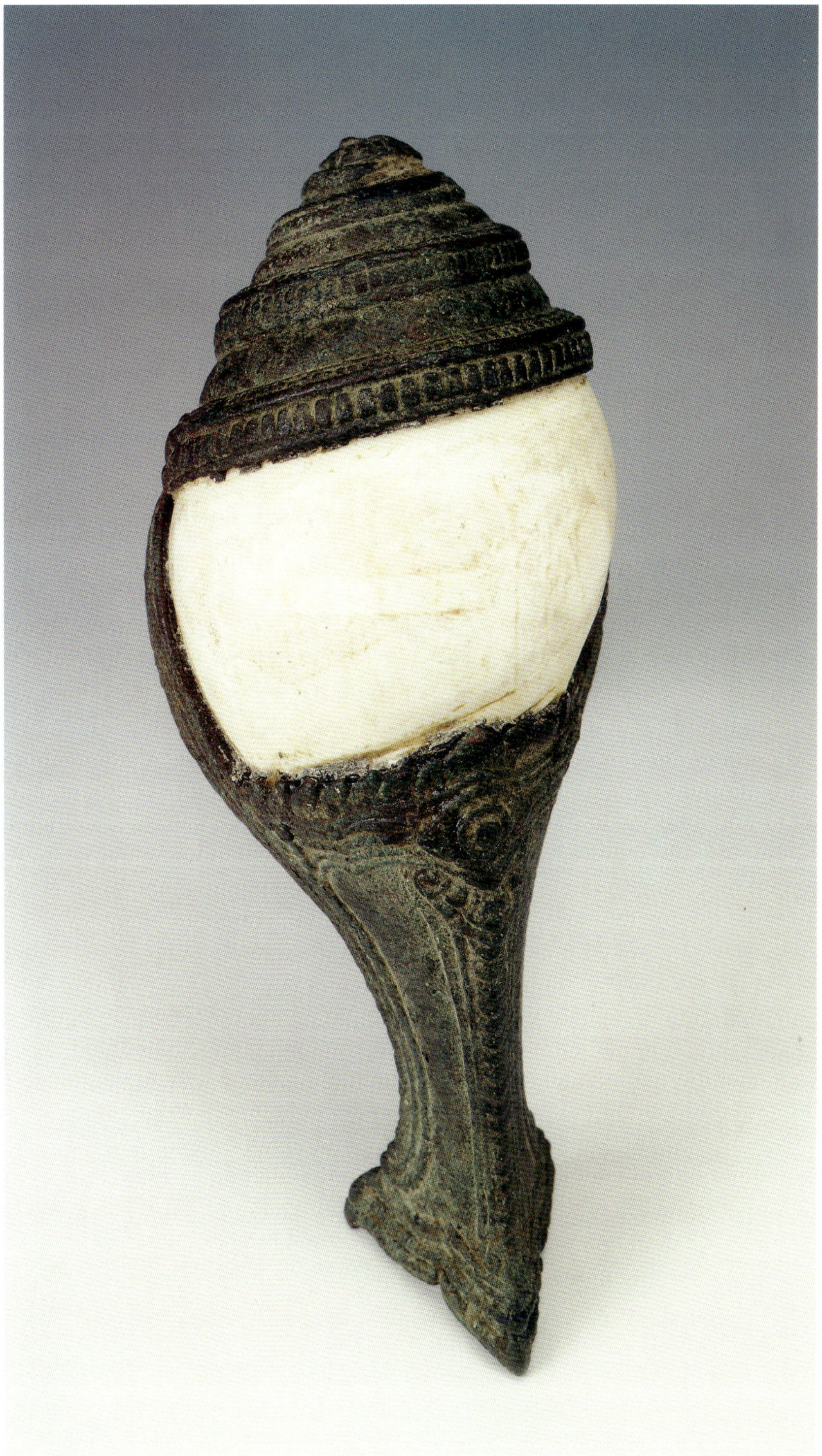

Plate 8 In both Hinduism and Buddhism, the conch (l. 24 cm) was used for ritual purposes and in battle, to rally the troops. AAM

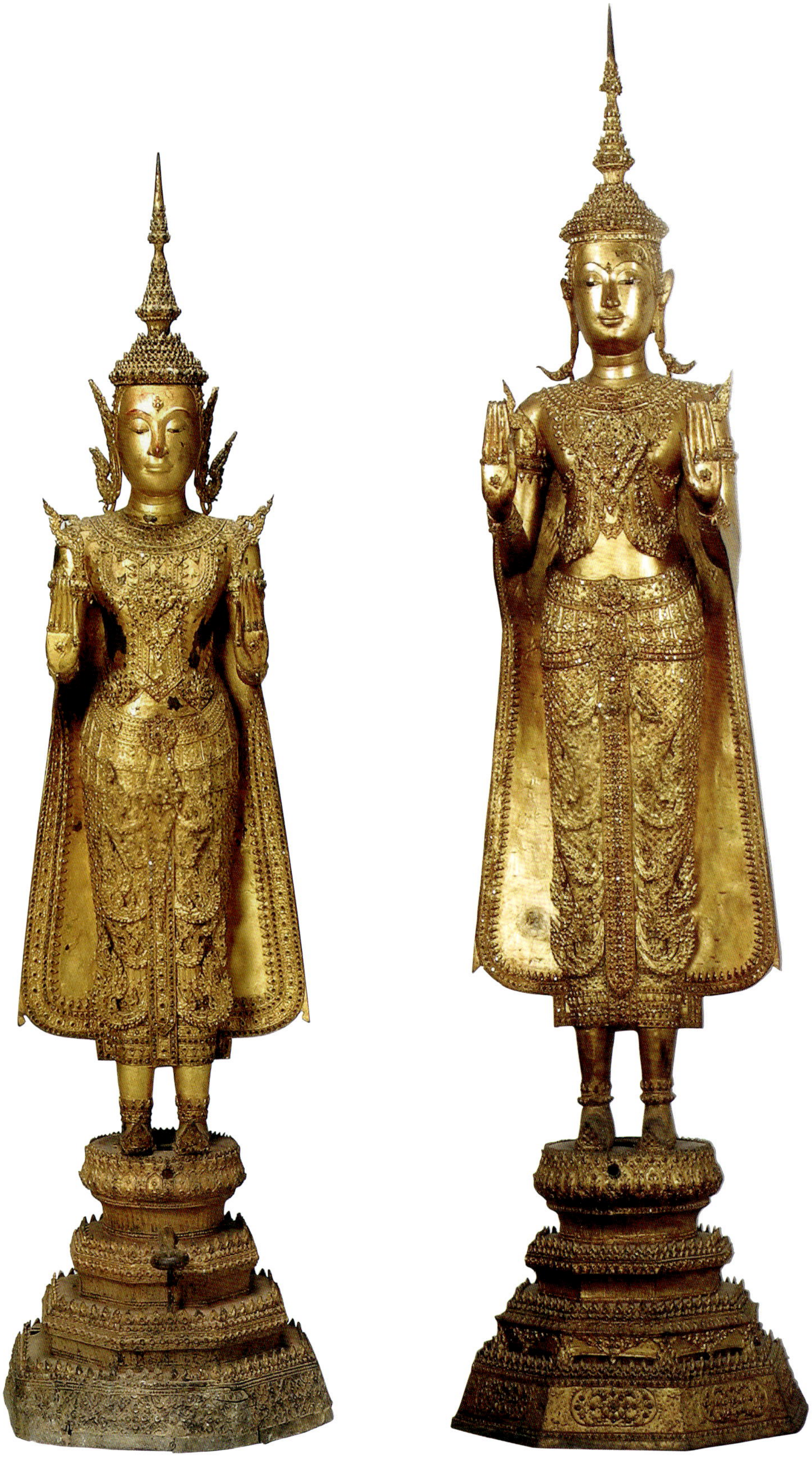

Plate 9 Adorned images of the Buddha (left, h. 120.5 cm; right, h. 178 cm) were popular during the Bangkok period (1782–present). His jewels refer to his royal lineage. AAM

Apparently Miss Duke was fond of this example, as she had it photographed at her home, Shangri La. One of the buildings for which she had architectural plans drawn, the Royal Pantheon of Wat Phra Kaeo, Bangkok, has freestanding *kinnara* around its base. She probably intended to display this piece, and the three others in the collection, around her replica in a similar location. (The collection also includes a group of small temple replicas [Figure 2, p. 11] of a type that are mounted on posts around the *ubosot* of Wat Phra Kaeo; these were probably intended to be placed near the Thai Village replica of that temple.) The placement of auspicious figures such as this one in the compound of a Buddhist temple enhances the sacred quality of the space. Other fantastic creatures, such as *makara* (crocodiles), *naga*, and *garuda*, are carved on the gables below the roof or on the eaves themselves. Most of this architectural sculpture was lost when Ayutthaya was razed.

The early kings of the Bangkok period, Rama I and Rama II of the Chakri dynasty (1782–1824), consciously followed precedents set in art and architecture of the Ayutthaya period, as they attempted to link their dynastic claims to the past. Many Buddha images survived the Burmese destruction of Ayutthaya in 1767 and lay in the debris of the destroyed cities of central and north Thailand. Rama I brought 1,200 Buddha images to Bangkok, where they were installed in the new temples and monasteries of that city. Ayutthaya artists had revived the iconography of the standing adorned Buddha with two hands raised.[13] Like the Khmer example discussed above (Plate 5, p. 28), this imagery probably refers to the time he showed himself in his glory to Jambupati. Bangkok standing images are similarly depicted, with the Buddha dressed in royal attire and either one or both hands raised in *abhaya mudra* (the gesture that the Thais call "calming the ocean"; Plate 9). Dating these images is difficult, as they were stylistically similar throughout the nineteenth century.

Under King Rama III (1824–1851), Buddha images were generally crowned and adorned as they had been in the preceding period. During the reign of King Rama IV (1851–1868), when European culture became familiar, however, there was an attempt to humanize the Buddha, and he was depicted without an *ushnisha* (Plate 10), one of the marks of a great leader and the usual iconography for the Buddha.[14] Images created during Rama VI's reign generally wear monastic robes arranged in a series of narrow folds, but this example is elaborately adorned. Without the *ushnisha*, one might think him a monk,[15] but his right hand in earth-touching gesture *(bhumisparsha mudra)* is more common for a Buddha. An alternate interpretation may indicate he is an attendant of the Buddha, as attendants holding fans are depicted in this manner during this period.

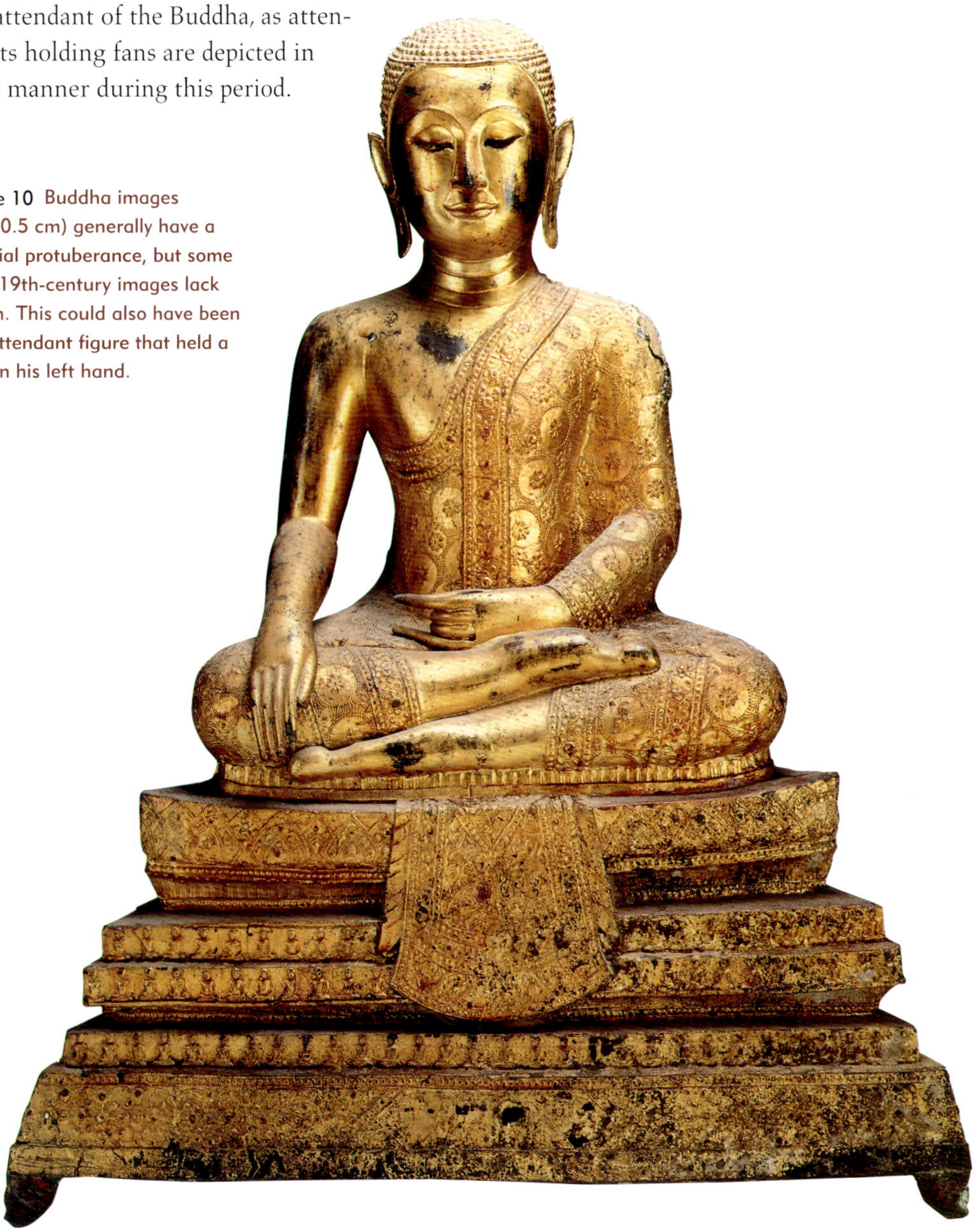

Plate 10 Buddha images (h. 70.5 cm) generally have a cranial protuberance, but some late 19th-century images lack them. This could also have been an attendant figure that held a fan in his left hand.

below **Plate 11** In Thailand, devotees (h. 54 cm) are often placed attending an image of the Buddha. Frequently they represent his disciples Moggallana and Sariputta. WAM

right **Plate 12** The monk Phra Malai accumulated sufficient merit to be allowed to visit heaven and hell and to tell of all he had seen. In this sculpture (h. 49.5 cm), inhabitants of hell beg him for assistance. Thailand. AAM

When an individual makes an offering or donates an image to a temple, the act gains merit for the donor and, in his generosity, for all sentient beings as well. The acquisition of merit through the donative process is the simplest way that a layperson can assure a better life in his next incarnation. This act of charity *(dana)* is performed in the practice of placing multiple images and offerings around the central figure on an altar. These gifts may be Buddha images or offerings of food, lotuses, and incense, the latter more transient offerings given in multiples of three in honor of the Buddha, the teachings *(dhamma)*, and the monastic community *(sangha)*.

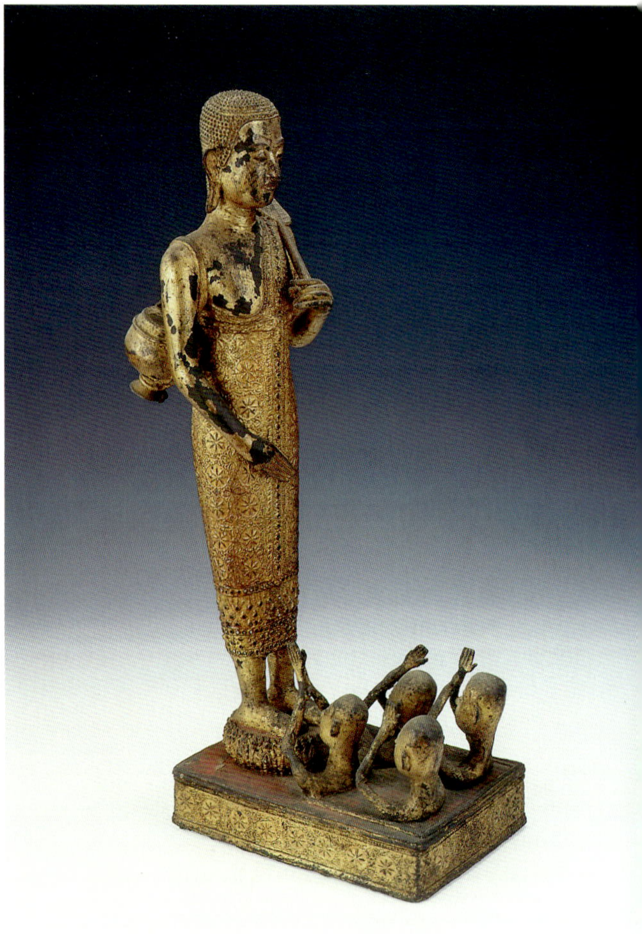

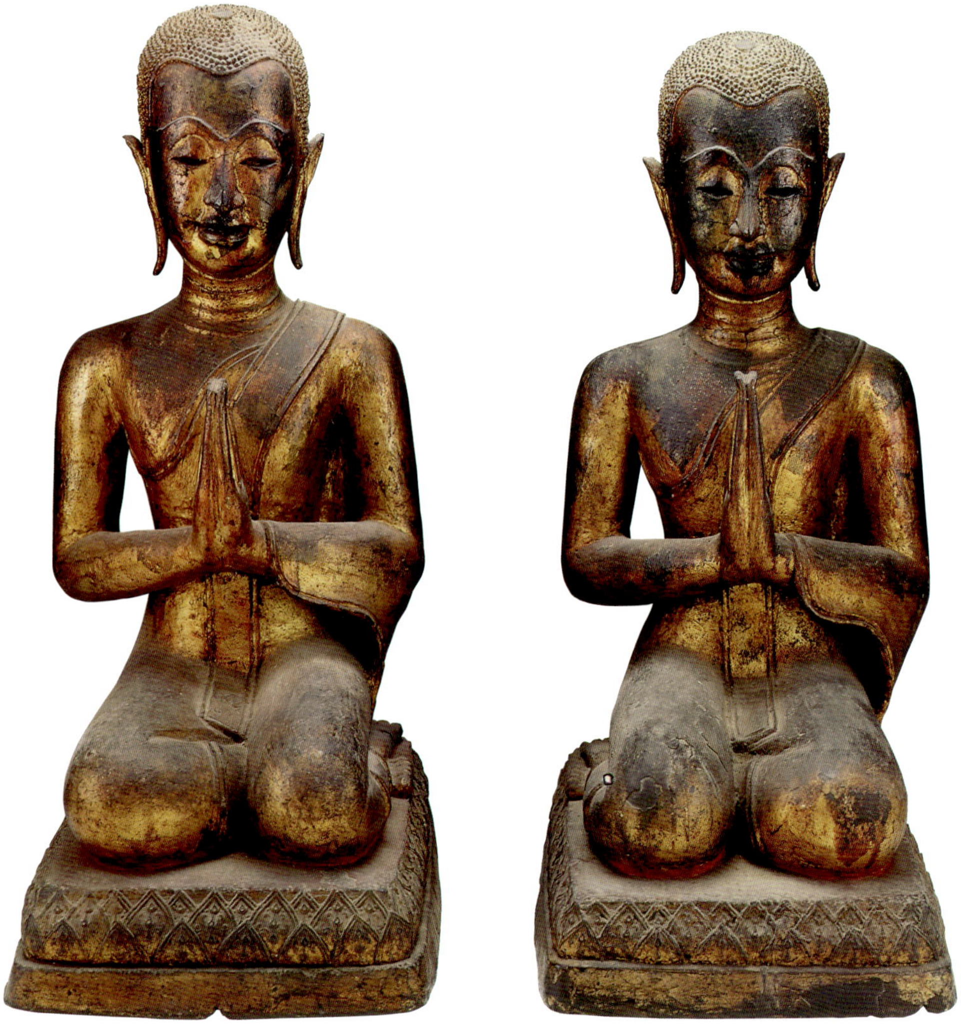

Devotees and attendants are prominently placed before a central Buddha on an altar (Plate 11). Pairs of attendants are often intended to represent Sariputta and Moggallana, his two most dedicated disciples, who were converted to Buddhism when they heard the Buddhist creed "Whatever proceeds from causes, their causes have been stated, as also [the means of] their cessation." During the Bangkok period in central Thailand, attendants were generally cast in bronze or brass, then gilded. Like images of the Buddha, they would be among the gifts donated to a temple. These two monks press their hands together in the gesture of respect and salutation *(anjali mudra)* to pay obeisance to the Buddha; the simplicity of their clothing and the bases upon which they sit suggest a date during the early Bangkok period.

Not all imagery is limited to the Buddha and his attendants; a favorite story of the nineteenth century tells of the monk Phra Malai whose accumulated merit allowed him to visit the many hells, then ascend to Culamani Chedi in Tavatimsa heaven, where he discoursed on what he had seen. The tale, coming from a Sinhalese source, is often depicted in manuscript painting. In sculptural representations (Plate 12), Phra Malai wears his monk's robe and carries his alms bowl over his shoulder, while at his feet, the beseeching damned stretch their arms toward him. There is a separate hell for each evil deed one commits; for instance, adulterers are driven naked up thorn trees by ferocious dogs that bite at them from below, while large birds pick at their eyes and flesh from above.

Bronze is the usual medium for Bangkok-period sculpture, but the tradition of woodcarving asserts itself in images such as this Buddha (Plate 13), whose jewelry, headdress, clothing, and the base upon which he stands are worked in repoussé metal. The sweet and delicate face indicates Burmese influence, which is interesting, as the details of the robe and headdress suggest a date in the late nineteenth century, somewhat distant from the eighteenth-century Burmese incursions into Thailand. Two stylistically related images are placed on the tall altar bearing the Emerald Buddha in the *ubosot* of Wat Phra Kaeo, and we might surmise this piece would also have been placed on the altar replicating that temple, though no papers have yet been found that describe exactly where the Duke Collection's individual objects were intended to be placed.

The abundance of hardwoods in Thailand and Burma provided the materials for artisans to create wood carving for all purposes. Architectural decoration includes doors, window frames, eaves and the struts supporting them, gables, and details of the interior. The Thai houses purchased for the planned Thai Village Project were not as heavily embellished as religious buildings, but their furnishings provided surfaces that welcomed detail. The collection includes many of these finely carved furnishings, which would have filled the interiors of the Thai houses.

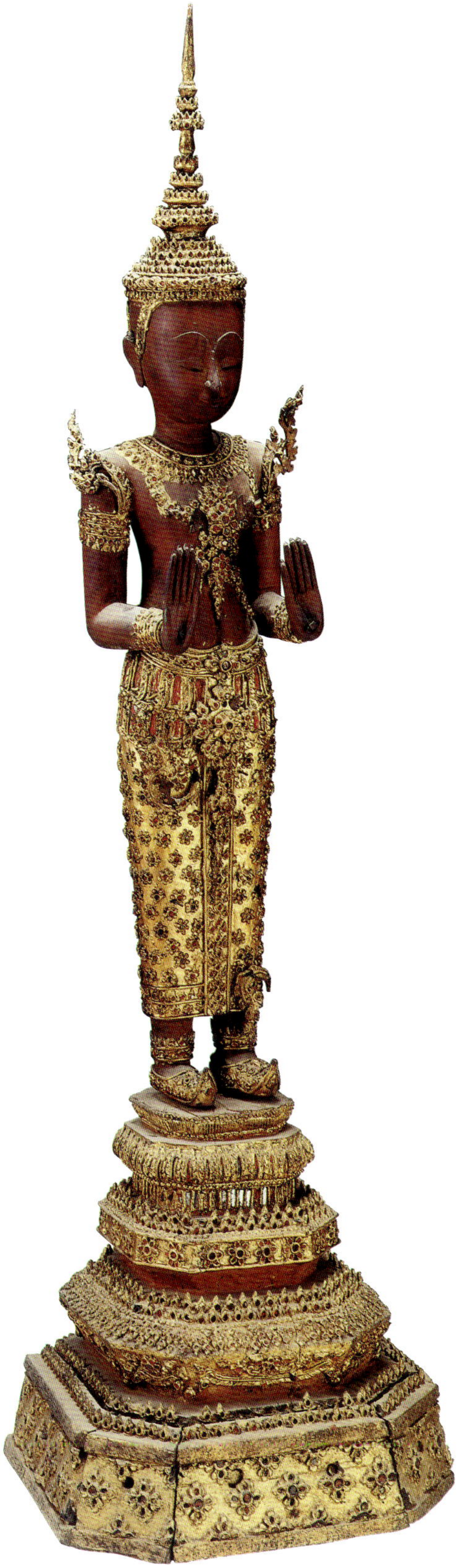

Plate 13 A wooden Bangkok-period Buddha (h. 86.5 cm), with metal used for his clothing and headdress, is close in style to two Buddhas on the altar of the Temple of the Emerald Buddha, Wat Phra Kaeo, Bangkok.

right **Plate 14** A Thai woman would sit on the floor or on a low platform to avail herself of a mirror, often elaborately carved and gilded like this one. AAM

below **Plate 15** Chinese-style motifs were popular in Thailand during the 19th century. The Buddha images (average h. 132 cm) on and around this Chinese-style bed (h. 226 cm) are Burmese in the Mandalay style of the 19th century.

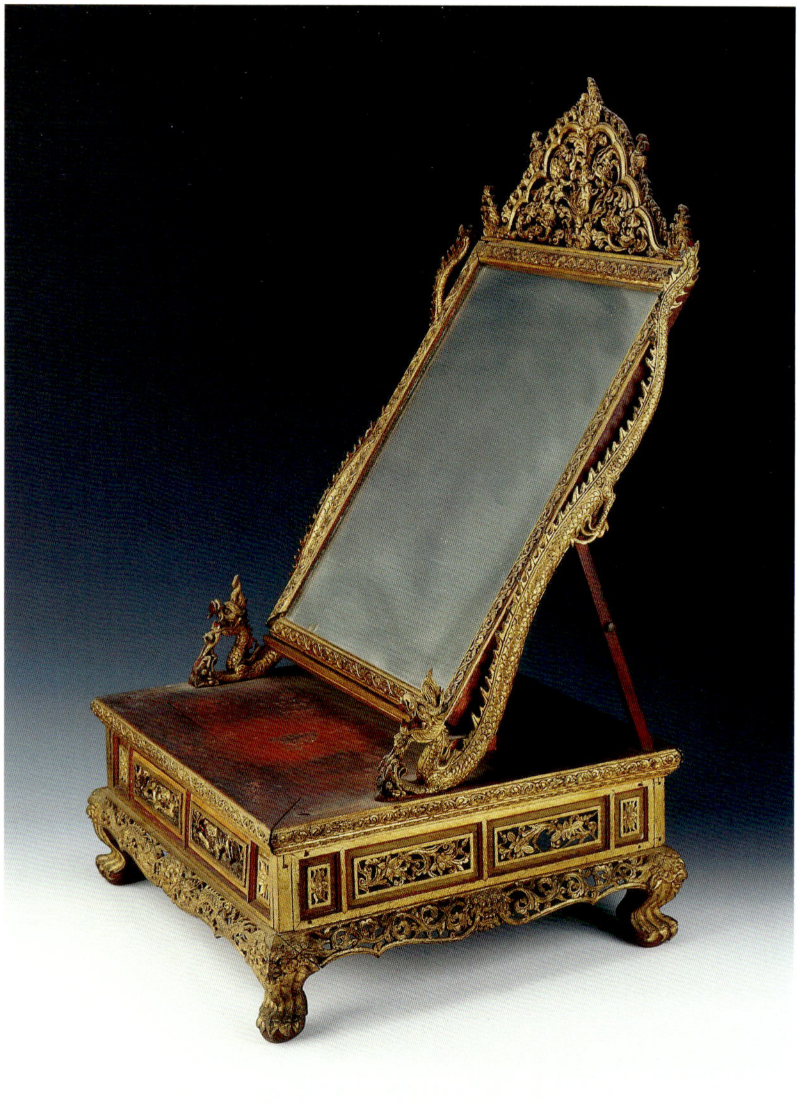

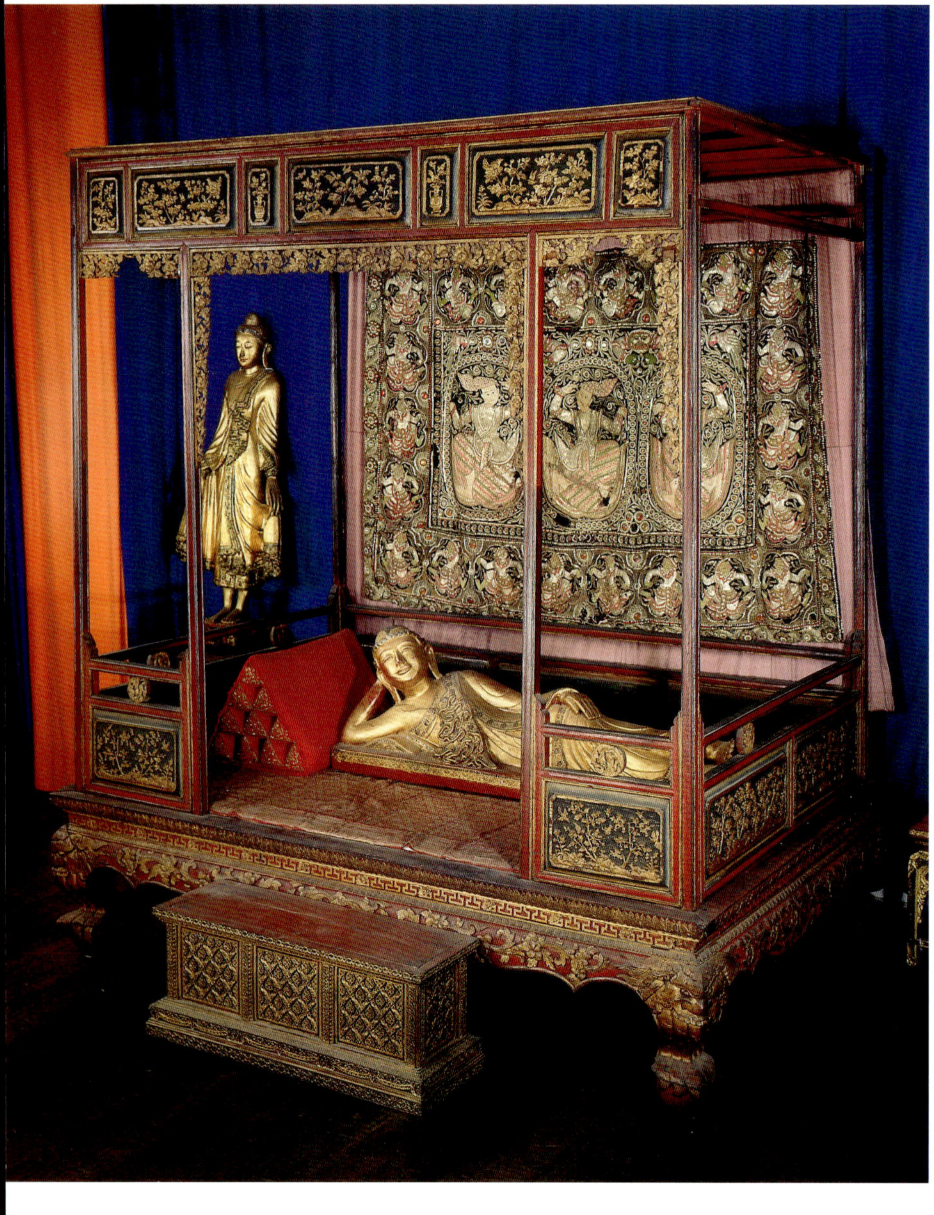

An aristocratic woman's boudoir would have held a mirror (Plate 14) for her daily toilet. Placed on a low wooden platform (similar to the platform under the Burmese altar [Plate 27, p. 49]), the mirror might have been accompanied by a rack for hanging a towel or face cloth (see Plate 56, p. 80, for such a rack) and other toiletries. Before assimilating Western influence, the Thais did not use chairs but instead sat or knelt on a cushion on the floor, or in this case, on the platform in front of the mirror. Animal motifs are incorporated into the details of the carving. The *naga*, looking very much like a Chinese dragon, swoops down along the edge of the mirror, and small lion heads emerge in the details of the base as well as the lion foot. The openwork on the lower frame is also indicative of Chinese influence, and this, taken with the dragon *naga*, suggests a mid nineteenth-century date, when both Western and Chinese motifs were embraced.

A piece most certainly of this time is the Chinese-style bed (Plate 15) that Miss Duke displayed, surrounded by nineteenth-century Burmese Buddhas, in the Coach Barn. Clawed lion feet support the piece, which is intricately carved with floral motifs, fretting, and landscapes on the base and the canopy. Red and black lacquer and gilding accentuate the carved details. A more discreetly decorated, though intricately carved bench (Plate 16) was also displayed in the Coach Barn. The overall floral medallion pattern of the backrest, with its inlaid glass and deeply cut flowers, contrasts with the broader carving on seat and legs and may indicate the back and base were carved at different times.[16]

Plate 16 Furniture is often elaborately carved, like the fine backrest and base of this Thai bench (l. 189 cm). AAM

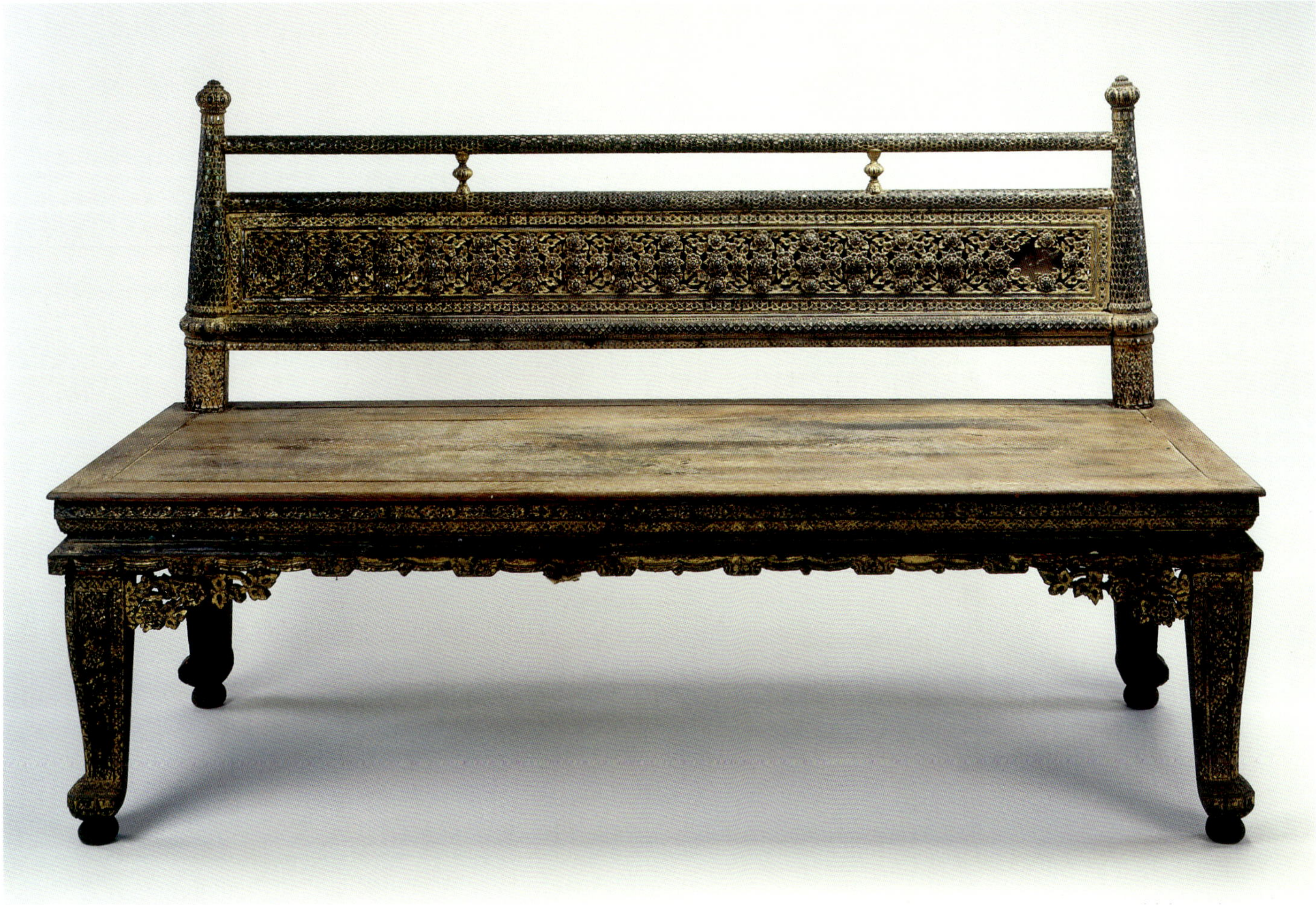

Plate 17 Thai manuscript cabinets can be painted, lacquered, or carved. This one (h. 216.5 cm) has scenes of the Himaphan forest. WAM

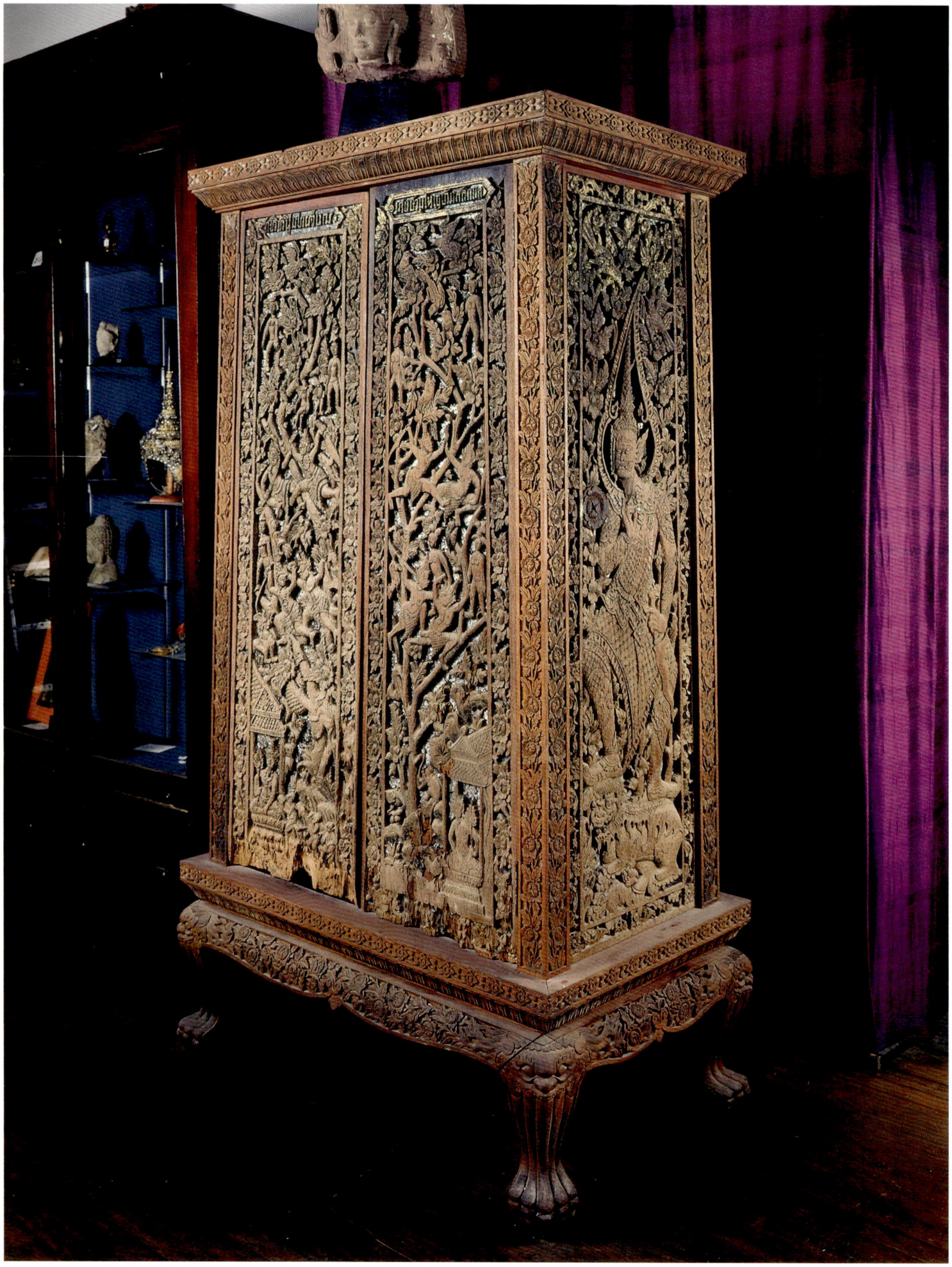

The intention in furnishing the Thai Village was to recreate a typical village, although these elaborate pieces of furniture from upper-class homes or palaces would have indicated a prosperous urban, rather than rural, setting. It would have been necessary to include some of the religious art in the houses, even though both the large open pavilion, the *ubosot*, and the Royal Pantheon would have provided for their display.

One other type of furnishing that incorporated fine carving is the cabinet with shelves and two doors that swing out. These practical containers found a place in both temples as storage for manuscripts, and in the home, for clothing and household items. Cabinets produced for the home were sometimes given to a temple, indicating the difficulty in identifying the provenance of many pieces. One large carved cabinet in the Duke Collection (Plate 17) incorporates a scene of Himaphan forest where a magic wishing tree, thick with fruit of young maidens, grows. It has been suggested that the cabinet doors originally functioned as doors to a room and have been refitted to the cabinet; thus they may be from the Ayutthaya period.

LAN NA SCULPTURE

A different sculptural tradition evolved in northern Thailand. Historically, the inland areas of Southeast Asia form a cultural and artistic tradition separate from that of the coastal regions. Their remoteness from international trading centers preserved a continuity of traditional culture that remained relatively untouched into the nineteenth century. The area was first ruled by Thai peoples in the thirteenth century, when King Mengrai established the kingdom of Lan Na, the land of a million rice fields, which extended from Upper Burma into Laos. The Buddhist monasteries had links to monasteries in Sri Lanka and northern India, and the sculpture from the fourteenth and fifteenth centuries reflects their influence. A bronze, kneeling devotee (Plate 18) of the sixteenth to seventeenth centuries[17] illustrates how the earlier, fuller figure type was replaced by an attenuation of body and limbs that continued into subsequent periods.

In northern Thailand, neighboring peoples exerted their influence, in particular the peoples of Yunnan, in southern China, and the Burmese, who ruled the area from the mid sixteenth century until 1774. At that time, the Tai peoples of the region, assisted by the Siamese, broke from Burmese rule and reestablished the independent state of Lan Na. Underpopulation in the region and a desire of the Tai princes to establish a formidable kingdom led to the resettlement of peoples from Laos, Burma, and the contiguous region of Sipsong Pan na (Xishuangbanna Autonomous Prefecture) in Yunnan Province, China.[18] Like the peoples

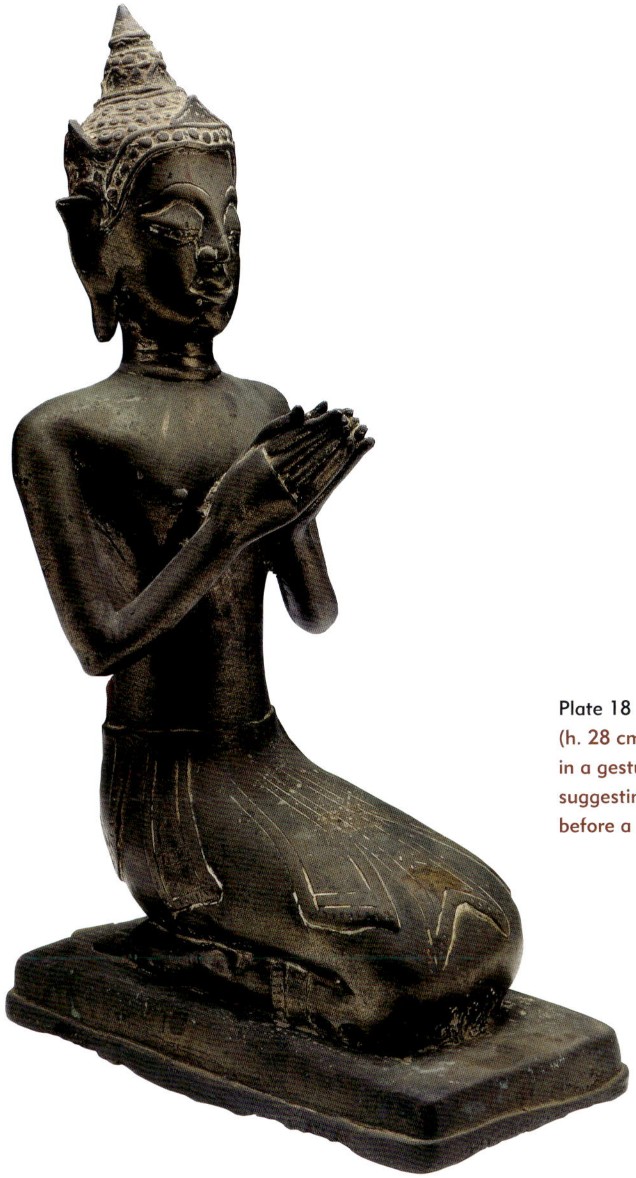

Plate 18 This Thai figure (h. 28 cm) holds his hands in a gesture of obeisance, suggesting he was once placed before a Buddha. AAM

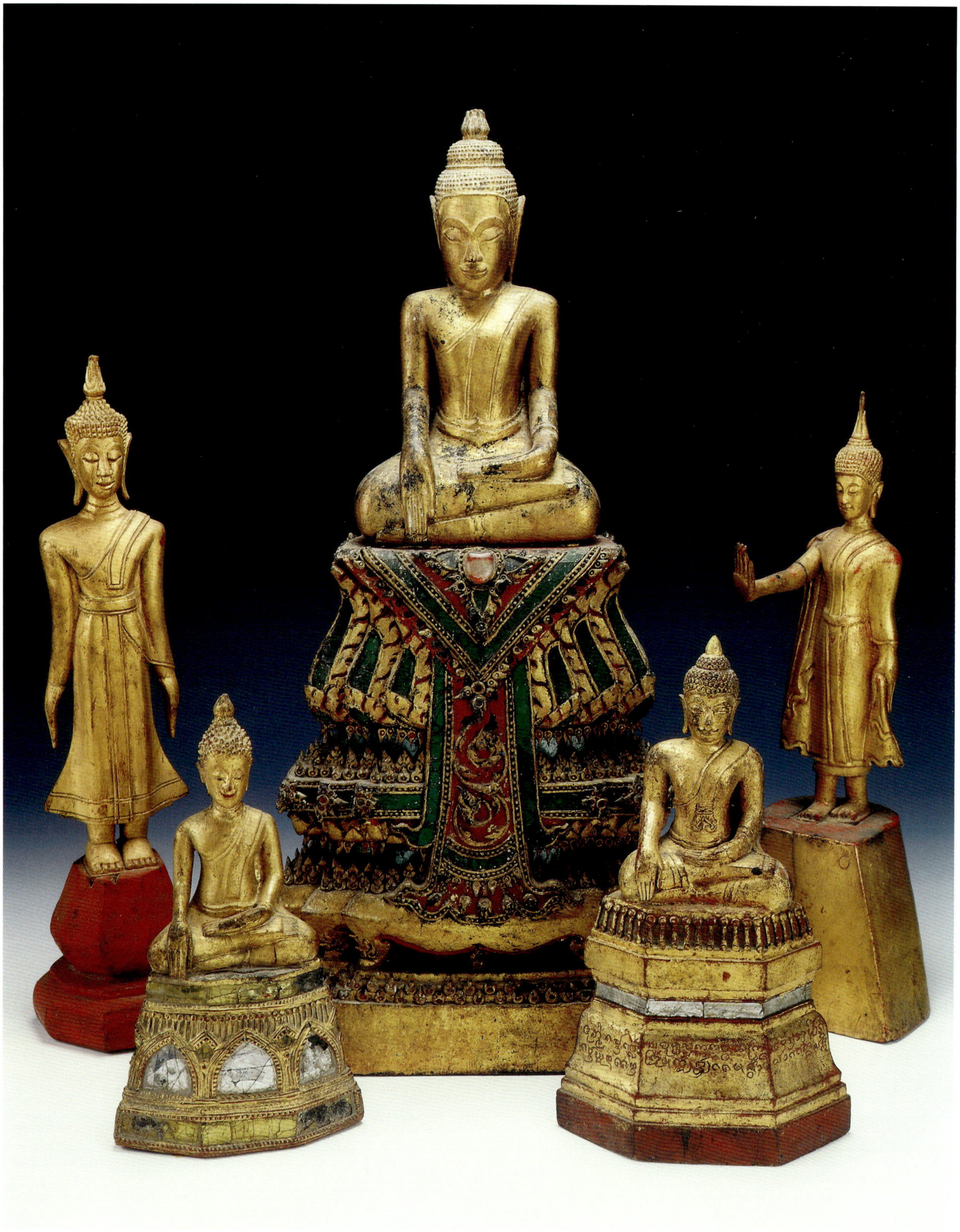

Plate 19 Small northern Thai wood sculptures of the Buddha (average h. 31 cm), inscribed with wishes for the attainment of merit by the donor, were given to temples. WAM

from Lan Na, they belong to the Tai-Kadai linguistic group and share customs and artistic antecedents.

Just as the kings of the Chakri dynasty (who remain the monarchy today) were asserting their legitimacy by building the city of Bangkok, so the Lan Na princes rebuilt the city of Chiang Mai. Much of the artistic remains in the north dates to the past 200 years. Wood was used extensively in the construction and decoration of monasteries, just as it was in Burma, the Shan States, and Laos, for hardwoods were abundant. A Lan Na chronicle, the *Tamnan Phra Kaen Chan*, cites the Buddha's permission to create wooden images in his likeness.[19]

Small sculptures of the Buddha in a variety of poses and gestures (Plate 19), and larger images, elaborately decorated and draped (Plate 20), adorned the altars of temples. Some sculptures are inscribed with dedications that include the date, the name of the donor, and then text such as: "I, Thao Wiset Bunsung, being the commissioner, establish this Buddha image together with my wife, sons, and daughters to uphold the religion assigning [the merit] to father and mother."[20] Since the act of creating an image or commissioning one accrues merit, it is not surprising to find that the principal image of any temple would have been surrounded by a multitude of Buddhas. Women and men without sons often sponsored at least one Buddha image during their lifetimes.[21]

Given the large size of the tall, thin Buddha with hands at his sides in a gesture known as 'calling for rain' in Laos and 'opening of the three worlds' in Thai, we might assume a wealthy person had commissioned it (Plate 20). He wears elaborate clothing that mimics the stiff felt or quilted formal attire of a Burmese king. Another stylistic influence is suggested by the unusual iconography of the 'calling for rain' pose, which was popular and seemingly developed in Laos. The use of inlaid glass, seen on the jeweled bands hanging over his clothing, is common throughout Burma, Laos, and northern Thailand.

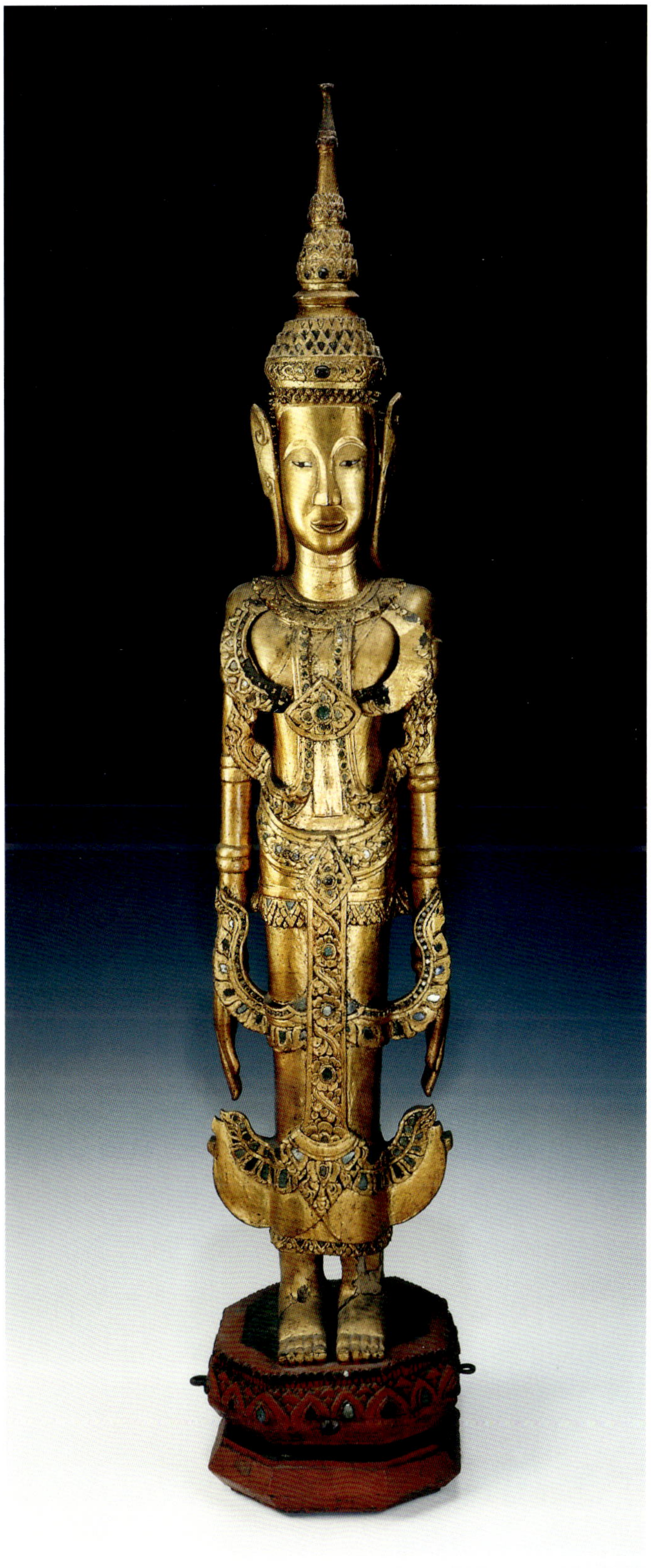

Plate 20 This northern Thai Buddha (h. 162 cm) holds his hands at his sides in a gesture known as 'calling for rain.'

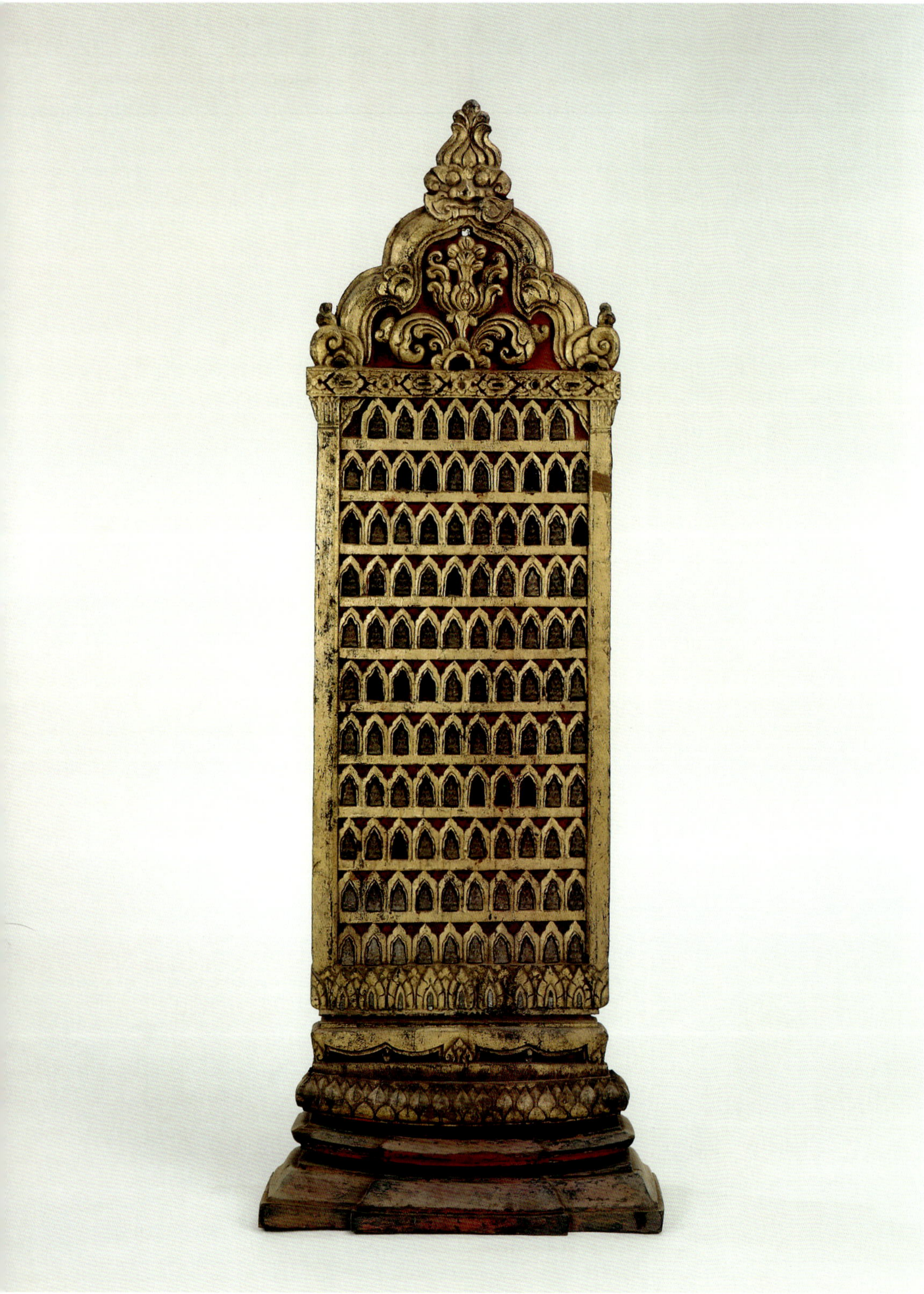

Another common sculptural form is the votive tablet *(phra phim)*, which is stamped using a clay, wood, or metal mold and damp clay. Tablets from a Theravada country, such as Thailand or Burma, generally feature an image of the Buddha. A monk or other pious individual can quickly accrue a quantity of merit by commissioning tablets, and this was probably the original intention of their makers. The tablets were often placed in a reliquary in the act of consecration. In Thailand in the nineteenth century, however, these small, portable tablets were adopted as amulets that protected the wearer from all types of evils and misfortune.[22] The apotropaic function of the votive tablets reflects the commingling of local spirit worship and Buddhism. By the seventeenth century, the Thai set these tablets in elaborate freestanding frames (Plate 21), which were placed in the temple before the altar, along with other offerings and images.

Another type of furnishing placed before the altar in front of the principal image, and also characteristic of the north, is the *sattaphan* or candleholder (Plate 22). The holder can be of any size, but it always supports seven candles, a possible reference to the seven mountains surrounding Mount Meru, considered the *axis mundi* or the center of the universe in Buddhist (and Hindu) cosmology. Intertwined *naga* characterize Lan Na candleholders, but floral motifs replace snakes in this example. The ubiquitous devotional figure, the *theppannom*, dominates the panel, hands pressed together in a worshipful pose. He bears lotuses, while below, the embodiment of the mythical planet Rahu swallows the moon, causing an eclipse, and monkeys attempt to thwart him by grabbing his elbows.

Plate 21 Votive tablets of stamped clay are considered auspicious throughout the Buddhist world; the making of them is an act of merit. In Thailand, votive plaques are sometimes set into stands (h. 115 cm) to be placed before an altar.

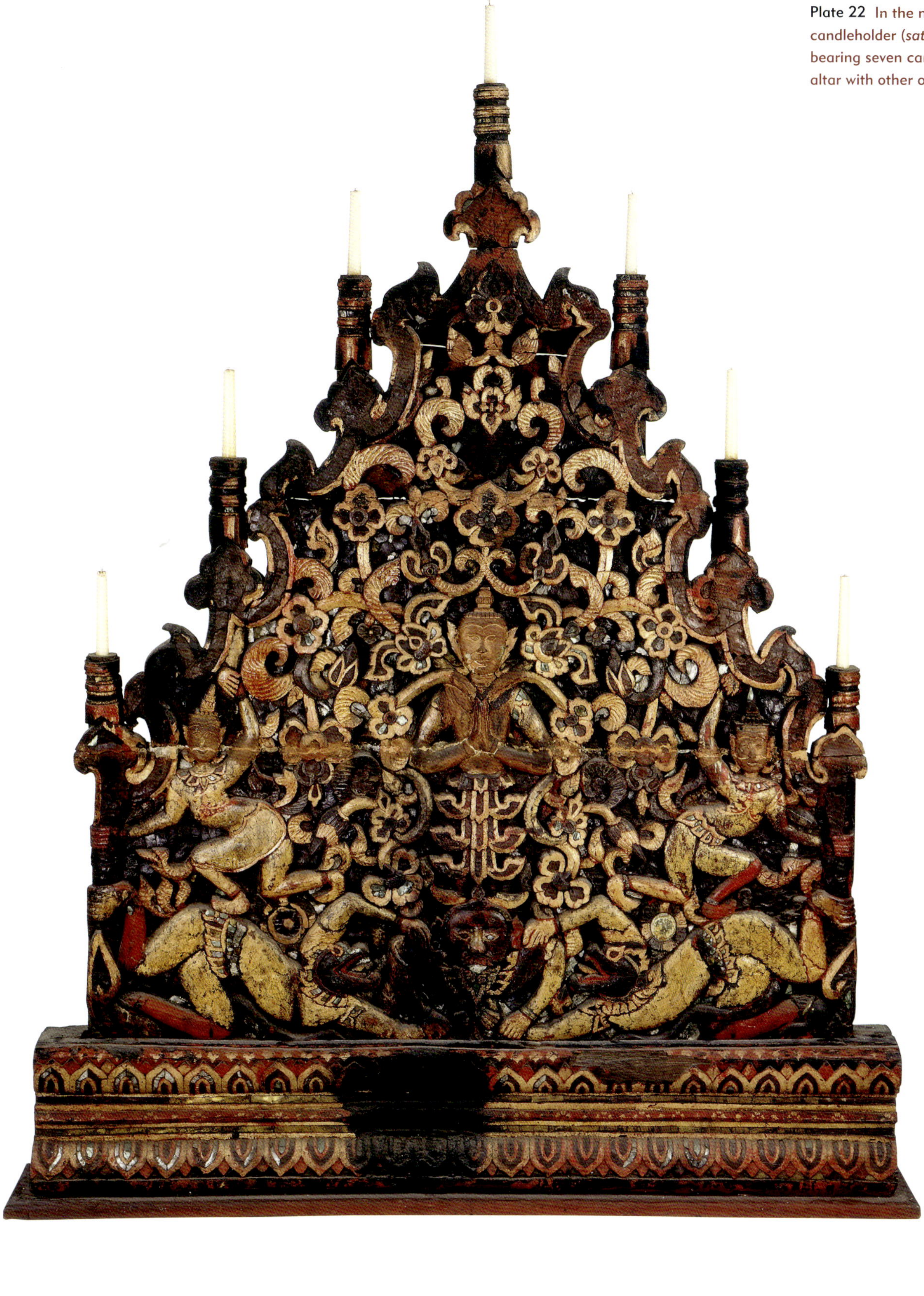

Plate 22 In the north of Thailand, a candleholder (*sattaphan;* h. 185.5 cm) bearing seven candles is set before the altar with other offerings. WAM

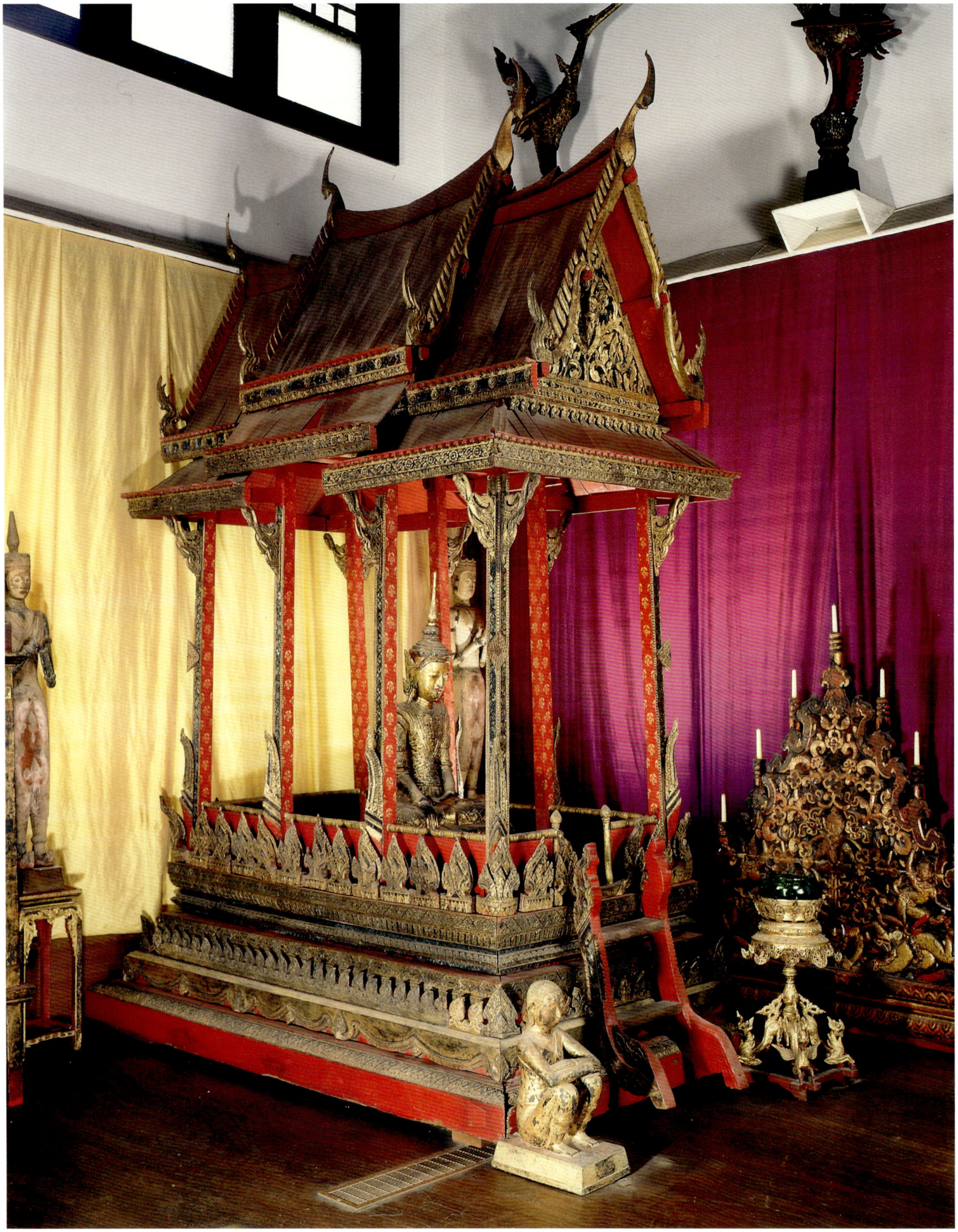

Since both monks and laypeople sit on the floor of the temple, little furniture is needed other than cabinets for the manuscripts and a pulpit *(thammat)* where a monk sits to deliver a teaching or to lead the monks in a chant. Often these *thammat* are tall architectural structures in the form of a temple (Figure 12), like this example from central Thailand, and large enough to allow for more than one chanting monk to sit inside. Four dramatic *thammat* are included in the Duke Collection and, like this one, have been used as platforms to display sculpture in the Coach Barn in New Jersey. Black and red lacquer and carved surfaces enliven the base and the eaves of the roof, and the roof finial *(cho fa)*, a birdlike element, characteristically finishes its ridge and eaves. In the north of Thailand, this creature is considered to be a combination of swan and elephant, though it also seems to have *naga* antecedents. Although the tall proportions of the *thammat* differ from that of a northern Thai building with a roof that sweeps lower to the ground, the construction of the roof, with its multiple levels, is typical.

A more unusual *thammat* in the collection is a low seat (Plate 23) of eight-sided construction on which a single monk or abbot would sit to give his teachings. Fashioned of wood, it is decorated with red and black lacquer, gilt, and inlaid glass. Two gilt figures offering lotuses stand amid a floral pattern on the backrest, a pattern reminiscent of that on the candleholder.[23]

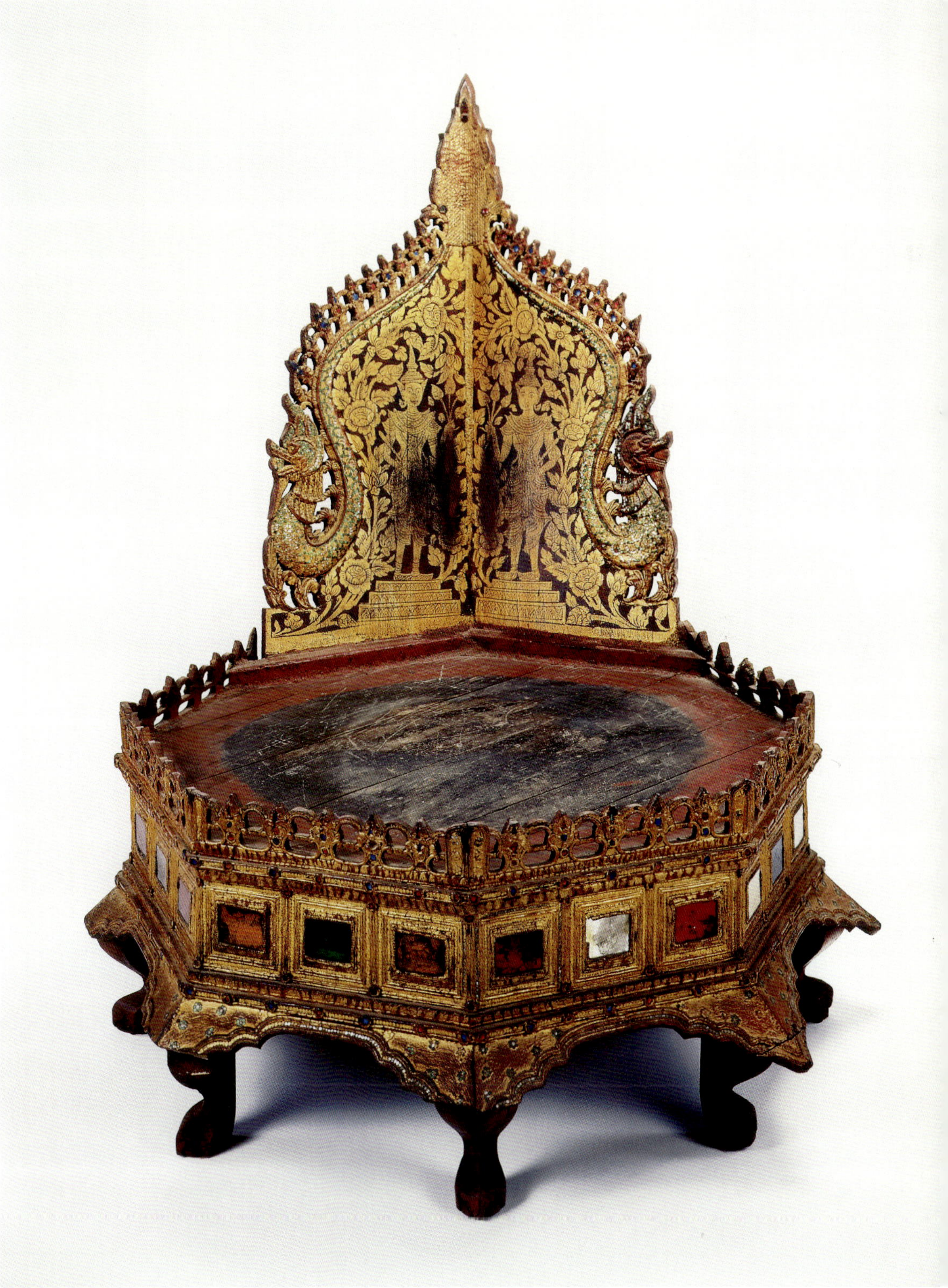

opposite **Figure 12** In central Thailand, the pulpit (*thammat;* h. 428 cm) can take many forms. There are four tall architectural examples in the Doris Duke Collection.

right **Plate 23** An abbot or monk giving instruction would have sat in this *thammat* (h. 38.5 cm) from the north of Thailand.

Plate 24 In the north of Thailand, the steps or the risers leading up to a pulpit (*thammat;* average h. 42 cm) are often carved in the shapes of animals.

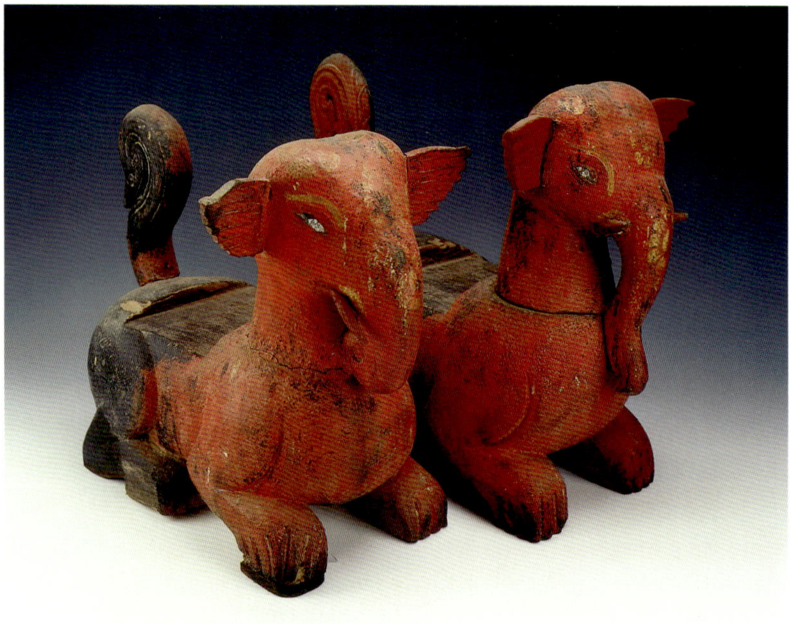

Plate 25 In northern Thailand, manuscript chests (h. 92 cm) with raised lacquer decoration *(thayo)* hold the sacred texts of a monastery.

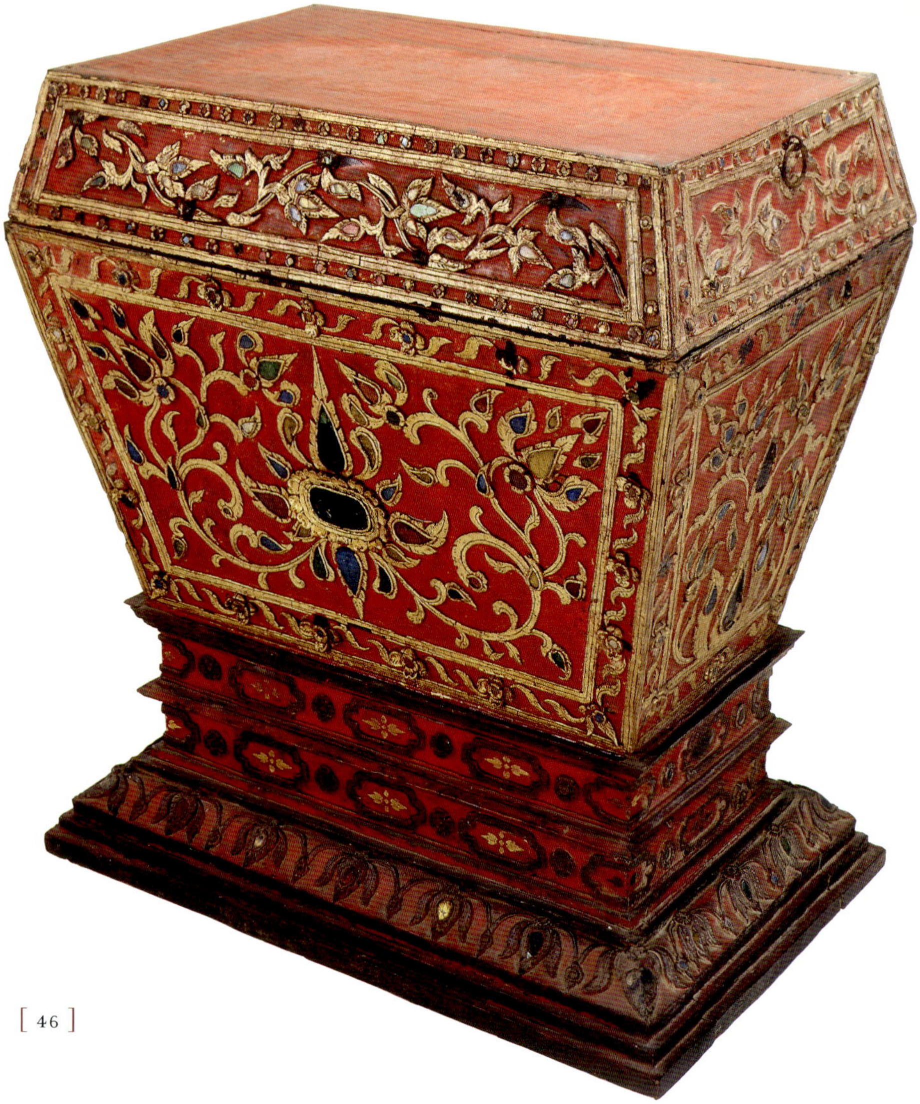

Some *thammat* have a more elevated base than this one, and they require steps to mount. These steps may be carved in the shape of animals or with supports of animals on either side of each step (Plate 24). The artist captures a lighthearted playfulness in these carvings of elephants, an animal greatly respected in Southeast Asia both for its great strength and for its role in many folktales and *jatakas*.

The other piece of furniture necessary to the monastery is the manuscript cabinet. The cabinets (Plate 25) produced in northern Thailand are radically different from the elegantly decorated examples from the central and southern areas of the country, which will be discussed in the chapter on painting (see Plates 31 and 47–50, pp. 56 and 70–73). The placement of the chest on a pedestal relates to pinched-waisted thrones used for images of the Buddha in Burma. Created of wood, they may be carved but more often include raised reliefs of *thayo,* a putty of lacquer sap mixed with clay, sawdust, or ash, a technique commonly used in Burma. Inlaid glass is also applied in abundance, in broad patterning that achieves more in the way of gaudy ostentation than delicacy. The tops of the chests are left unfinished, suggesting a cloth or some other object was placed on top. Burmese influence, in the style of the sculpture, material, and techniques, links the artwork of northern Thailand more closely to that of Burma than to the more urbane works of central Thailand.

BURMA (MYANMAR)

The Pyu peoples of northern Burma and the Mon of the south were the dominant forces in Burma until the tenth century. Then in 1057, King Anawrahta of Bagan, in central Burma, laid seige to the Mon city of Thaton, returning triumphant with the king, his artisans, and a set of the *Tipitika,* the sacred texts of Buddhism. Establishing Buddhism as the state religion, he began—and subsequent rulers continued—a building program that resulted in a city of thousands of temples and *chedi.* At the end of the thirteenth century, Bagan experienced a period of rapid decline, possibly as a result of Kublai Khan's incursions into Burma, but more probably because of a laxity on the part of the kings and the increased power of the religious elite.[24] With the decline of Bagan, the next three centuries saw a confusing series of changes of capitals and powers, ending in the eighteenth century in upper Burma in the area surrounding present-day Mandalay. (The Duke holdings of Burmese art date exclusively to the eighteenth to twentieth centuries.)

At the end of the eighteenth century, King Hsinbyushin invaded and leveled Ayutthaya, the capital of Thailand. Like King Anawrahta in the eleventh century, he returned home with members of the Thai royal family and dozens of artisans, whose work influenced that of Burmese artists. With the frequent change of capitals, a result of astrological predictions and calculations, artisans were constantly employed with new building projects and with reconstructing buildings, which were dismantled and moved from one location to the next. Monasteries were built in wood, like the palaces, and adorned with extensive carving; Buddha images and *nat* (indigenous spirits)—made of marble, bronze, wood and dry lacquer—along with crafts in a variety of media, filled the temple compounds. After King Hsinbyushin's death, his son Bodawpaya and subsequent rulers began a period of conflict with the British, which ended with the British conquest in 1885.

The Burmese practice Theravada Buddhism and propitiate the *nat,* who are known to be volatile and easily offended. In the eleventh century, King Anawrahta, in his zeal to promote Buddhism as the national religion, banned *nat* worship, but he soon realized he was alienating the people from the very religion he propounded. Rescinding his order, he allowed images of the thirty-seven *nat,* who are believed to live on Mount Popa near Bagan, to be placed in a building on temple grounds. It is a measure of the adaptability of Buddhism that *nat* shrines remain a powerful presence in Buddhist establishments to this day. *Nat,* a word related to the Sanskrit word for 'lord,' are nature spirits tied to specific locations or drawn from legendary or actual historical personages.[25] The most frequently propitiated spirit is the Mahagiri *nat,* who protects the household and is displayed in the southeast corner of a house as a coconut wrapped in a red and white cloth (Figure 13). Aung-zwa-ma-gyi, formerly a soldier in the royal army of Bagan at the end of the twelfth century, was raised to

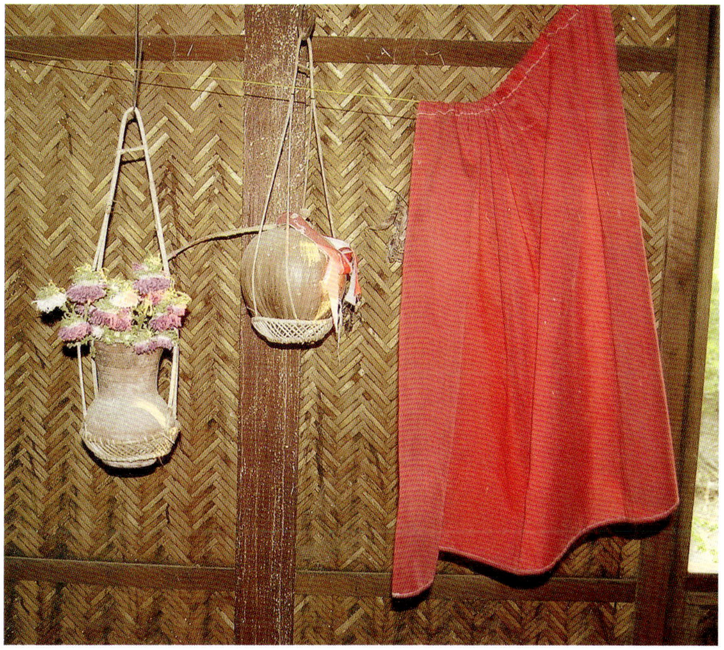

Figure 13 The Mahagiri *nat* is the most important of the indigenous spirits of Burma and is worshiped in the form of a coconut in most households. This one is from Minnanthu Village, Bagan.

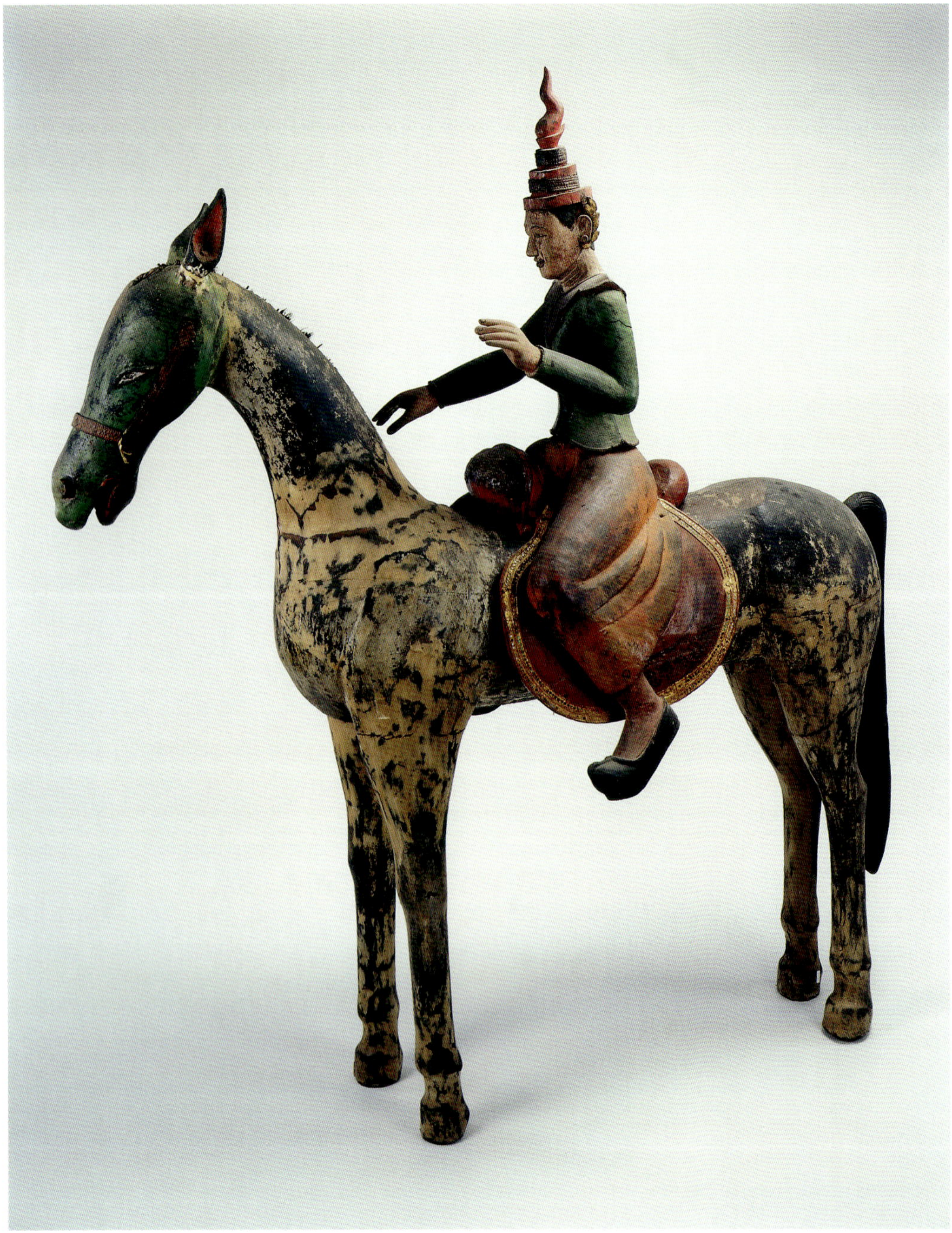

Plate 26 Aung-zwa-ma-gyi is a historical figure who achieved the status of a spirit (*nat;* h. 152.5 cm) in 12th-century Burma.

the status of *nat* after serving his crown prince faithfully. *Nat* are identifiable by various attributes, and he wears a uniform and is depicted on a white horse (Plate 26). When King Anawrahta made Buddhism the national religion, he had the foresight to include the Buddha as the supreme *nat*.

Images of the Buddha have been made throughout Burma since the religion first made its way to the area in the sixth century, but the Mandalay-style Buddha (taking its name from the last Burmese capital before the period of British rule) has become the quintessential example of Burmese art (Plate 27). The sweet, childlike face, elaborately layered and folded drapery, and the entire surface, brilliant with gold and inlaid with sparkling glass, combine to form an image both ethereal and fantastic. To the Westerner, its golden jewels seem to contradict the monastic vow taken by the Buddha, but to the Buddhist devotee, this great personage is deserving of royal attire. Again, reference to his magical appearance before the heretic king Jambupati is made.

The most common iconography for the Mandalay Buddha shows him standing (Plate 15, p. 36); seated with his hand in earth-touching gesture (*bhumisparsha mudra,* Plate 27); or lying on his side in death, the *parinibbana* (Plate 15, p. 36). During the period when the collection was installed at Duke Farms, Miss Duke took particular care of this Buddha, carefully dusting it herself whenever she visited the Coach Barn.[26] She also favored one of the most dramatic and imposing objects in the Duke Collection, an altar in which the Mandalay-style Buddha is placed (Plate 27).[27] She had displayed it in the hallway to Shangri La during the years the collection was stored at her Honolulu estate (Figure 9, p. 19).

The installation of the altar in the Coach Barn incorporated Burmese and central and northern Thai Buddhas and attendants placed on finely carved offering tables laden with offering paraphernalia. Manuscript cabinets flanked the sides of the elaborate altar, the focal point in a room bursting with artworks. Miss Duke, a very spiritual woman, frequently placed incense, flowers, and lighted candles before this altar.[28]

Plate 27 An elaborate Burmese altar (h. approx. 345 cm) with a Mandalay-style Buddha (h. 51 cm).

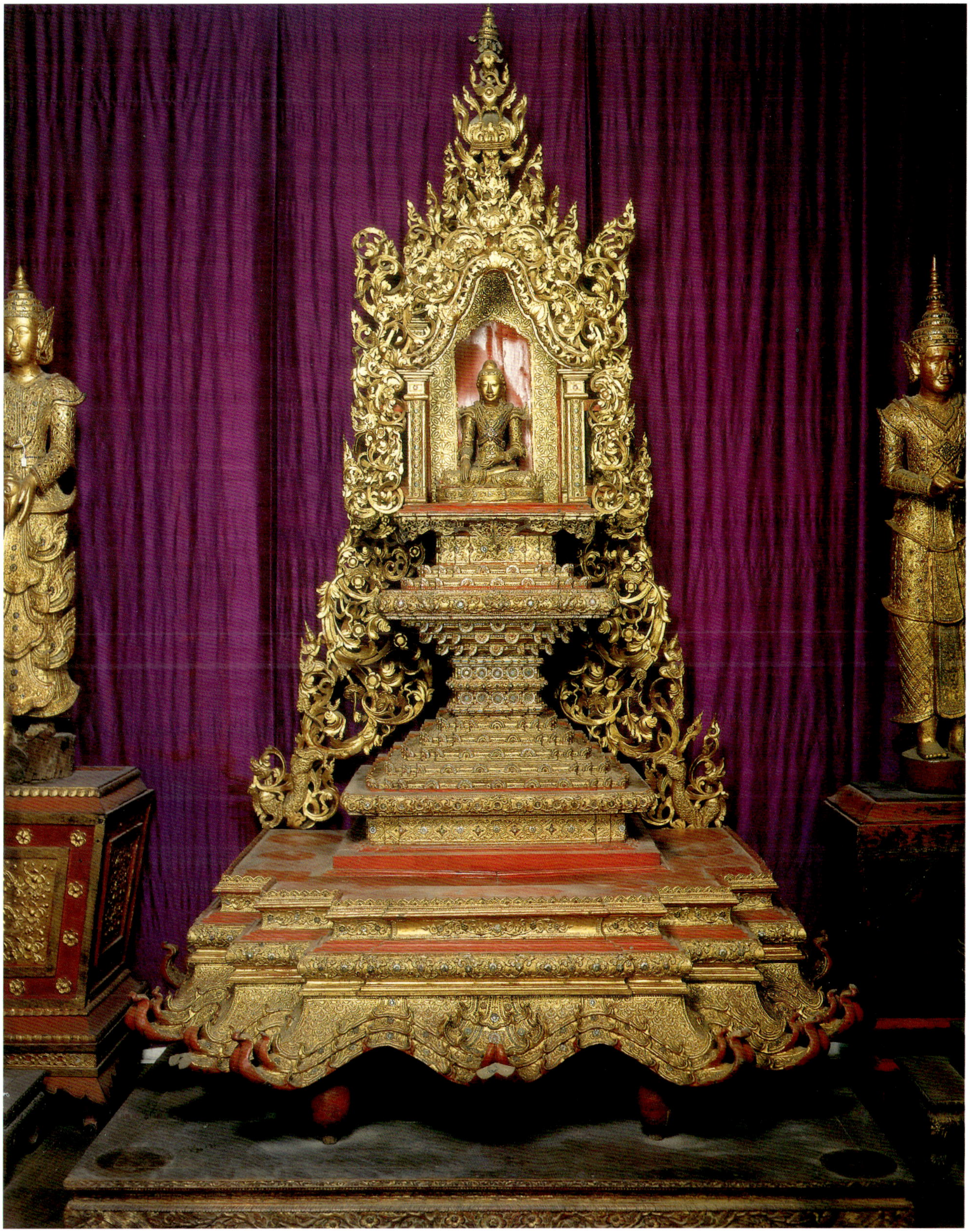

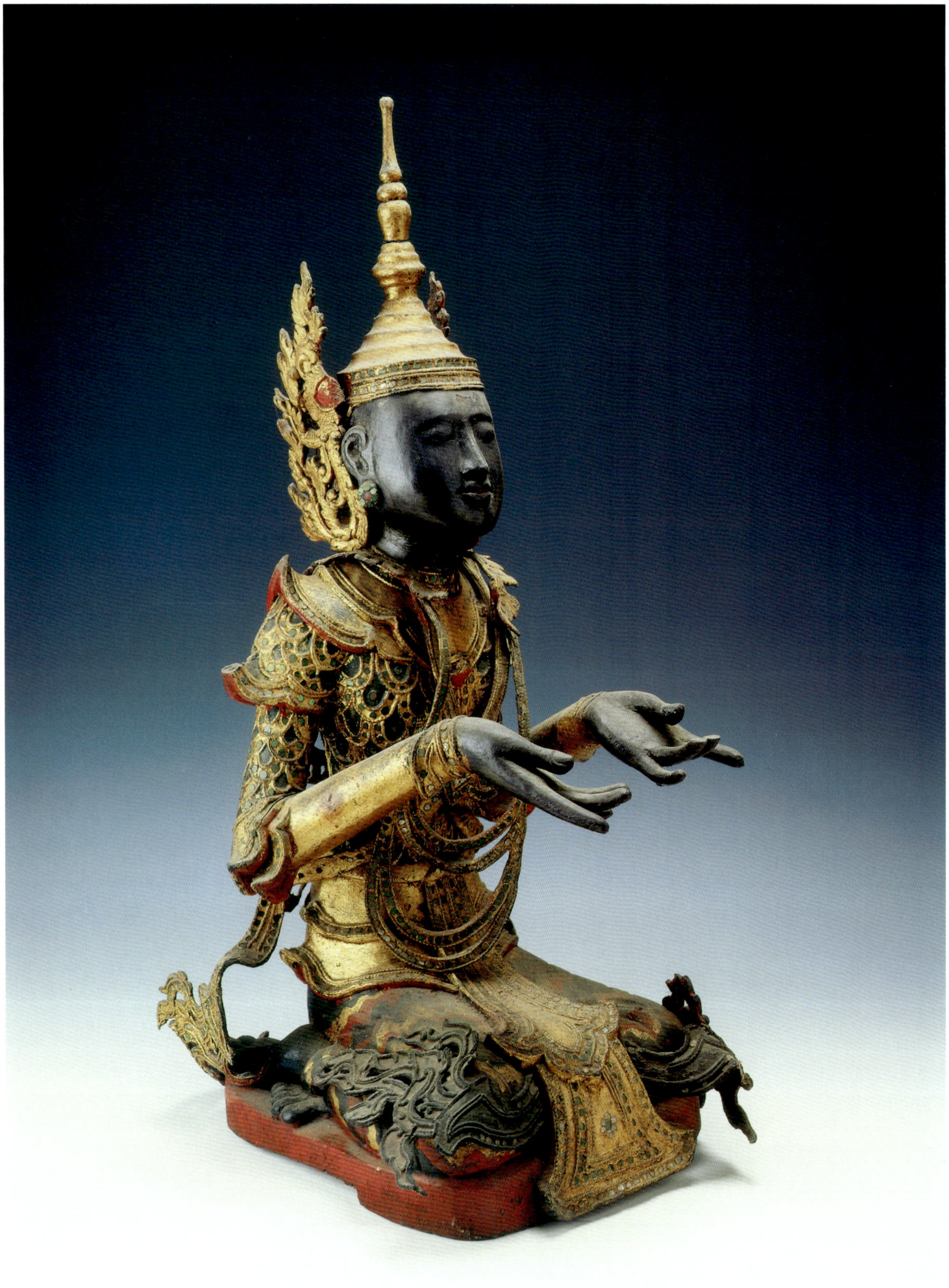

Plate 28 As in Thailand, the Buddhist altar in Burma includes images of devotees (h. 61 cm). This figure, with his flying draperies and sweet face, is particularly engaging. WAM

It was a fitting choice, for the variety of sculptures on and surrounding it effectively mirrors the breadth and depth of her passion for the objects she collected. Thrones of this type are still used in the temples surrounding Inle Lake in the Shan States on the eastern borders of Burma (Figure 15), though the center of production for these thrones seems to have been Mandalay.[29]

Bronze, wood, dry lacquer, and marble are the most common media for works of this later period, and in some instances, wood and marble are combined, the head and hands made of marble, and the body of wood. Other media are also combined (Plate 28).[30] The artist, not content with the three-dimensionality of the wooden figure, has added flying drapery of leather studded with glass, while investing this devotee with the guileless expression of one whose abode is Mount Meru. The Buddhist altar often includes multiple Buddhas and devotional figures; this sculpture would have been placed in front of and below the figure he revered.

Dry lacquer, a method developed in China and practiced throughout East Asia, is sometimes used to fabricate Buddha images (Figure 14 and p. 23). The earliest example known in Burma dates to the eighteenth century. The first step in making a dry-lacquer image involves producing a clay form. The artist then coated it with ash paste, covered it with a lacquer-soaked cloth, then coated that with *thayo*, a putty of lacquer sap and sawdust. Once the putty dried, the desired details could be tooled into the surface.[31] Images of quite large size were fashioned in this manner, most in Mon-ywa district. This Buddha is an excellent example of the possibilities inherent in the technique and of Shan taste, for the artists sold most of their images in the Shan States.[32] Many large lacquer images remain in the temples of the Shan States (Figure 15), where the people are of Tai descent. Burmese claim that the figure known as Nan Paya, in Salay, just south of Bagan, is the largest dry-lacquer Buddha in Burma; it is possible to walk inside this image. In Burma, artisans no longer create

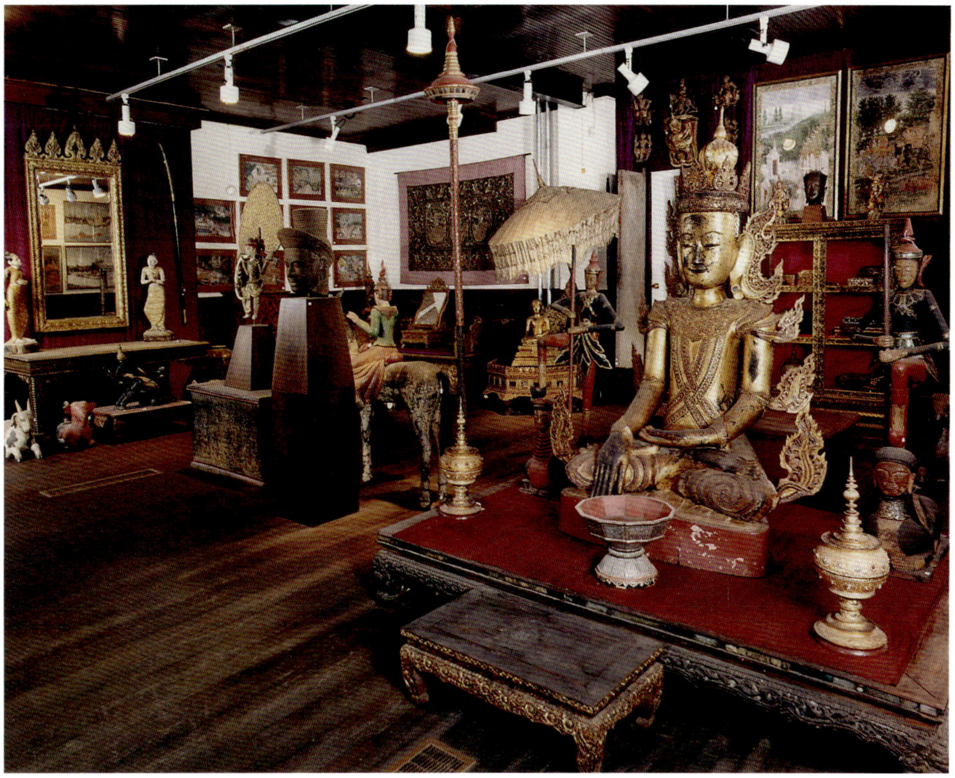

above **Figure 14** This large Burmese Buddha (h. 181.5 cm) is a fine example of Burmese use of dry lacquer. (Also see p. 23.) WAM

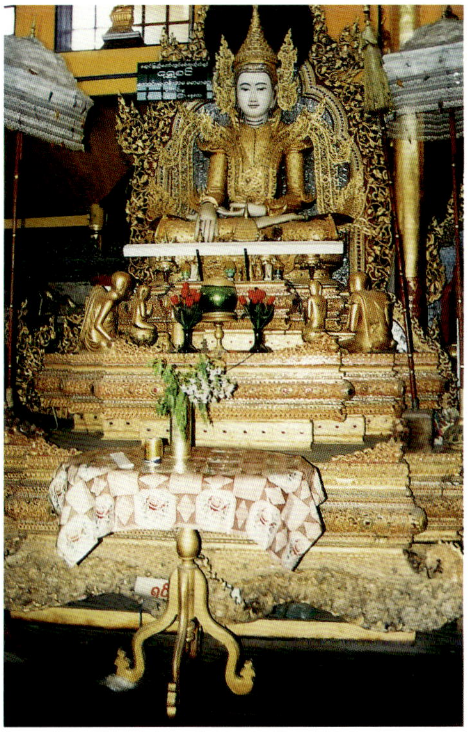

left **Figure 15** Thale monastery, Inle Lake, Burma. Buddha images and larger elaborate altars continue to be used at monasteries in the Shan States.

Plate 29 Standardized, graduated weights (average h. 13 cm) cast as elephants, birds, or lions, have been used for centuries in Burma. WAM

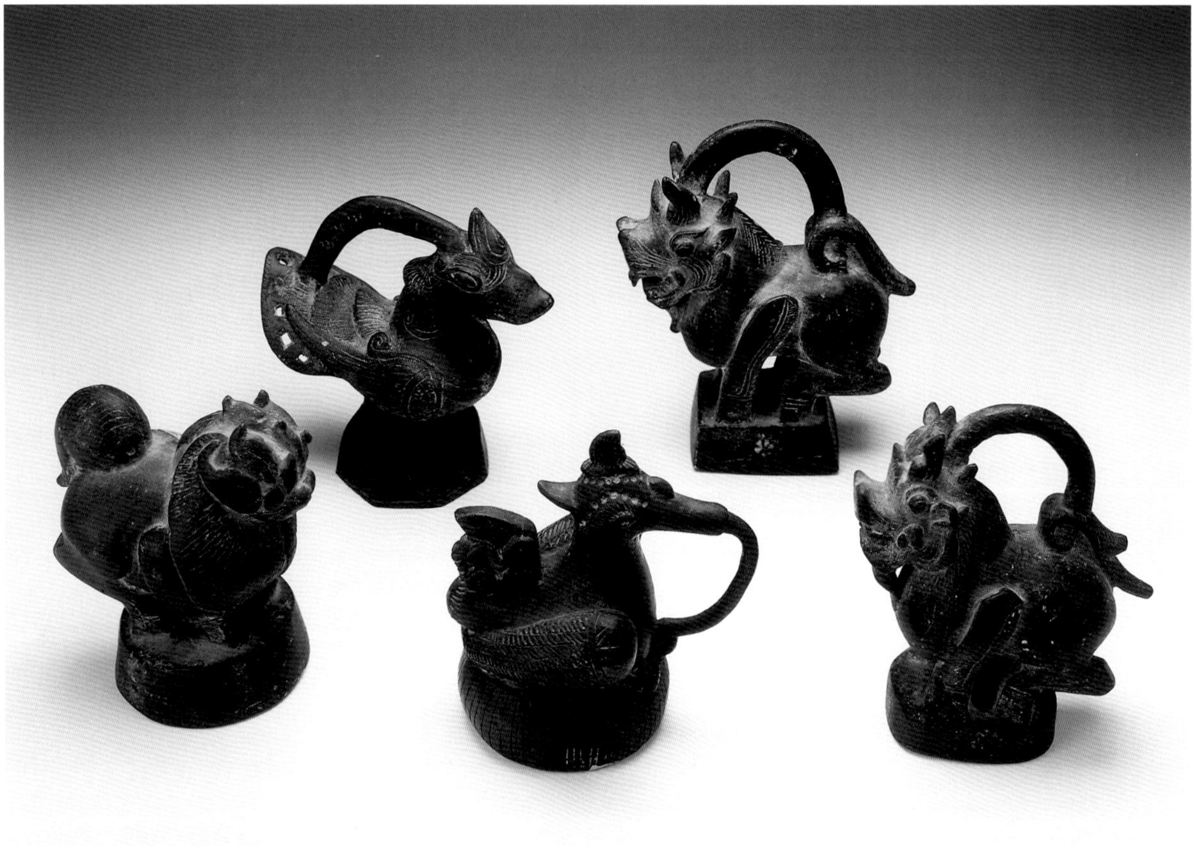

dry-lacquer images; use of the technique died out in the twentieth century.

Finally, a group of sculptures that served a practical purpose should be mentioned, as the Duke Collection includes quite a number of these delightful objects. Graduated weights of a feline, elephantine, or birdlike shape have been made in Burma since the fifteenth century for use in trade, though the practice of using them has died out in the past century.[33] These high-lead bronze standardized weights were fabricated under governmental controls; chronicles tell us that in the eighteenth century, the use of weights not made in the palace was a criminal offense.[34] Although certainly mass-produced for a mundane purpose, the sculptural quality of the animals has an obvious appeal (Plate 29). The high, sloping hexagonal base of the bird (back left) indicates that it is a nineteenth-century product, while the smaller bases of some of the other weights indicate an earlier date in the seventeenth to eighteenth centuries. Each of the weights in this group is from a separate set.

NOTES

1. DDCF Archives, SEAAC.8, inventory of art objects; date of purchase 5/20/60.

2. Donald Swearer, *The Buddhist World of Southeast Asia* (New York: State University of New York, 1995), 6.

3. David Chandler, *A History of Cambodia* (Boulder, Colorado: Westview Press, 1983), 16.

4. The flaring, ridged crown of this example relates to other bronzes from Phimai, though the facial features are not so bold as those. See Hiram W. Woodward, Jr., et al., *The Sacred Sculpture of Thailand: The Alexander B. Griswold Collection, The Walters Art Museum* (Bangkok: The Trustees of the Walters Art Museum, 1997), plates 70, 73, and 74, pp. 77 and 79.

5. Hiram W. Woodward, Jr., has suggested emanated Buddhas such as these indicate both the Buddhas of the past and the Miracle of Sravasti; see "The Bayon-period Buddha Image in the Kimbell Art Museum," *Archives of Asian Art*, 32 (1979): 72–83.

6. The number of Buddhas is sometimes also twenty-four.

7. Textual evidence provides only two explanations for the crown. One is the Jambupati tale. The other lies in the practice of Vajrayana Buddhism (which we know was practiced in Southeast Asia, in particular at Phimai, at the time this piece was made), in which a crown denotes enlightenment.

8. A second sculpture in the Duke Collection, in which the aureole is detached from a crowned seated Buddha, includes the same small Buddha images in the flames.

9. It may have been carved in Suphanburi; for a comparison, see Woodward et al., *The Sacred Sculpture of Thailand*, 80, plate 75.

10. 'Tai' refers to speakers of the Tai language group. 'Thai' refers to citizens of Thailand.

11. For a discussion of these artistic traditions, see Woodward et al., *The Sacred Sculpture of Thailand*.

12. Cited by Dirk Van Der Cruysse (trans. Michael Smithies), *Siam and the West 1500–1700* (Chiang Mai, Silkworm Books, 1991), 52; Cornelis van Neijenrode, *Vertoog van de gelegenheid des koninkrijks Siam, 1621* (Account of the situation in the kingdom of Siam, 1621), in *Kroniek van het Historisch Genootschap gevestigd te Utrecht* (Chronicles of the Historical Society of Utrecht, 1871), vol. 27, 279–318.

13. Woodward et al., *The Sacred Sculpture of Thailand*, 233.

14. M.C. Subhadradis Diskul, *Art in Thailand: A Brief History* (Bangkok: Amarin Press, 1986), 30.

15. He might be interpreted as an image of Phra Malai, as is sometimes depicted in painting when he is discoursing with the gods in heaven. For an example of Phra Malai, with his right hand in a similar gesture and seated on a throne, see Henry Ginsburg, *Thai Manuscript Painting* (London: The British Library, 1989), plate 25.

16. See Naengnoi Punjabhan and Somchai Na Nakhonphanom, *The Art of Thai Wood Carving: Sukhothai, Ayutthaya, Ratanakosin* (Bangkok: Rerngrom Publishing Co., Ltd., 2535 B.E. [1992]), 188, for another example. Forrest McGill feels that the back and seat of the bench were constructed together.

17. For a dated Buddha (1509) of similar though more elaborate dress, see Ping Amranand and William Warren, *Lanna Style, Art and Design of Northern Thailand* (Bangkok: Asia Books Co., Ltd., 2000), 46. For comparable devotees, see Theodore Bowie, ed., *The Arts of Thailand: A Handbook of the Architecture, Sculpture and Painting of Thailand (Siam), and a Catalogue of the Exhibition in the United States in 1960–61–62* (Bloomington: Indiana University, 1960), plates 112, 137; and M.C. Subhadradis Diskul et al., *The Suan Pakkad Palace Collection* (Bangkok: Princess Chumbhot of Nagara Svarga, 1982), figure 31.

18. Susan Conway, *Silken Threads, Lacquer Thrones: Lan Na Court Textiles* (Chicago: Art Media Resources, 2002), 26. Throughout its history, war in Southeast Asia was waged to obtain laborers and increase population. In this instance, regional cities such as Chiang Mai, depopulated by warfare, had fallen into neglect.

19. Sanguan Chotisukharat, "Phra Kaen Chan Legend," *Conference on Lanna Thai Legends*, 2514 B.E. [1971] 66–68, as cited in Naengnoi Punjabhan, Aroonrut Wichienkeeo and Somchai Na Nakhonphanom, *The Charm of Lanna Wood Carving* (Bangkok: Rerngrom Publishing Co., Ltd., 2537 B.E. [1994]), 110.

20. Hans Penth, *Kham charuk thi than phra phuttharup nai Nakhon Chiang Mai (Inscriptions on the bases of Buddha images in the city of Chiang Mai)*, (Bangkok: Samnak Nayok Ratmontri [Office of the Prime Minister], 1976), 171, translated by Hiram W. Woodward, Jr. Example dates from 1920.

21. Naengnoi Punjabhan et al., *The Charm of Lanna Wood Carving*, 110–11.

22. For a lengthy discussion of votive tablets in Thailand, see M.L. Pattaratorn Chirapravati, *Votive Tablets in Thailand: Origins, Styles, and Uses* (Kuala Lumpur: Oxford University Press, 1997).

23. For a six-sided pulpit decorated with a devotional figure carrying flowers from Wat Rong Ngae, Pua District, Nan Province, see Naengnoi Punjabhan, *The Charm of Lanna Wood Carving*, 141.

24. Michael Aung-thwin, *Pagan: The Origins of Modern Burma* (Honolulu: University of Hawai'i Press, 1985), 28.

25. Maung Htin Aung, *Folk Elements in Burmese Buddhism* (Rangoon: U Hla Maung, 1959), 96–97. See also Sylvia Fraser-Lu, *Burmese Crafts, Past and Present* (Kuala Lumpur: Oxford University Press, 1994; reprint 2002), 5–7.

26. Cupie Singh, personal communication, 9/02.

27. For a similar altar, see John Lowry, *Burmese Art* (London: Her Majesty's Stationery Office, 1974), plate 1.

28. Cupie Singh, personal communication, 9/02.

29. Sylvia Fraser-Lu, personal communication, 10/02. She also pointed out that Burmese altars do not seem to be arranged in a systematic manner, unlike the Thai altar.

30. A similar figure, dated approx. 1850, is illustrated in Lowry, *Burmese Art*, plate 4.

31. Fraser-Lu, *Burmese Crafts: Past and Present*, 244. Ralph Issacs and T. Richard Blurton, *Visions from the Golden Land: Burma and the Art of Lacquer* (London: British Museum Press, 2000), 102.

32. Sylvia Fraser-Lu, personal communication, 10/02, and idem, *Burmese Crafts: Past and Present*, 244.

33. Donald Gear and Joan Gear, *Earth to Heaven: The Royal Animal-Shaped Weights of Burma* (Chiang Mai: Silkworm Books, 1992). See also Fraser-Lu, *Burmese Crafts: Past and Present*, 135.

34. Gear and Gear, *Earth to Heaven*, 10.

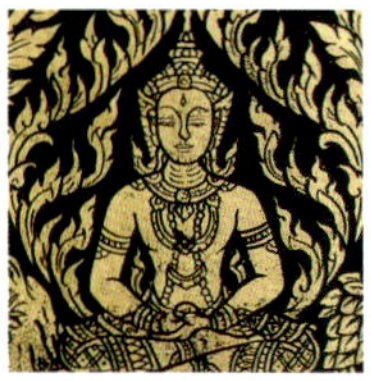

Painting

When Doris Duke and James Cromwell stopped in Bangkok on their honeymoon in 1935, we know that she visited at least one *wat* (Thai temple compound), probably Wat Phra Kaeo (Figure 8, p. 18). This visit would have been her first introduction to Thai painting, as murals adorn the interior walls of Thai temples from floor to ceiling. At Wat Phra Kaeo, she and Cromwell would have viewed scenes from the life of the historical Buddha and *jataka* tales along the side walls, the temptation of Mara above the entry doors, and the Traiphum (the three worlds of heaven, earth, and hell of Buddhist cosmology) behind the altar. Although the use of painted temple banners died out during the latter part of the twentieth century, in 1935, Miss Duke may well have seen them hung from the ceiling before the main altar at another temple.[1] She may not have seen smaller paintings on cloth during that first trip, but a photograph taken in 1957 assures us she saw them then (Figure 16). Given the approximately 200 paintings she purchased for the Southeast Asian collection, we can assume she had become enamored of these lovely though fragile works of art.

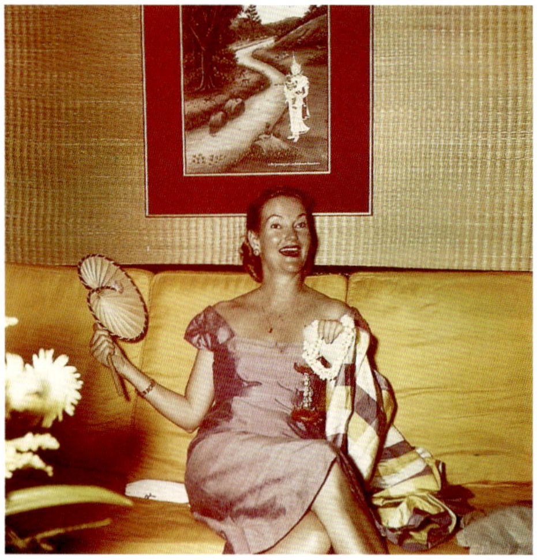

Figure 16 Doris Duke at the home of François Duhau de Bérenx in Bangkok in 1957. Behind her hangs a Thai painting.

Although little painting earlier than the seventeenth century survives in Thailand, we are able to identify a painting tradition that dates back to sketches painted or incised on temple bricks during the Dvaravati period (sixth–eleventh centuries). Today, vividly imagined and richly colored murals cover the interior walls of the ordination hall *(ubosot)* and the assembly hall *(wihan)* of the *wat*. Restored and repainted over the centuries, few of these works date earlier than the nineteenth century.

Constructing a history of painting done on perishable materials proves even more difficult, for damage by insects, the harshness of the climate, and the destruction of Ayutthaya in the eighteenth century have left us with little. One banner painting on cotton from Chedi Wat Dok Ngon in the north of Thailand has been tentatively dated to the mid sixteenth century, but it is not until the founding of Thonburi (1768–1782), followed by the establishment of Bangkok across the river in 1782, by Rama I of the Chakri dynasty, that larger numbers of paintings come to exist.

above detail, Plate 49, page 72

opposite Plate 30 Small Thai manuscript chests (l. 66.5 cm) house accordion-folded illuminated manuscripts made of *khoi* paper. Ivory markers identify the manuscripts. AAM

One way in which the Chakri kings could establish the supremacy of their dynasty was to continue previous traditions, both in the arts and in governance. They constructed temples and furnished them with the appropriate accoutrements: artists painted murals, adorned manuscript cabinets (Plate 31) with black lacquer and gilt to house the sacred texts (Plate 30) illuminating them with scenes from religious and secular works, and painted cloth temple banners *(phra bot)*. The style and motifs of these various works attest a continuation of the

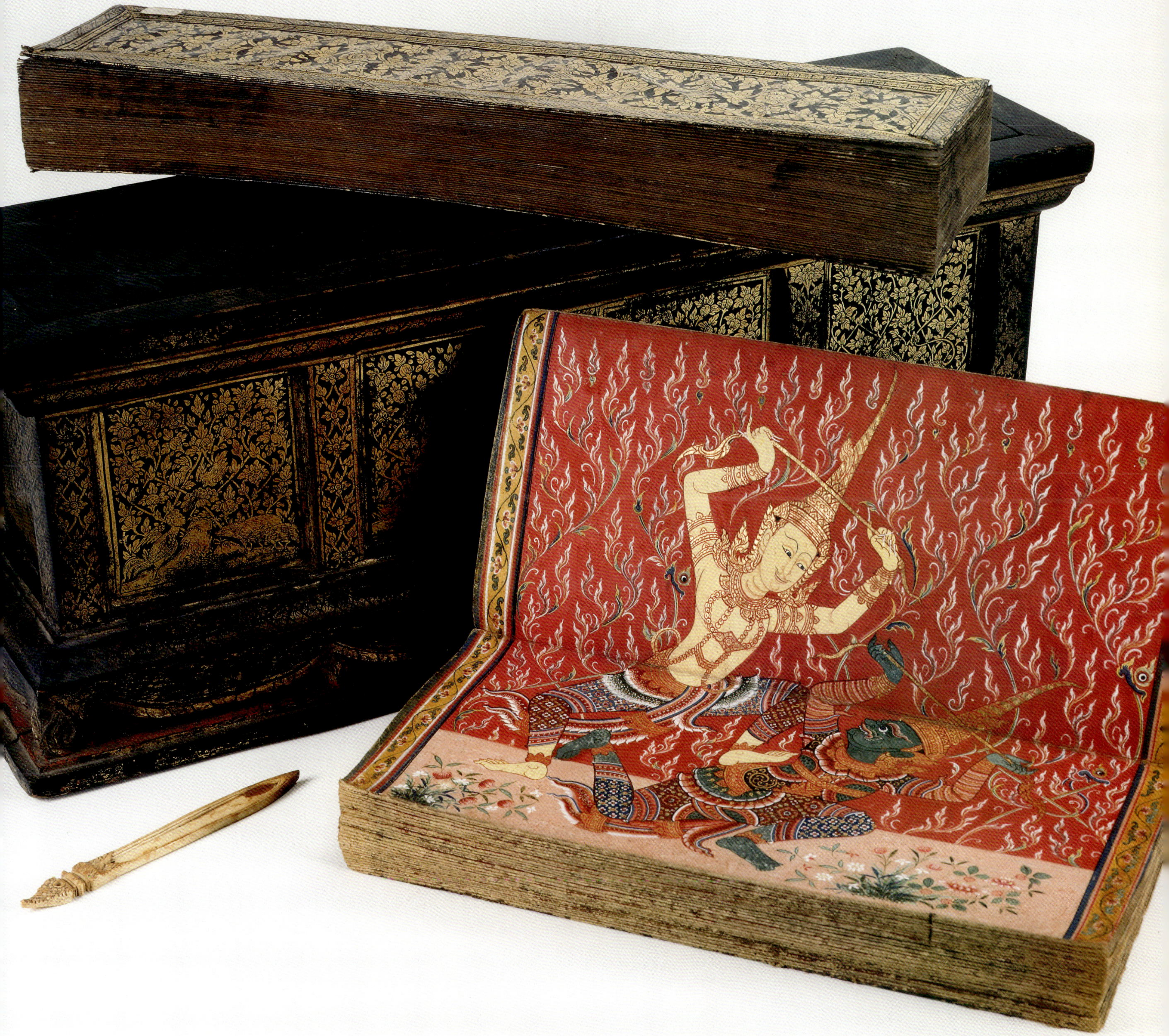

Plate 31 Thai manuscript cabinets like this one (h. 156 cm), decorated in black lacquer and gold leaf, housed sacred texts in Buddhist monasteries.

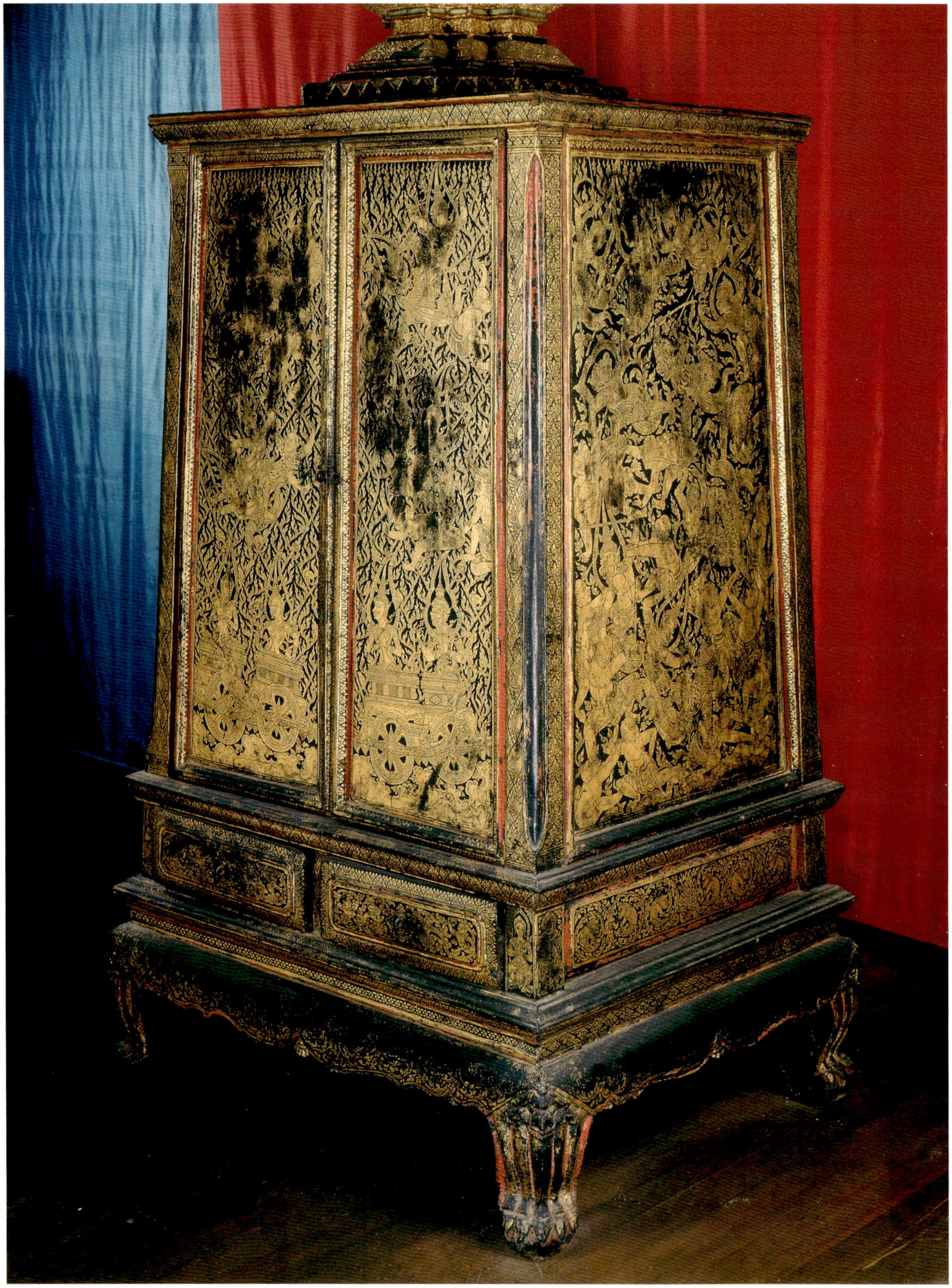

artistic traditions of the Ayutthaya period, and the sophistication of the objects indicates the refinement that these arts had attained during that period.

Each of the Duke Collection's particularly fine Thai paintings was created for a religious purpose, and all date to the eighteenth through twentieth centuries. Few Western collectors in the 1960s saw the importance of these paintings, which were hung in temples during appropriate ceremonies.[2] Some, as long as 3 meters, would have been arrayed around the altar, while others, in sets of thirteen, were hung along the walls or outside the temple on temporary walls specially raised for the occasion. Their condition is always a problem, as they were painted with tempera that has tended to wear and which cracked when the paintings were rolled for storage.

The long vertical banners are impressive, both in size and in their often bold depictions of the Buddha. The thirty long banners in the Duke Collection exhibit a range of types and iconography, though the Buddha is the primary feature of all of them. He sits on a throne, his hand raised in a gesture of teaching *(vitarka mudra)* as monks, arrayed in horizontal bands, listen attentively; he descends the ladder from Tavatimsa heaven where he has been preaching to his mother; he stands on a lotus and is attended by monks.

In many examples, the lower half or third of the banner includes or expands upon a scene from the Buddha's life. In one example (Plate 32), an adorned Buddha is attended by two devotees and below, instead of scenes from the Buddha's life, two demons fight Hanuman the monkey general of the *Ramakian*. The relationship between Hanuman and the Buddha is tenuous at best, but the monkey is a favorite of the Thai people, his role in this great Indian epic greatly expanded in their version of the story.[3] Below the boldly portrayed Hanuman and combatants, the artist has depicted worshipers at two reliquary mounds. This painting hung in an early installation in the Coach Barn (Figure 17), as did others. Their fragility must have become apparent, however, for in the more recent installation at the Coach Barn, only paintings on wood or framed cloth paintings have been hung.

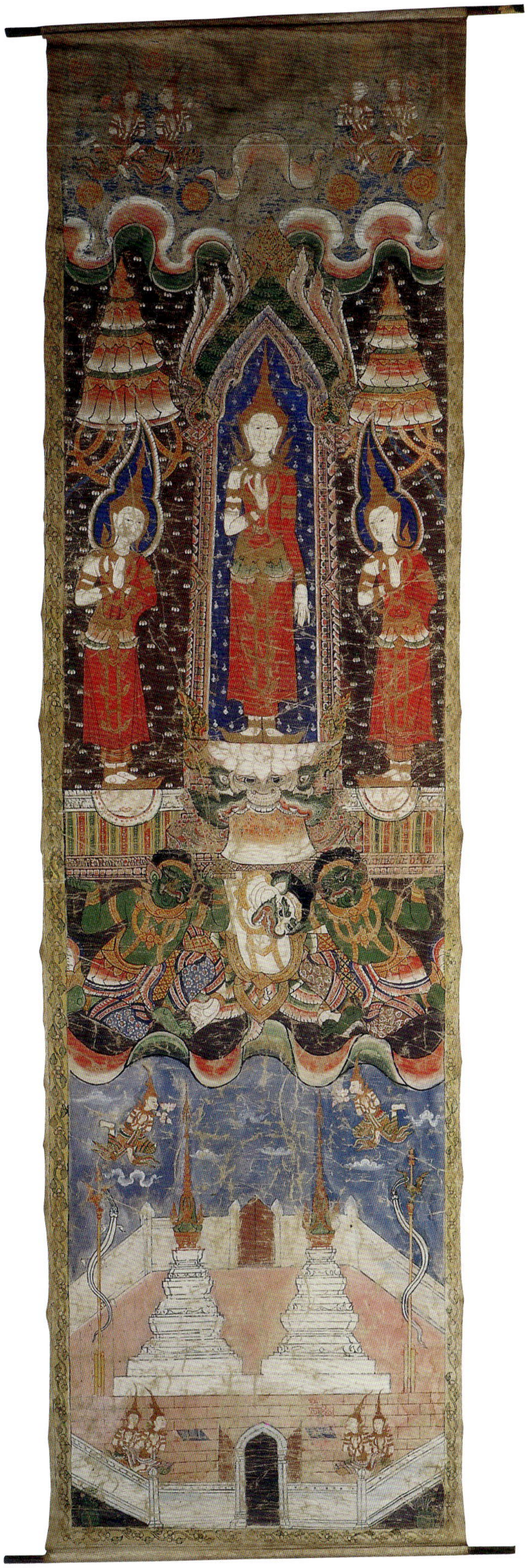

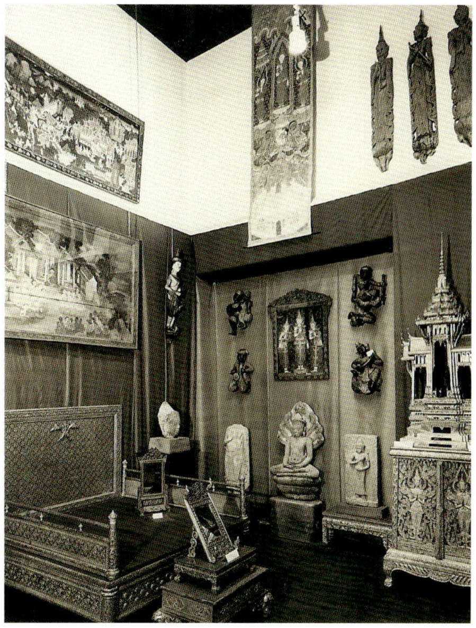

above **Figure 17** This 1970s installation in the Coach Barn, Duke Farms, Hillsborough, New Jersey, includes the banner painting of Plate 32. In recent years, banners have not been hung in the Coach Barn, possibly because of their fragility.

left **Plate 32** Two demons fight Hanuman, the monkey general of the *Ramakian*, below an adorned Buddha with devotees (h. 297 cm). Thailand. WAM

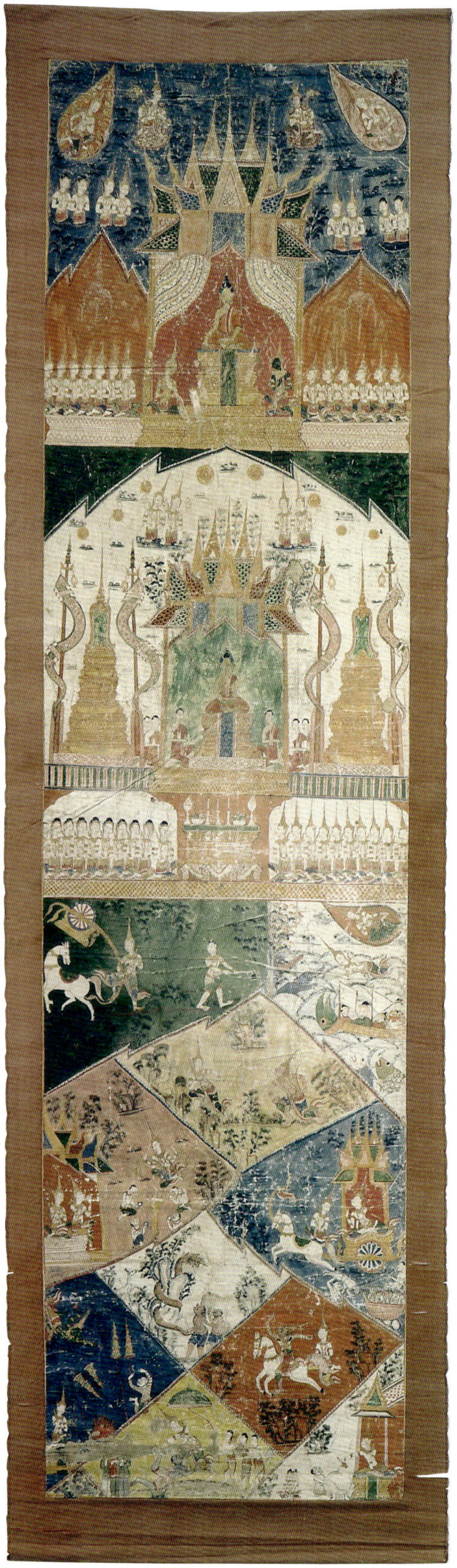

Plate 33 The last ten life stories of the historical Buddha *(Thotsachat)* were popular subject matter for both temple murals and the banners (h. 352 cm). Thailand. AAM

Following his enlightenment, the Buddha ventured forth and performed various miracles, then proceeded to Tavatimsa heaven to preach to his mother and the gods (see p. 9). Finishing his teachings, he descended to earth accompanied by Indra and Brahma. This late nineteenth-century painting, though marked by the ravages of time, still shows the wonderful skill of the artist, who makes the transition from the heavens—replete with flying musicians and monks, celestial palaces, and accordioned stairs—to the hell scene below. There, huge boiling pots are fueled with human carcasses, and the hellish repast features the same. Two naked adulterers climb a thorn tree, while a dog bites at them from below. The contrast between glorious heaven, the destination of those whose actions are good, and the consequences of bad actions would seem all the more emphatic to the worshiper, who would be able to examine the hell scene hanging closer to eye level in all its detail.

The lower portion of another painting (Plate 33) includes a representation of the *Thotsachat,* the last ten life stories *(jataka)* of the Buddha's previous existences.[4] Theravada Buddhists particularly revere these stories, part of the Pali canon, as they represent models of behavior. Named for these principal characters, they describe the perfection of ten important virtues: Temiya, renunciation; Mahajanaka, courage; Sama, devotion; Nimi, resolution; Mahosadha, wisdom; Bhuridatta, perseverance; Canda-Kumara, forbearance; Narada, equanimity; Vidhura, truthfulness; and Vessantara, charity. Each of the small lozenges at the bottom of this painting includes a key episode from one of the ten tales, the story unidentifiable to those unfamiliar with Buddhism but easily understood by the regular temple-goer (see detail, p. 59).

In an earlier time, Bhuridatta the *naga* (serpent) and an ascetic of great powers, had sheltered a lowly hunter in his grand palace, then offered him the use of a magic jewel when the hunter departed. Grateful for his luxurious stay, the hunter refused the jewel. Later regretting this action, the hunter led the Brahman Alambayana (who had unwittingly obtained the jewel and did not know its powers) to Bhuridatta. Alambayana agreed to give Bhuridatta the jewel, once

Detail of Plate 33 with the *Bhuridatta jataka*, in which the Buddha was a snake in a previous life. Thailand. AAM

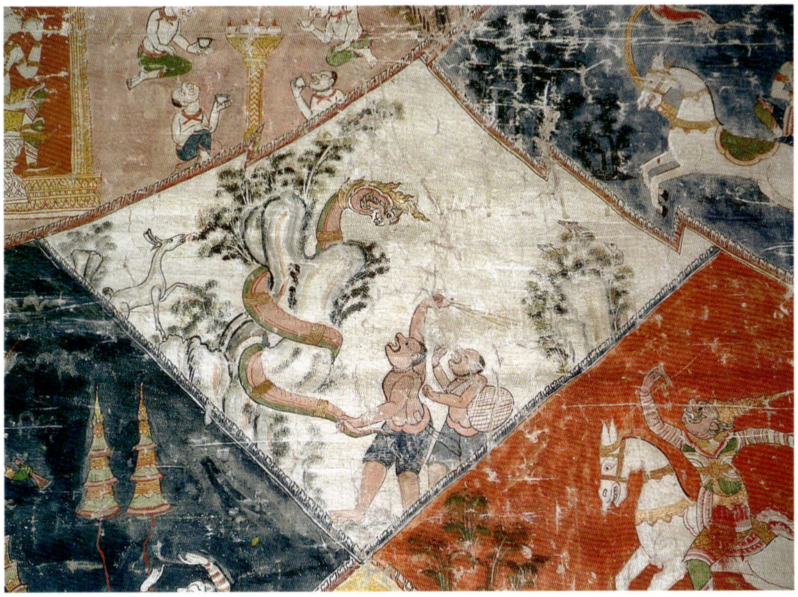

he had control over the powerful serpent. Showing great perseverance and resolution in his asceticism, Bhuridatta continued his fasting and did not resist when Alambayana caused him great pain by cruelly crushing his bones to make him fit into a bag. The Brahman then carried him to town, where he forced the *naga*, still unresisting and pliant, to entertain an audience. Eventually Sudassana, Bhuridatta's brother, saved him, thwarting Alambayana by taking the form of a youthful ascetic and exposing him to the king.

The devout Buddhist needs only a single scene to identify the tale, and here it is one described in the Pali text: Bhuridatta coils around an anthill, where he performs his daily asceticism, as Alambayana clasps his tail. His upraised hand grasps the magic jewel, which will fall into a crack in the earth when the hunter, shown here reaching for it, takes it into his hand. Bhuridatta's royal status is emphasized by the bands of gold that encircle his body, and his fierce dragonlike head adds grandeur to his form. Instead of symmetrically organized registers to enclose the *Thotsachat*, the artist has employed a series of lozenges set in zigzag lines, the zigzag pattern a device used by the mural painters of the Ayutthaya, Thonburi (across the river from Bangkok and an earlier site for the Chakri dynasty's capital), and in the early Bangkok periods to distinguish one scene or group of celestial beings from another.[5] During the Bangkok period, the *Thotsachat* often forms part of the mural program inside the *bot* (ordination hall) or *wihan*. We cannot be certain whether this example supplemented a program lacking in these stories, or had no relationship to the overall program of the temple painting, but rather reflected the taste of the donor.

Sets of smaller paintings, thirteen in number, of the Vessantara *jataka* (Plates 34–36) were to be hung during a ceremony called the *Thet Mahachat*, or recitation of the Great Life, which lasts a full day and a night after the rains retreat during the twelfth lunar month (November).[6] Thirteen monks recite the thirteen stanzas of the tale, an act that bestows great merit upon all who listen to the complete rendition. Generally the thirteen works (each representing one of the stanzas) were painted on cloth; this set is exceptional in the use of wood and the fact that they appear to have been framed at the time of their making. Epitomizing the perfection of charity *(dana)*, the tale resonates in the lives of Southeast Asian Buddhists, for it is through charity that the layperson can most readily acquire merit and thus improve his karma. It is the most frequently depicted of all the *jataka*.

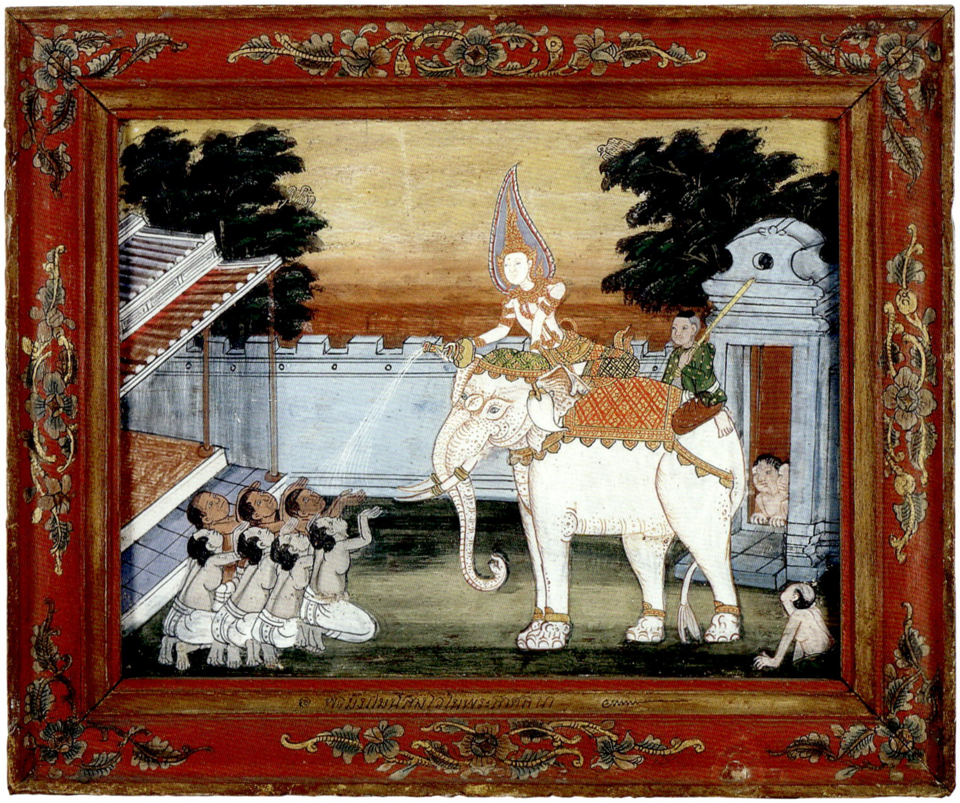

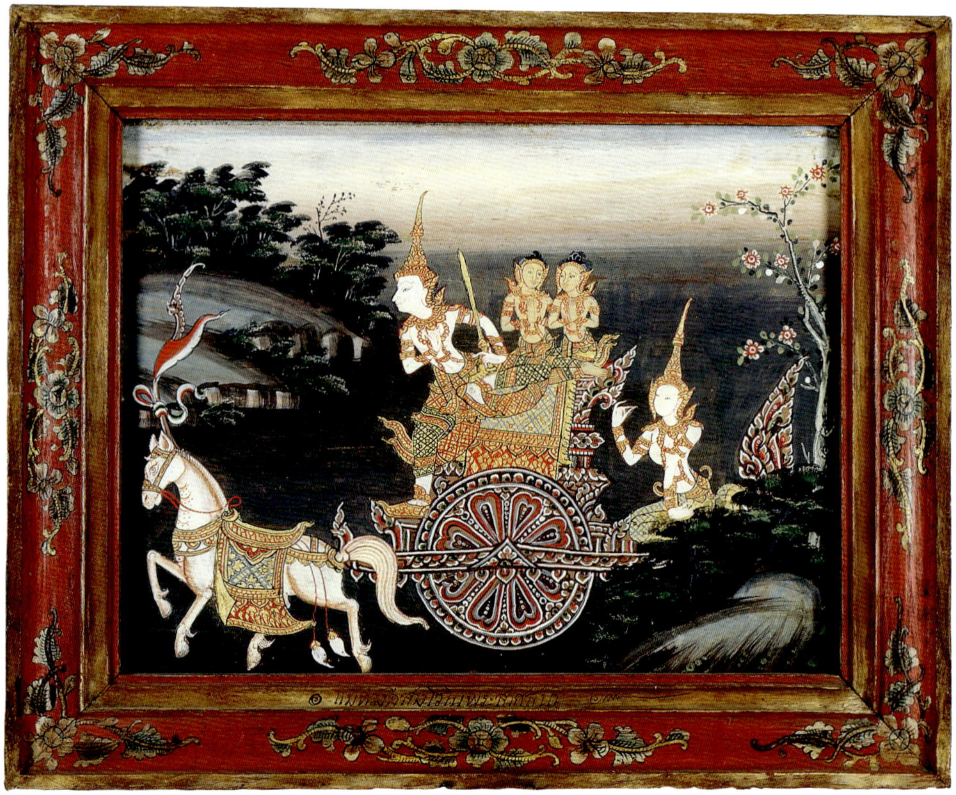

The episodes unfold as follows: Indra, king of the gods, sends Phusati to earth to give birth to Prince Vessantara. The King of Kalinga sends eight Brahmans to ask the adult Prince Vessantara for his kingdom's white elephant, hoping ownership of the lucky elephant will end a lengthy drought. After Vessantara gives them the elephant, his father's subjects are furious, and his father is forced to exile him, his wife Maddi, and their two children (Plate 34). On their trip to the forest, the prince generously grants another group of Brahmans' request for the horses, and next the chariot in which he and his family ride (Plate 35). Vessantara eventually gives his children to the Brahman Jujuka, a pathetic character, and stops short of giving away his wife only because the god Indra intercedes. Jujuka takes the children to the capital, where their grandfather, the king, recognizes them and buys them from Jujuka, who squanders his newfound wealth and dies of overindulgence. Prince Vessantara and his entire family are then reunited, and the visual rendition in Thailand and Laos ends with a procession back to the palace (Plate 36).

Stylistic elements in this set suggest a date in the second half of the nineteenth century. Traditional Thai painters showed little interest in placing their characters in complex landscapes or rendering a scene in one-point perspective. Not until the mid nineteenth century did Western influence make itself felt, an influence evident in this painting in the shading of rocks and hills, the relatively realistic depiction of the trees, and the interest in space in the palace enclosure. The inclusion of foreigners in the procession celebrating Vessantara's return to the palace and their antiquated garb typify the depiction

above **Plate 34 The Vessantara *jataka*, the story of the penultimate life of the Buddha, is the most popular topic for small Thai and Lao paintings on cloth *(phra bot)* and occasionally wood paintings (h. 44.5 cm). Here, Vessantara gives away the white elephant. WAM**

below **Plate 35 Vessantara and his family are exiled to the forest (h. 44 cm; from the same set as Plates 34 and 36). WAM**

of outsiders in paintings of this period. Traditional aspects are also apparent in the treatment of the royal family, with their refined demeanor and elegance, in contrast to the roughness of the commoners; the flattening effect of the gilt surfaces; and various iconographic features, such as Vessantara's pouring water over the hands of the Brahmans to symbolize his gift of the elephant.

This same story is depicted in another format in northeastern Thailand, in horizontal banners of lengths up to 120 feet. As in the sets of paintings, the banner commemorates the *Thet Mahachat* recitation of the Vessantara *jataka.* The day before the recitation, village elders carry the scroll through the village (Figure 18) to the *wat,* where it is hung as the sets of paintings are hung, intended to provide a visual cue to the tale being recited.[7] Again, the story includes thirteen scenes, though the artist does not systematically separate them, but instead elaborates different elements in the story. The section shown here (Plate 37) represents an early episode in the tale, with Vessantara, in the lower panel, pouring the water that symbolizes a gift. To the right of that scene, Vessantara, his wife Maddi, and the two children are shown inside the palace, and to the far right, the Brahmans scramble onto the elephant. The artist has given free rein to his imagination; he shows two of the men flinging their luggage onto the animal's back as they struggle to not be left behind.

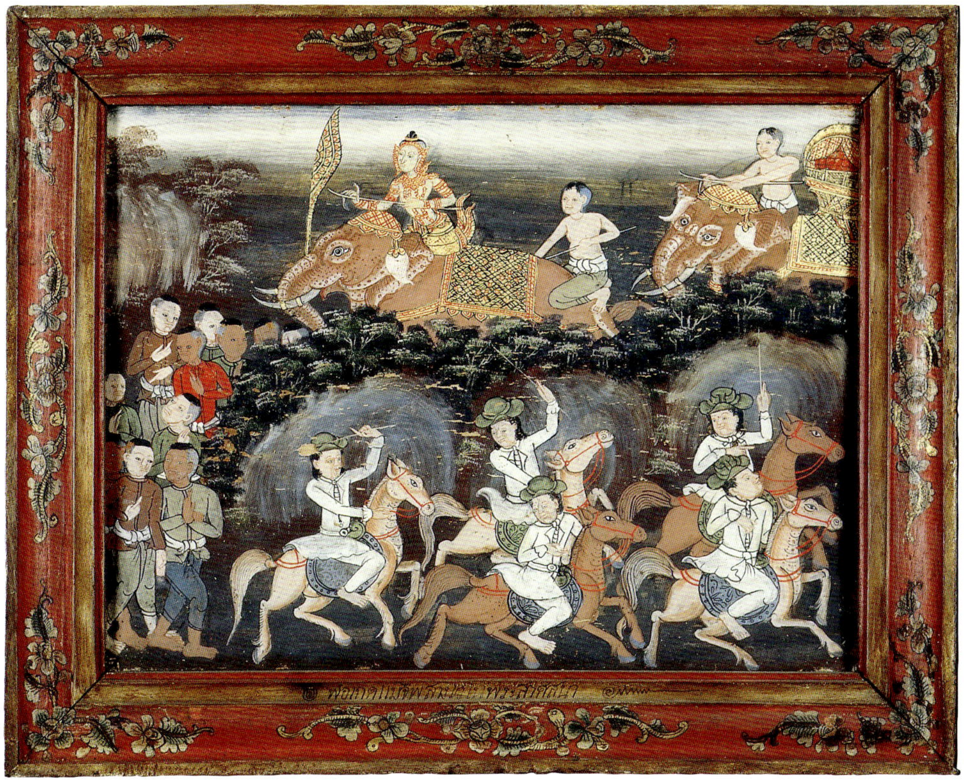

above **Plate 36** Vessantara, having perfected his charity, returns to the palace with his family (h. 46 cm; from the same set of paintings on wood as Plates 34 and 35). WAM

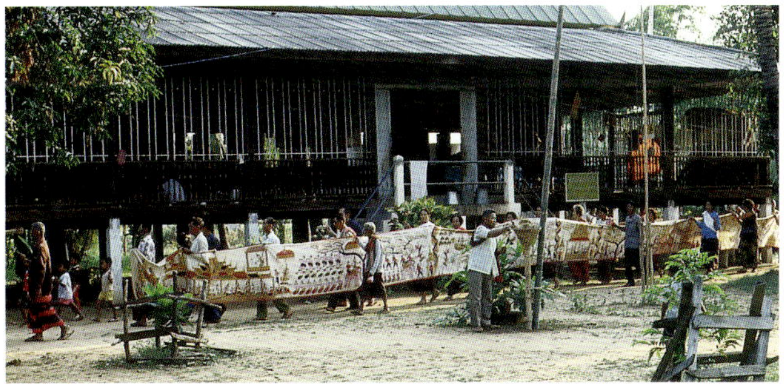

middle **Figure 18** The unrolled Vessantara *jataka* painted scroll *(Phaa Phrawaet)* carried three times clockwise around the temple meeting hall after being paraded through the village of Baan Dong Phong, Amphur Muang, Kohn Kaen Province, Thailand, March 1982. © Leedom Lefferts.

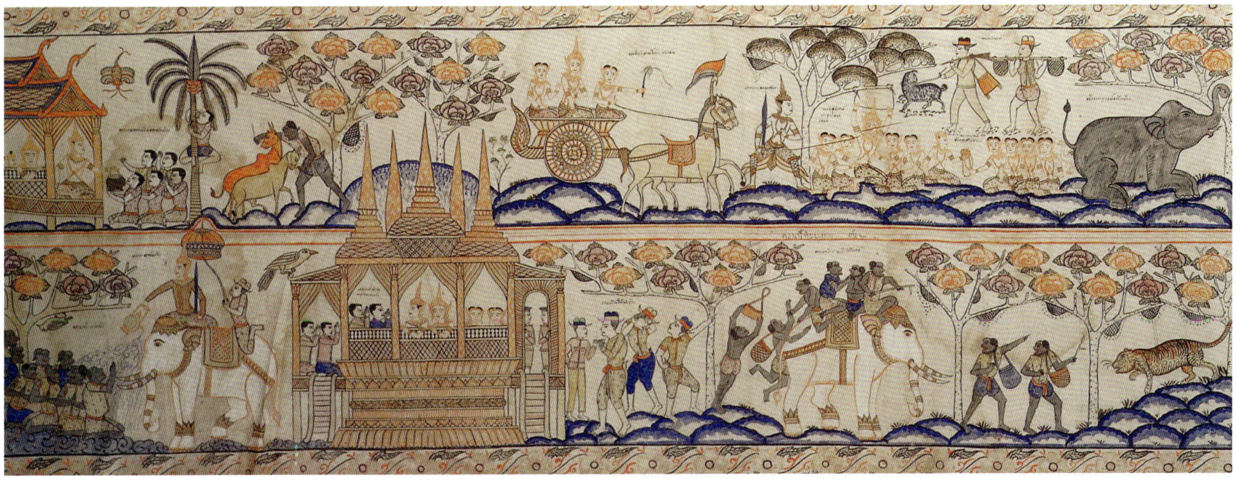

below **Plate 37** Banners (total length 2032.5 cm) of the Vessantara *jataka*, used in the northeast of Thailand, are sometimes more than 120 feet long. In this section, Vessantara gives away the white elephant (lower register), and food, drink, women, and slaves (upper register). WAM

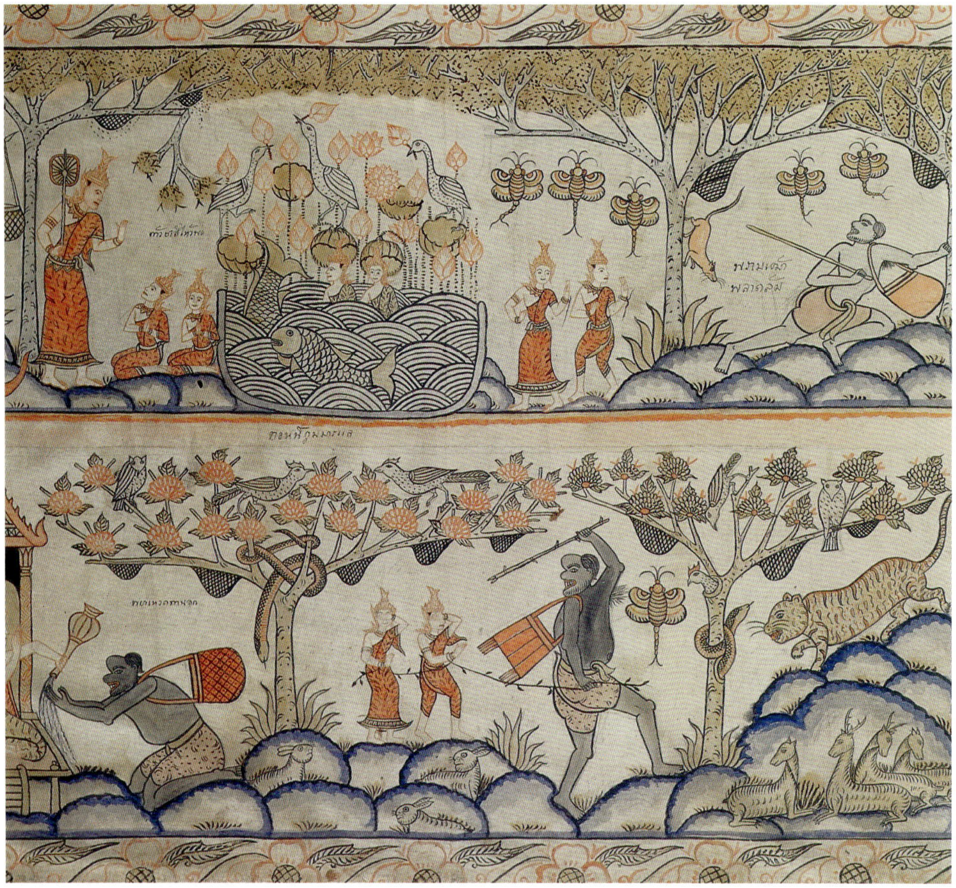

Plate 38 Section of another banner (total length 1937 cm). In the perfection of his charity, Vessantara gives the Brahman Jujuka his children, but they hide in a pond. Thailand. AAM

The narrative does not continue in a systematic, linear fashion, from either left to right or bottom to top; in this section, the upper level contains the next episode. After Vessantara gives away the white elephant, the people insist his father exile him, but Vessantara is allowed to stay in his palace one more night: "And when the night was at an end, and the sun rose next day, then King Vessantara began his gifts to give away."[8] He gave food and drink, elephants and horses, and, as illustrated in the upper right, 700 women beautifully adorned, "each standing in a car,"[9] and an additional 700 slave women. As one would expect, Vessantara's charity is emphasized throughout the painting. A charming detail that transpires later in the story (Plate 38) shows Vessantara dressed as a hermit, telling his children that he is giving them to the Brahman Jujuka. The unhappy children run from their father and hide in a nearby pond overgrown with a mass of lotuses and teeming with aquatic life. Again the artist emphasizes Vessantara's charity, but does not miss an opportunity to elaborate and add drama to the everyday details.

Like sculptures of the Buddha, paintings were commissioned by Buddhist followers who hoped to gain merit by their production. Occasionally they commissioned paintings on wood, which were hung as permanent displays in buildings in the temple compound. Like the cloth works, they served a didactic purpose, reminding both monks and the laypeople of the life and previous lives of the Buddha. Most of the examples in the Duke Collection are scenes from the life of the historical Buddha, like this depiction of his quelling the elephant Nalagiri (Plate 39).

In a number of his 547 lives, the Buddha was tormented by his evil cousin Devadatta, who sought his downfall. Even after the Buddha had attained enlightenment, Devadatta continued to harass him. Here he preaches to the rampaging elephant Nalagiri, whom Devadatta had set on a course to trample him. When the elephant caught sight of the enlightened being, he paid his respects and attentively listened to the words he preached.

Small paintings set in freestanding wooden frames (Plate 40) are among the religious objects adorning temples or the personal altar found in many Buddhist homes. Here two attendant monks pay obeisance to a Buddha image, which stands with hand raised in a gesture that means 'have no fear' *(abhaya mudra)*. The three appear to stand upon an altar adorned with fruit and flowers, while the carving, gilt, and lacquer of the stand add to the object's overall decorative quality. Rather than alluding to specific tales from the Buddha's life or previous lives, this painting illustrates a representation of him, thus serving an iconic rather than a didactic purpose, although other small framed paintings in the Duke Collection illustrate specific stories of the Buddha's life.

Freestanding altars *(attachan)*, with stepped shelves for an image of the Buddha (placed on the top shelf) and offerings (on the lower shelves), developed in the Ayutthaya period.[10] Like the freestanding framed paintings, they were more often adorned with iconic

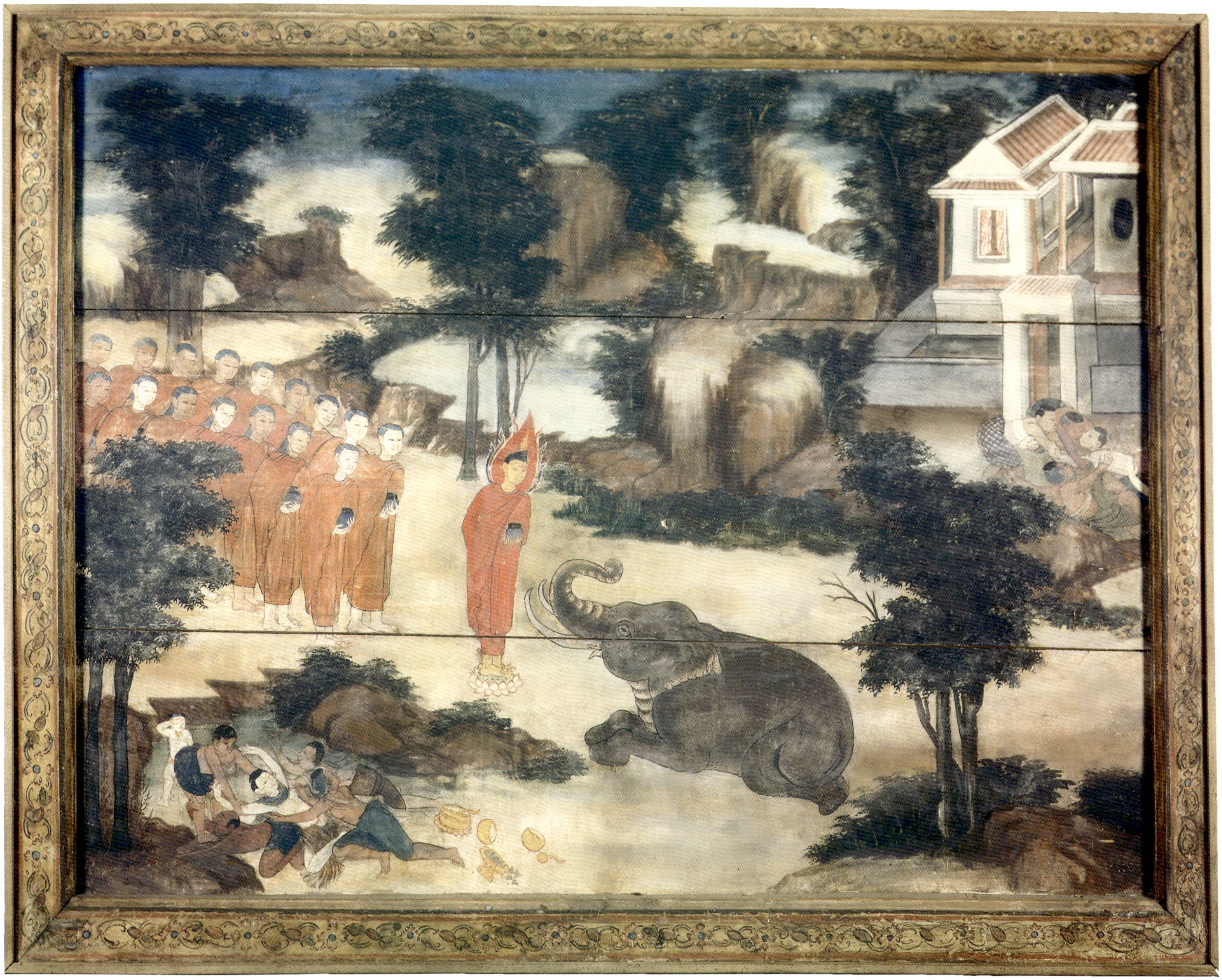

Plate 39 Large Thai wooden panel (w. 157.5 cm) with the story of the Buddha's taming of Nalagiri, a rampant elephant sent by Devadatta to destroy him. WAM

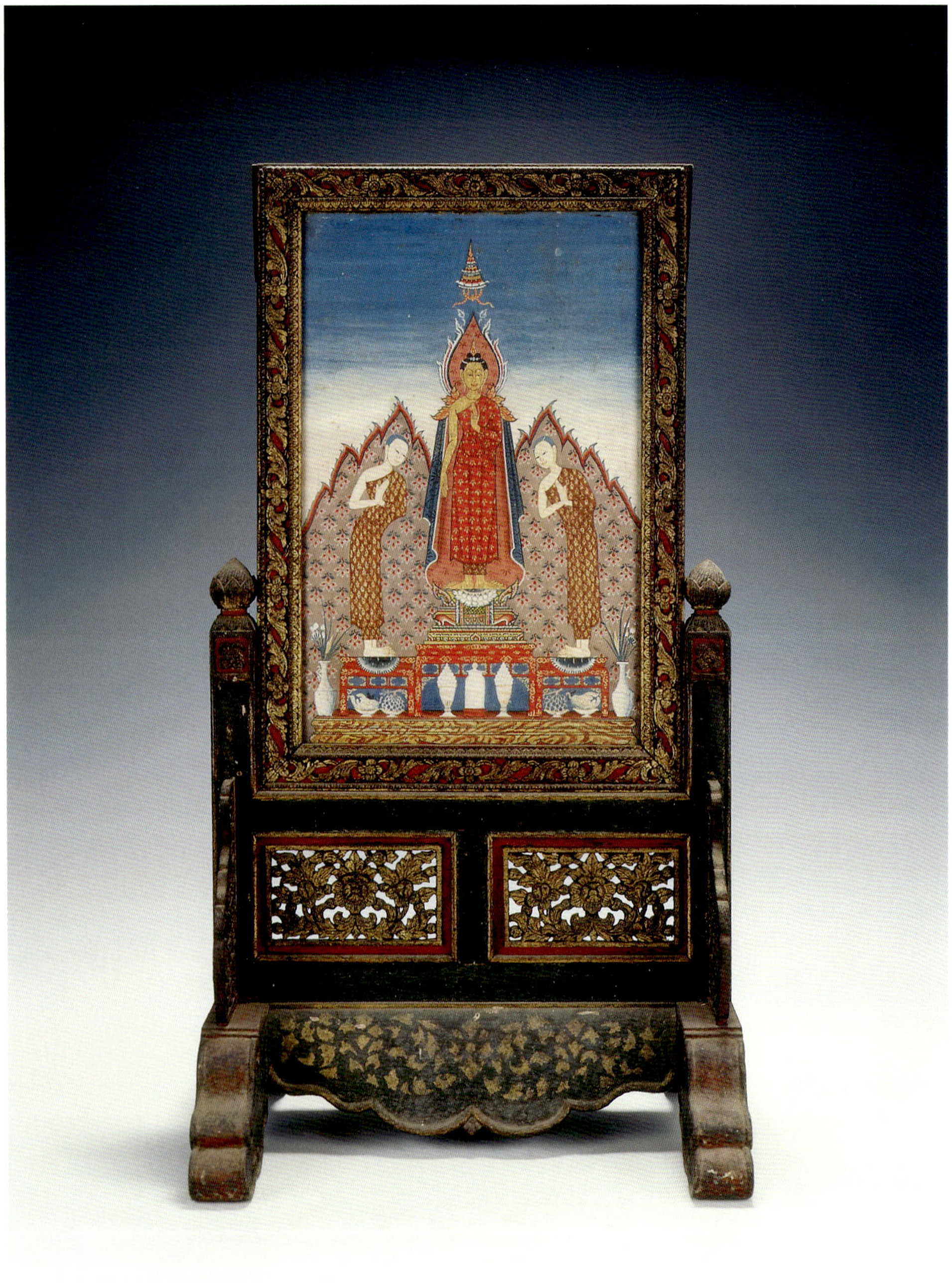

Plate 40 Small framed painting (h. 70 cm) of the Buddha and devotees. Thailand.

painted scenes (Plate 41). In a landscape of looming boulders and trees, the Buddha appears on a throne fronted with offerings, while a heavenly being and various princely figures pay their respects. The addition of the offerings creates the sense that the Buddha has not been painted as a living person but rather that the worshipers revere an image of the Buddha. Setting a scene within a landscape was a mid nineteenth-century development based on Western models. There was also an increase in Chinese-style decoration in the 1820s and 1830s, such as the bird-and-flower motifs of the carving of the *attachan,* so a late nineteenth-century date seems probable for the piece.

An artist, whether painting on wood or cloth, or making murals, used tempera, which has not fared well in Thailand's heat and humidity. He also painted with tempera made of natural pigments when illustrating the manuscripts that play such an important role in the religious life of the *wat;* these paintings have fared better, since the manuscripts are closed, wrapped in cloth, and stored carefully in cabinets. Commissioning a religious manuscript or writing or illustrating one accrues merit to those involved, as does the reading of the text. Kept in monasteries, the books are read during ceremonies or removed from their cabinets for monks to study. Their paintings are frequently unrelated to the text, which quite often includes portions of the Pali *Abhidhamma,* treatises on various philosophical issues. Common subject matter for the paintings includes the *Thotsachat* and the story of Phra Malai, popular in the nineteenth century.[11]

Other topics for manuscripts are divination, cosmology, warfare, and elephants. Elephants, particularly the white elephant, achieved a semidivine status in Southeast Asia, representing the king's power and the strength of the state. The elephant also symbolizes the universal monarch *(cakkavattin),* in a secular and a Buddhist context. The manuscript illustrations of elephants include both mythological (Plate 42) and actual animals, and the texts describe deities associated with the beasts or the various characteristics of individual animals. This manuscript page illustrates

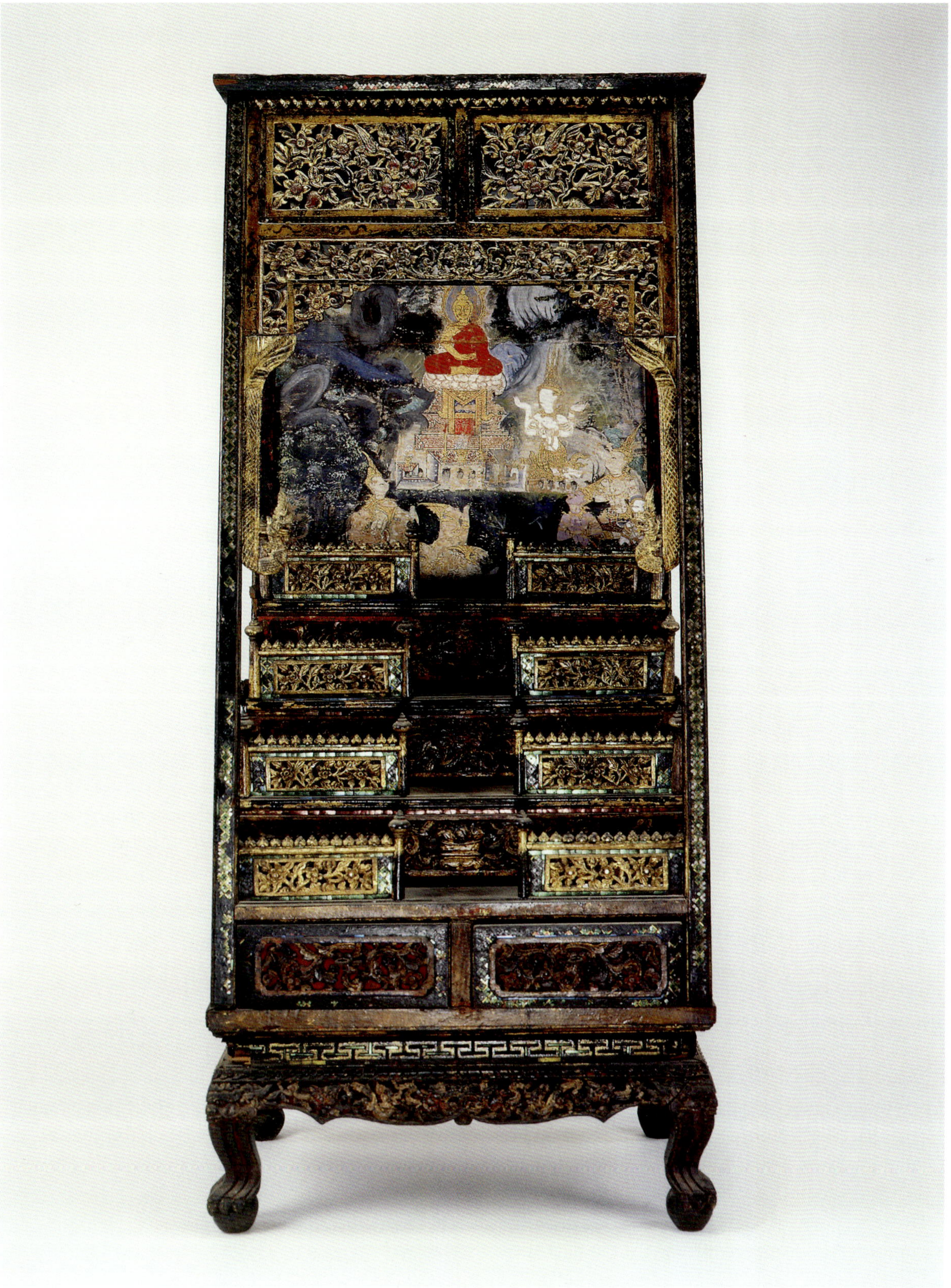

Plate 41 Freestanding altars (*attachan;* h. 152.5 cm) used in homes and temples are often painted.

Plate 42 The importance of elephants is attested in treatises (w. 36 cm) that include depictions of both real and imaginary elephants, such as this image of Erawan with his thirty-three heads. Thailand.

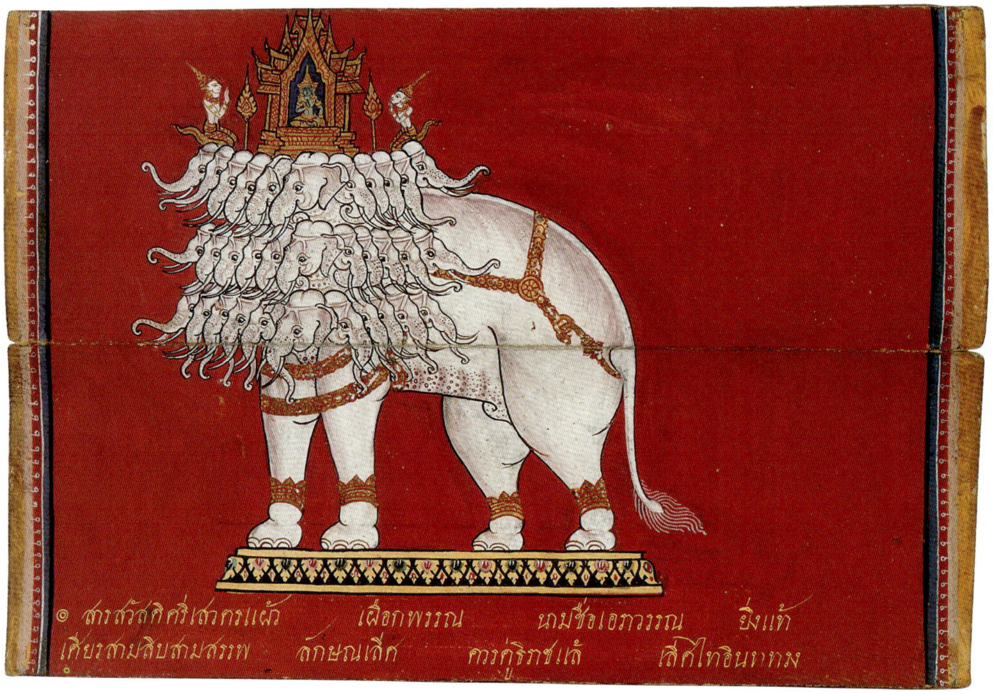

Indra, king of the gods, riding Erawan, his thirty-three-headed elephant mount. The writing on this page, in thin Thai script, suggests a nineteenth-century date.[12] Even rarer than the elephant manuscript are paintings of the *Ramakian.* This example does not include any text but instead shows large, bold, combative figures on brilliant grounds, in a style that suggests an early nineteenth-century date (Plate 43).

Thai Buddhist manuscripts are traditionally made from either palm leaves inscribed with a stylus (which are rarely illustrated) or accordioned lengths of *khoi (Streblus aster)* paper. Palm-leaf manuscripts are generally Buddhist, while the two-sided accordion books may also be secular. The most common format for these books places the script in the center of the page with paintings at either side (Plate 44). The elegant Thai script, derived from Indian-based scripts, was used for secular manuscripts, and the Cambodian script has traditionally been used for Buddhist texts.

The scripts provide useful clues to the dating of a manuscript. A thick-lettered form of Cambodian script was common in the eighteenth century, but a thinner script became popular in the nineteenth century.[13] Furthermore, the size of the manuscript may also indicate its age, for those of the seventeenth and eighteenth centuries tend to be smaller (9–10 cm high) than those made in the nineteenth century (14–15 cm high).[14] The style of the manuscript's painting changes along with its size; earlier illustrations are generally arrayed on a pale ground, with little attempt to delineate space.

By the early nineteenth century, the grounds were more brilliant and the figures larger. Chinese motifs were included, and increased attention to Western modes of illustration markedly altered the direction of all Thai painting in the mid nineteenth century. Landscapes became more elaborate and perspective more common, though some late nineteenth-century manuscripts continue to depict minimal landscapes, as does the manuscript with Phra Malai (see Plate 44). Because of his accumulation of merit, this monk was allowed to visit heaven and hell and described them to people so vividly that they could see those places.[15] The painter contrasts the women on the left, who provide food for the monk, with the emaciated figures on the right, who have discovered the consequences

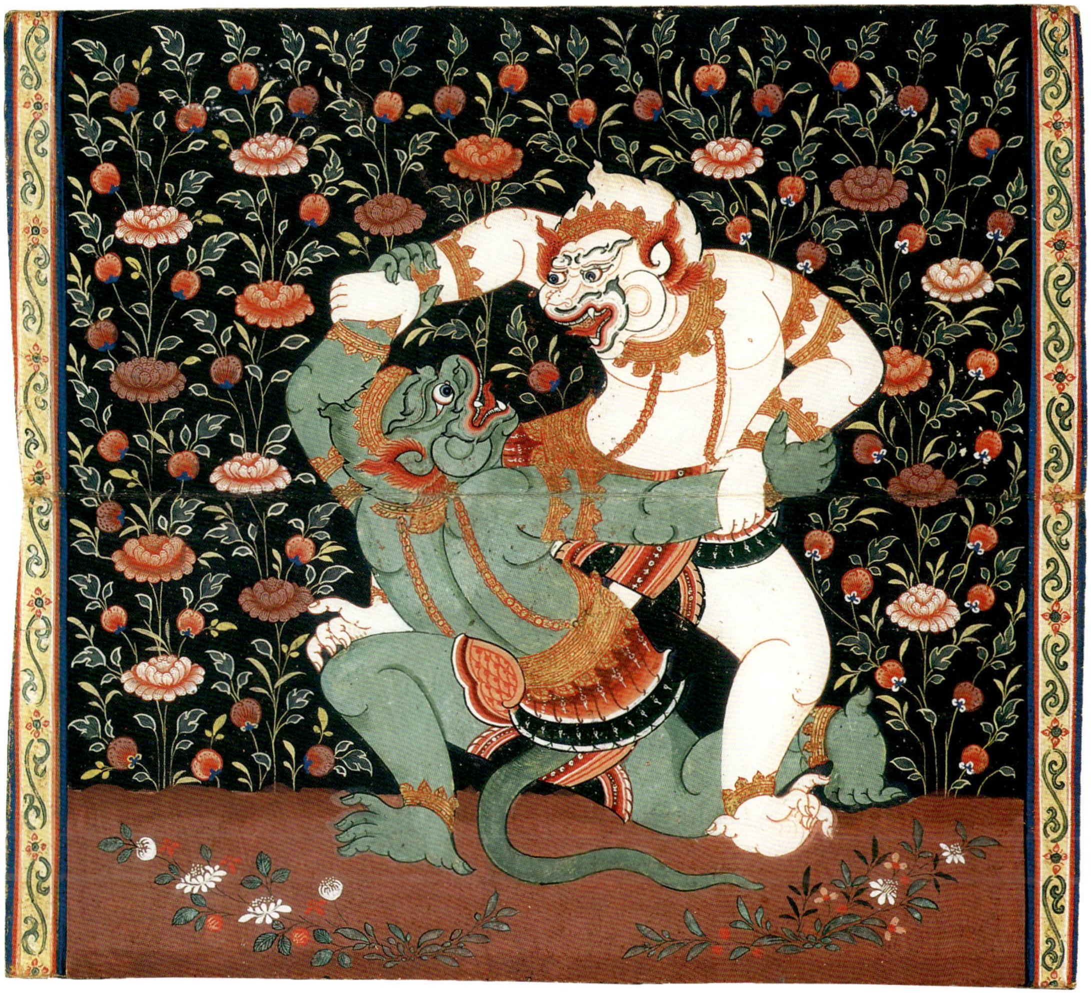

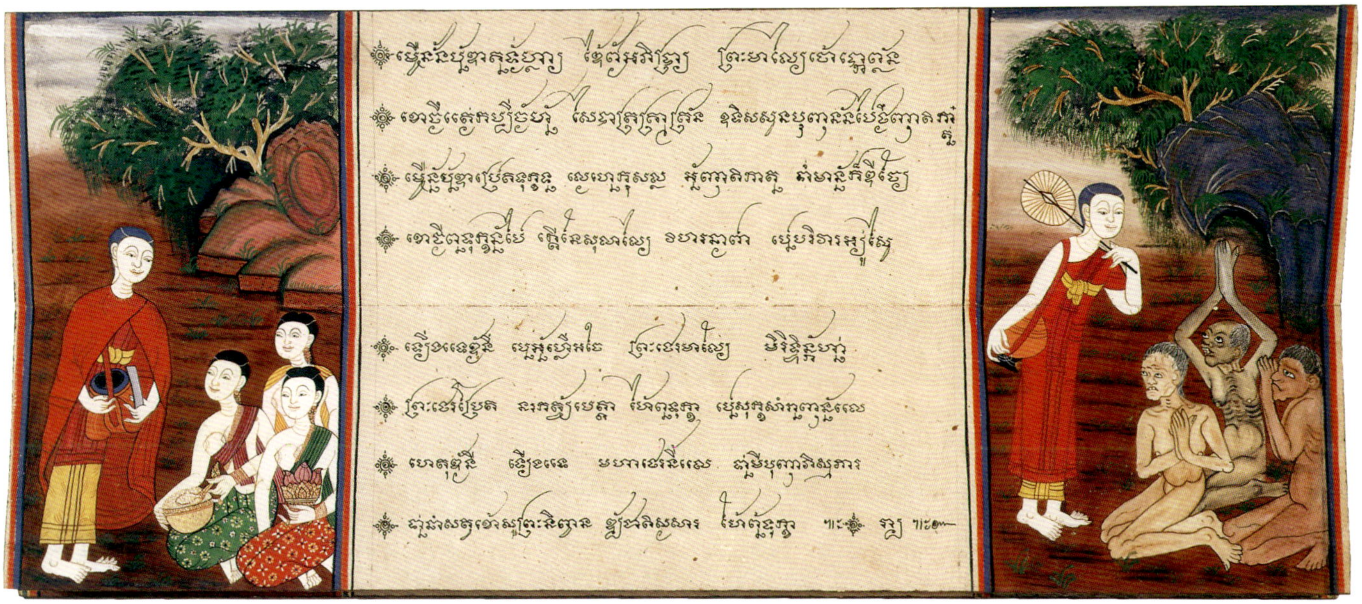

above **Plate 43** The great Indian epic, the *Ramayana* (Thai: *Ramakian*), is rarely reproduced in the paper accordion manuscripts of Thailand (w. 49.5 cm). WAM

below **Plate 44** The written word of illustrated sacred texts is generally placed in the center of the page, between two paintings. This Thai text (w. 68 cm) illustrates the story of the good monk Phra Malai. WAM

right **Plate 45** Burmese manuscripts of the *Kammavaca* (rules of the order; w. 56 cm) are written in square or tamarind script. This example has a fine ivory cover.

below **Plate 46** Burmese book chest (*sadaik;* h. 61.5 cm) decorated in raised lacquer *(thayo)*, gilding, and glass inlay.

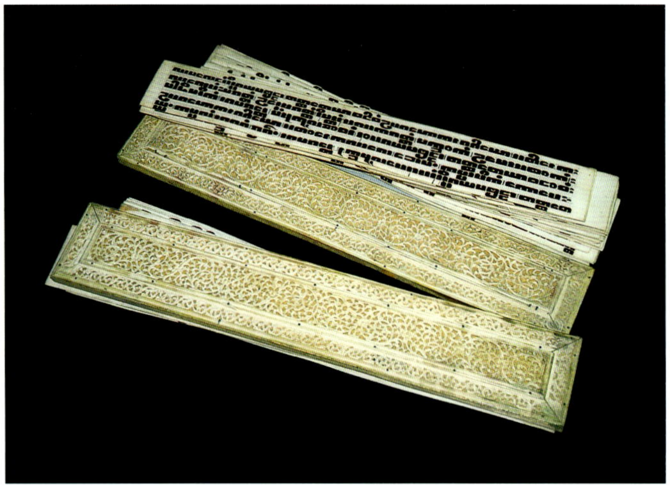

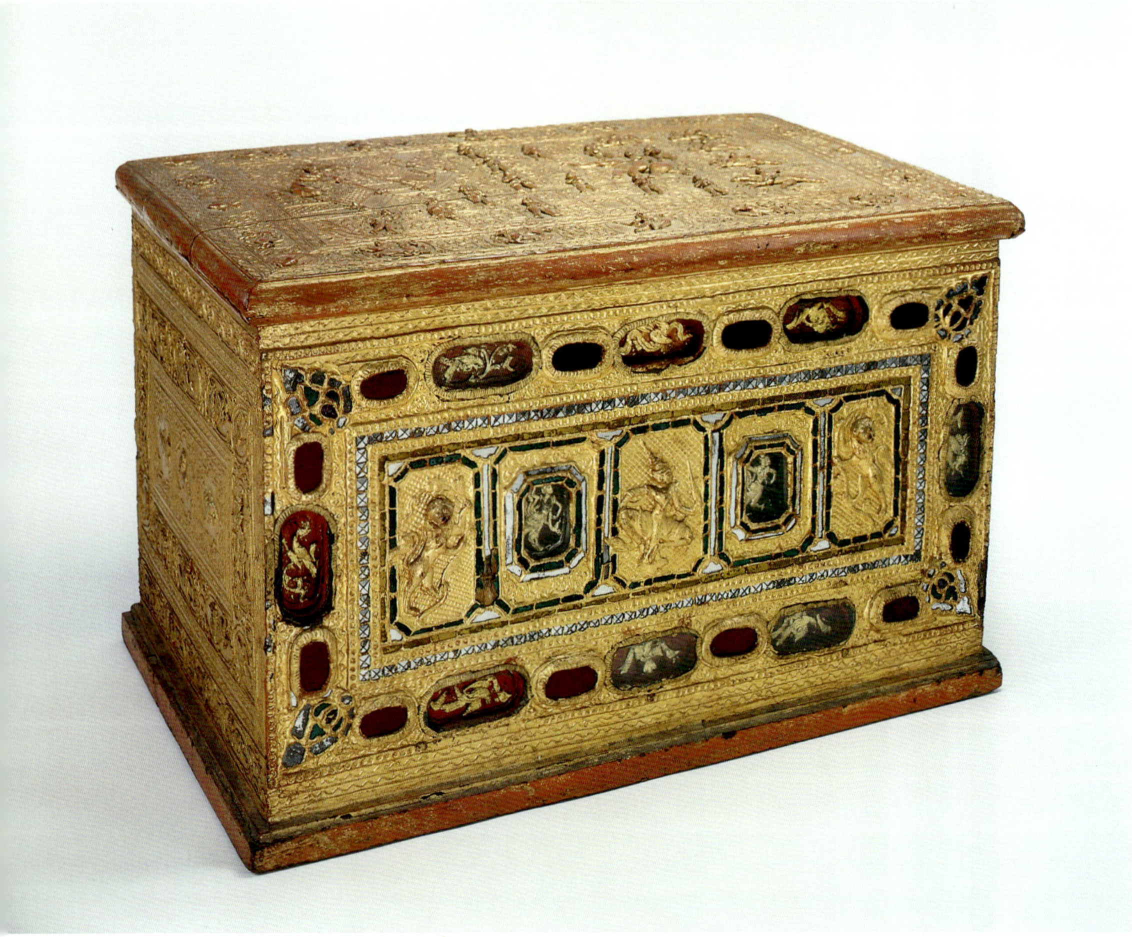

of evil action. The Phra Malai story is read at funerals to remind all of correct behavior and meritorious acts, and in the northeast, it is read prior to the reading of the Vessantara *jataka* at the *Thet Mahachat.*[16]

A similar painting tradition evolved in Burma. The Burmese painted the interiors of their temples during the Bagan period (ninth–fourteenth centuries), and some of these paintings remain in good condition, as the climate of that region is drier than that of central Thailand. Fragments of a banner painting depicting *jataka* tales aligned in registers, as they were in temple murals, were found in Temple 315, in Bagan, Burma, in 1984.[17] Unfortunately, this tradition of banner paintings is not represented in the Duke Collection. In more recent centuries, the Burmese have created painted manuscripts *(parabaik);* none of the Duke Collection's books, however, are of this type. Examples of Burmese manuscripts in the collection include an ivory-covered *Kammavaca* text (drawn from the *Vinayapitaka,* rules for monastic discipline) and lacquered and inlaid covers of palm-leaf manuscripts. The ivory-covered manuscript contains lacquered pages of square script (Plate 45). Traditionally, the pages are created by applying lacquer over the remnants of monks' robes to form a stiff page that is then inscribed.

In Burma and in the north of Thailand, an area long under Burmese rule and influence, books are stored in chests of a different form and decoration than the two-door cabinets of Thailand. Although not painted, their use and the graphic quality of their decoration dictate discussing them here. The shape of the Burmese chest, *sadaik* (Plate 46), most closely resembles a Western chest, rectangular with a top-opening lid. With their usual delight in elaborate decor, the Burmese artists apply a scene in low relief fashioned of *thayo,* a putty of lacquer sap mixed with clay, sawdust, or ash. The story is obscure; it may be a general reference to a battle scene between the Burmese and Thais[18] (see detail, Plate 46). The side of this chest includes not only flying figures of raised lacquer but also inlaid glass. From the end of the nineteenth century, the glass is mirrored, while earlier examples include glass backed with mercury-treated paper.

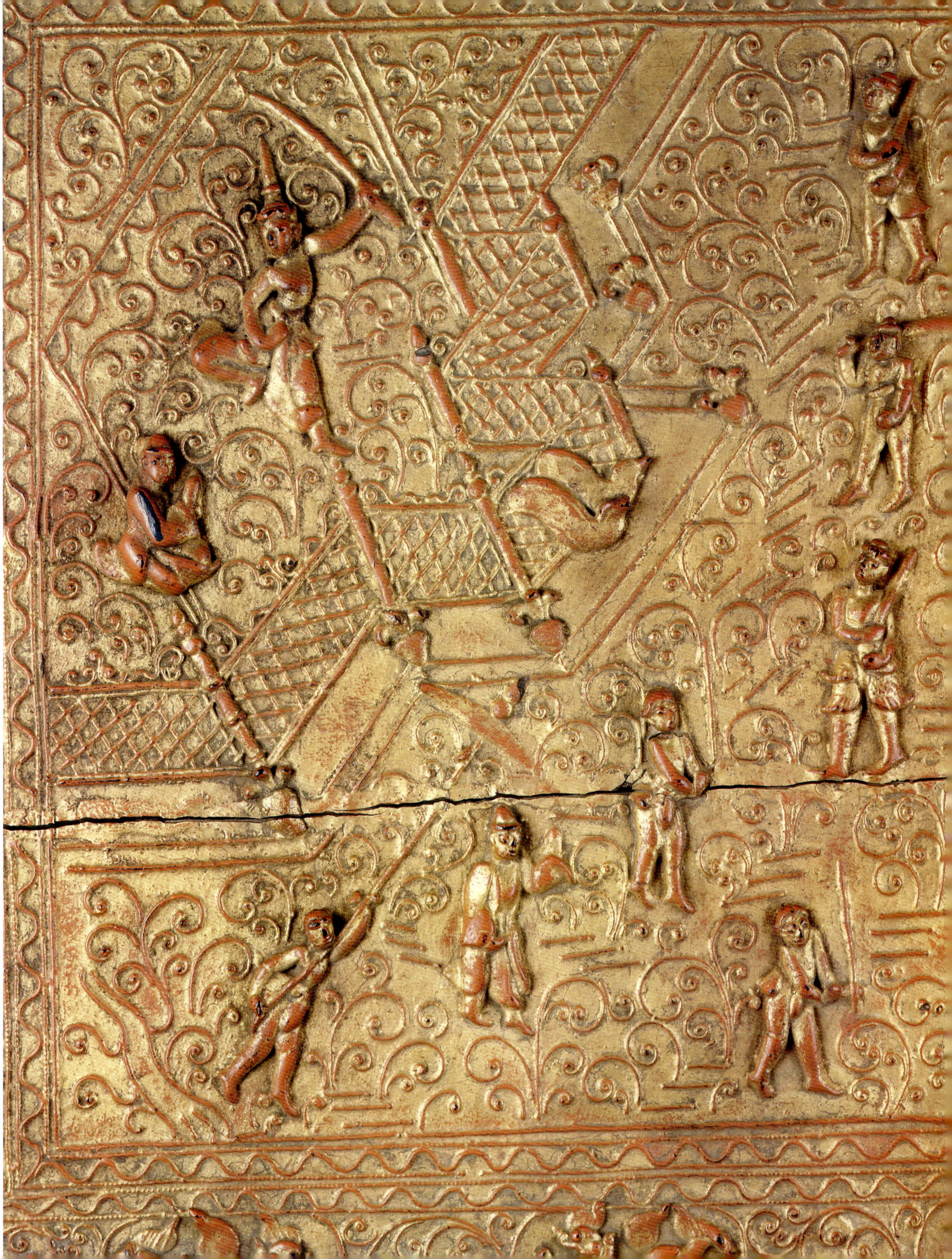

Detail of the chest lid of Plate 46. Reliefs rarely appear on the lid of a book chest; generally they are on the sides.

Plate 47 Black lacquer and gilt *(lai rot nam)* manuscript cabinets (h. 99 cm) preserve one of the most elegant of the graphic traditions in Thailand.

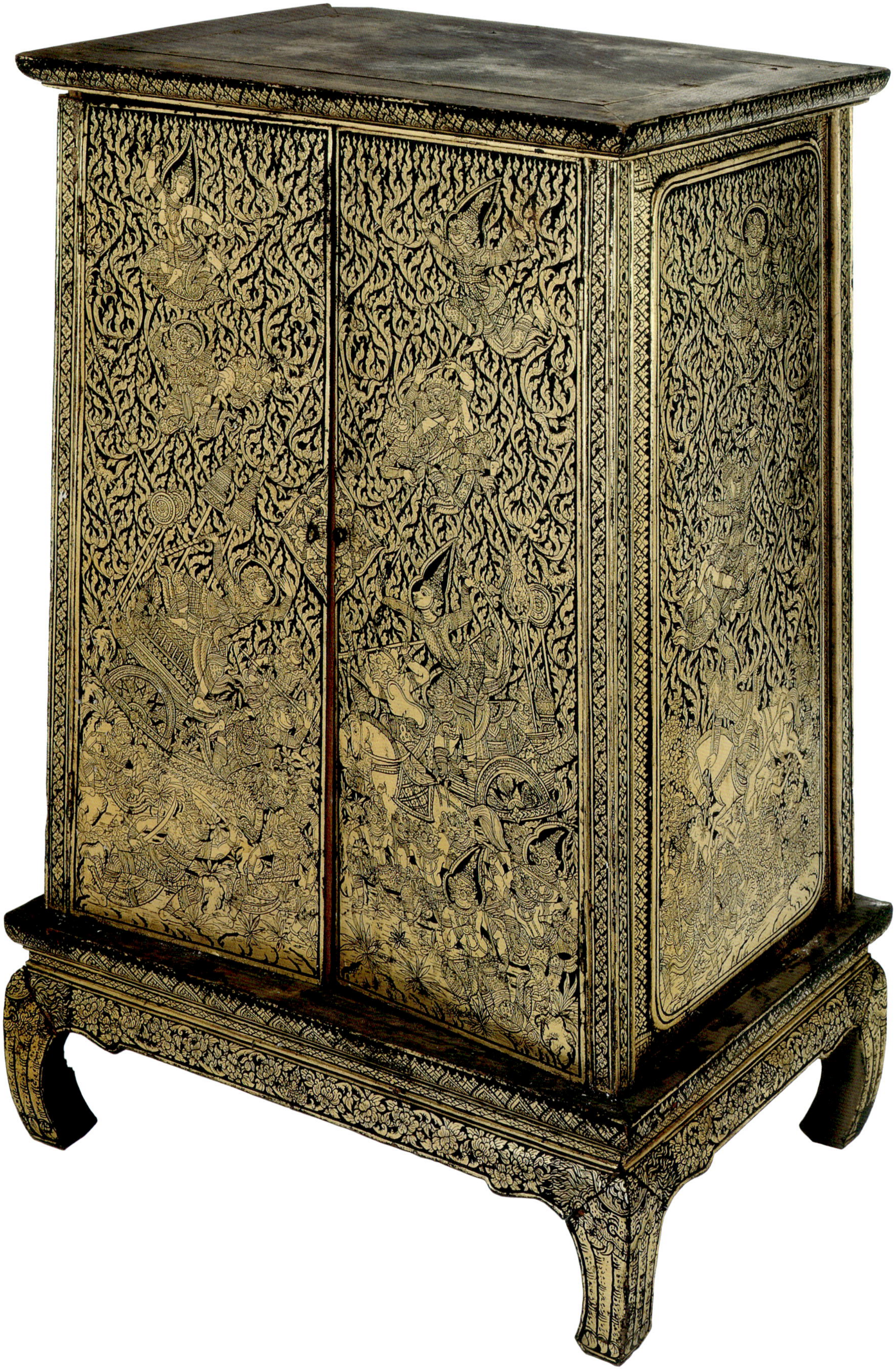

In larger Thai *wat*, a separate library, often built over water to deter termites and rodents, housed the manuscripts. But whether stored in a library or another building of the temple compound, the books were wrapped in cloth; marked, sometimes with an ivory marker; and placed in a box or cabinet for safe-keeping. In Thailand, where small boxes might hold a single book for a sermon (*hip phra thet*, Plate 30, p. 55), or larger cabinets (*tu phra thom*, Plates 47–50) the complete holdings of the monastery, the cabinets were often finely decorated with black lacquer and gold leaf. Few of these cabinets have made their way to the West. King Rama V (1868–1910) founded the Vajirayan Library in Bangkok, and many cabinets were donated at that time. Thus the Duke Collection, which includes over twenty cabinets (and twenty chests of varying sizes), represents the largest group of manuscript cabinets outside of Thailand.

The technique of applying gold leaf on a lacquer surface *(lai rot nam)* involves laying down three coats of lacquer (sap from the *Melanorrhoea usitata* tree, of the family *Anarcardiacae*), followed by a fourth coat of refined, thicker lacquer. After it is dried and polished, the design's outline, which has been drawn on paper, is pricked with a pointed instrument and pounced onto the surface. The artist then applies a yellow ink of orpiment mixed with sap from the *mah khwit* tree to the area that is to remain black. He then applies a final coat of lacquer, and before it dries completely, he covers the entire surface with gold leaf. A number of hours later, he thoroughly washes the surface with water, which rinses away the area previously covered with the yellow ink, and the gold leaf remains only on the intended design.

Ayutthaya-period manuscript cabinets are more sparsely decorated with gold leaf than those of the nineteenth century, when narrative scenes were incorporated into the designs. The subject matter on the cabinets, like that on temple murals, *phra bot*, and manuscripts, includes the *Thotsachat*, the *jataka*, the *Ramakian*, the life of the Buddha, and less frequently, the story of the good monk Phra Malai (Plate 48), who here preaches to heavenly beings at Culamani Chedi in Tavatimsa heaven in Indra's paradise. The narrative

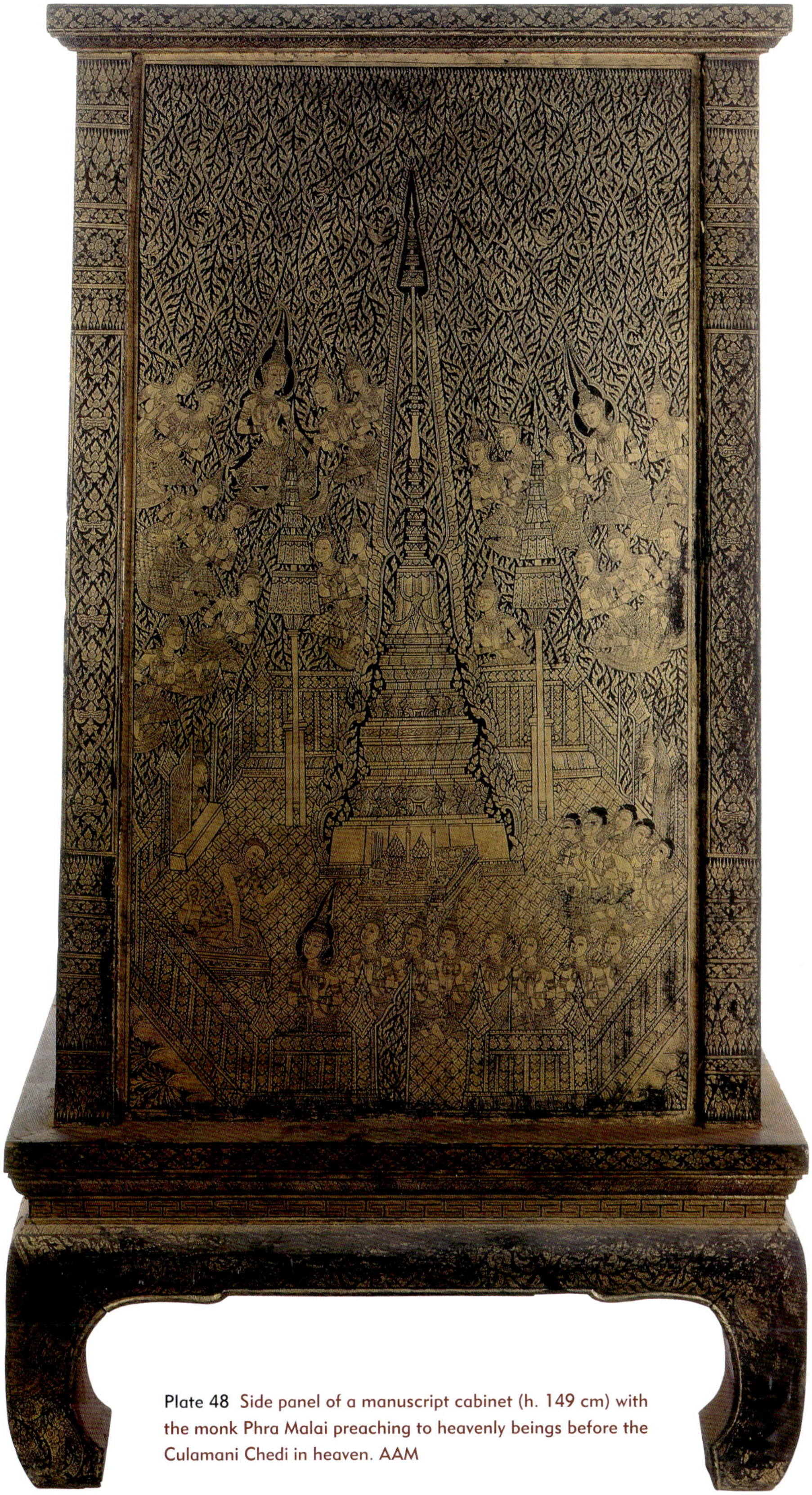

Plate 48 Side panel of a manuscript cabinet (h. 149 cm) with the monk Phra Malai preaching to heavenly beings before the Culamani Chedi in heaven. AAM

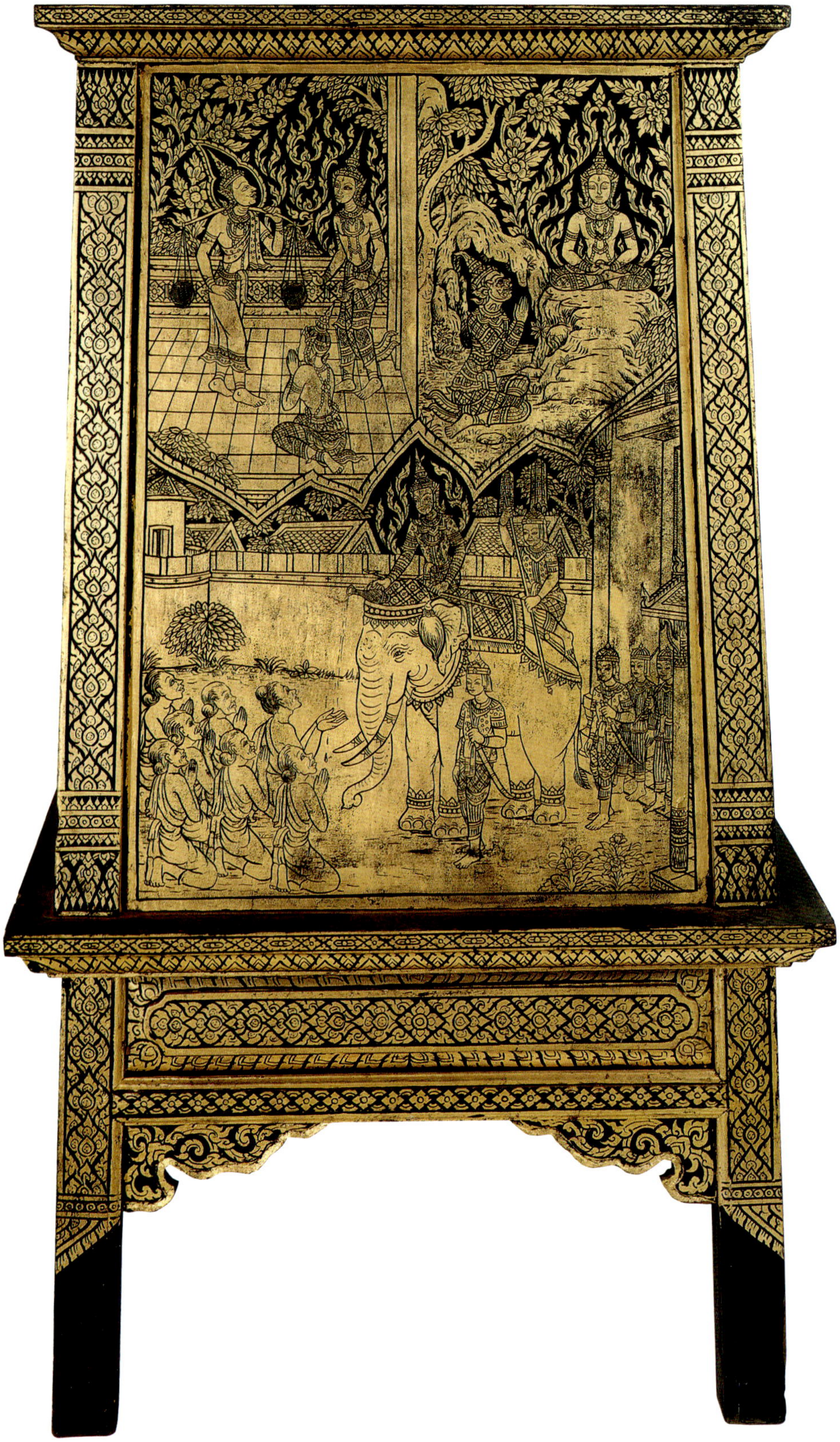

occurs in a swirling background motif *(lai kanok)* that combines vegetal and flame forms.

One small, late nineteenth-century cabinet in the Duke Collection is decorated with scenes of the last ten lives of the Buddha, the *Thotsachat.* Though lacking some of the detail of lacquer and gold leaf decor of earlier works, the depictions on the back of the cabinet (Plate 49) clearly describe the Nimi *jataka* (upper left), the Narada *jataka* (upper right), and the Vessantara *jataka* (below). The *bodhisatta* Nimi was a great king who was granted a visit to the heavens and hells, and returned to earth to tell his people of what he saw. In the Narada *jataka,* a false mendicant convinced the king that he need not live an upright life. His daughter, shocked at her father's subsequent waywardness, prayed to the heavens for help in returning him to his former goodness. Narada, the Brahma of that time, came to earth carrying two alms bowls suspended from the ends of a stick he carried over his shoulder and persuaded the king to uphold his duties. And in the last life illustrated, Vessantara makes his gift of the white elephant to the Brahmans.

The truncated pyramidal shape (Plate 50) of these cabinets is dictated by Thai architecture. The walls of a Thai wooden building are constructed on the ground, then raised not perpendicular to the floor but inclining inward at the top where they meet the roof. The lines of the furniture thus reflect and fit the slope of these walls. Some cabinets are carved in low relief (Plate 17, p. 38), while others are decorated with yellow, red, green, and black lacquer. Purely decorative motifs, such as flowers, animals (mythical or real), or landscapes, sometimes replace religious subject matter and may indicate that the cabinet was initially made for a secular purpose and later donated to a temple. At various points in time, Chinese-style decoration, without the overall *lai kanok,* was popular (Plate 50).[19] The decoration includes hunting scenes and animals in the Himaphan forest, which is identified by its trees that bear fruit of young maidens.

Plate 49 The tales of the last ten lives of the Buddha (Thai: *Thotsachat*) were sometimes depicted on manuscript cabinets (h. 91 cm). Thailand. WAM

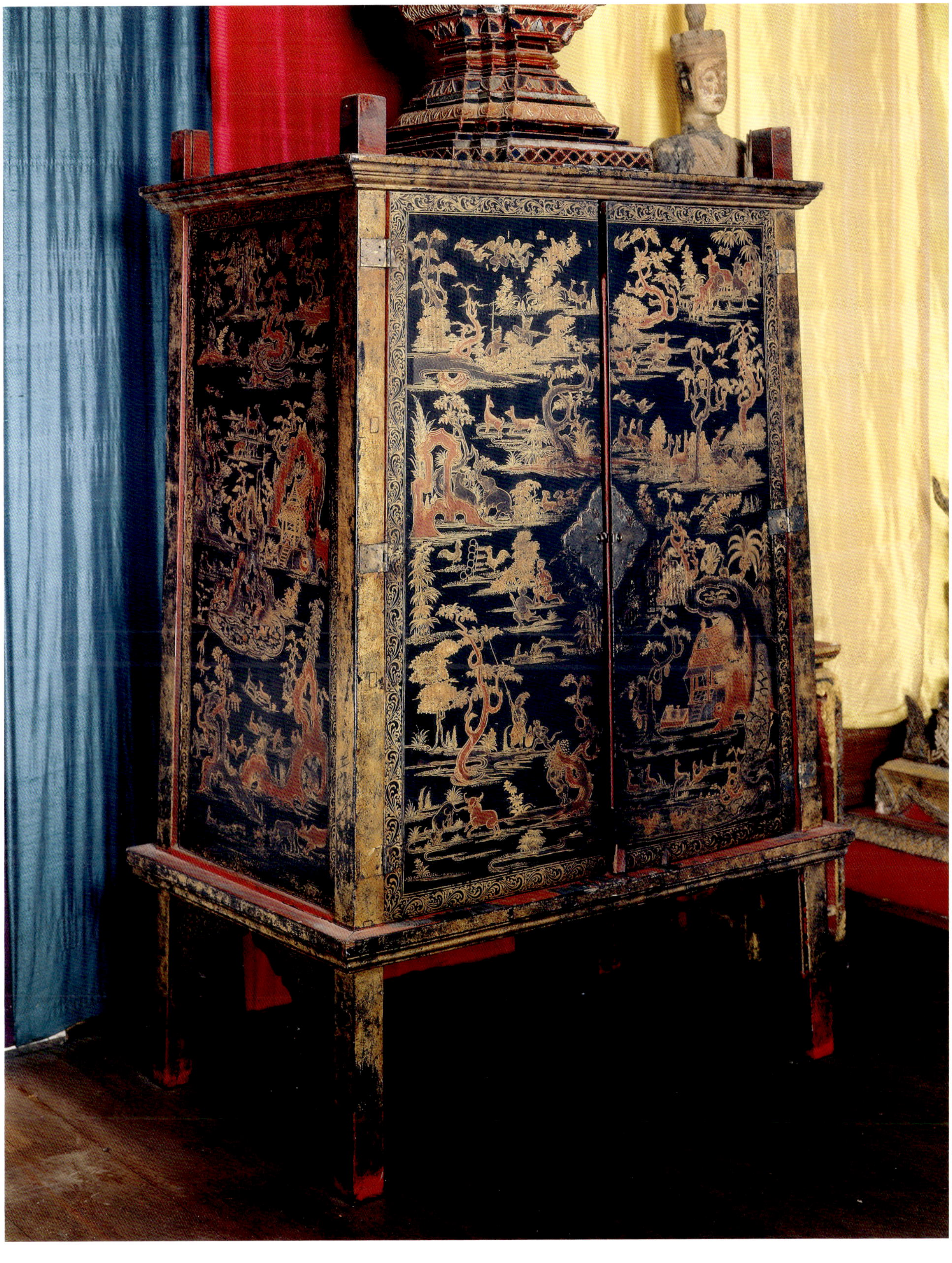

Plate 50 19th-century manuscript cabinet (h. 184 cm) with Chinese-style painting. WAM

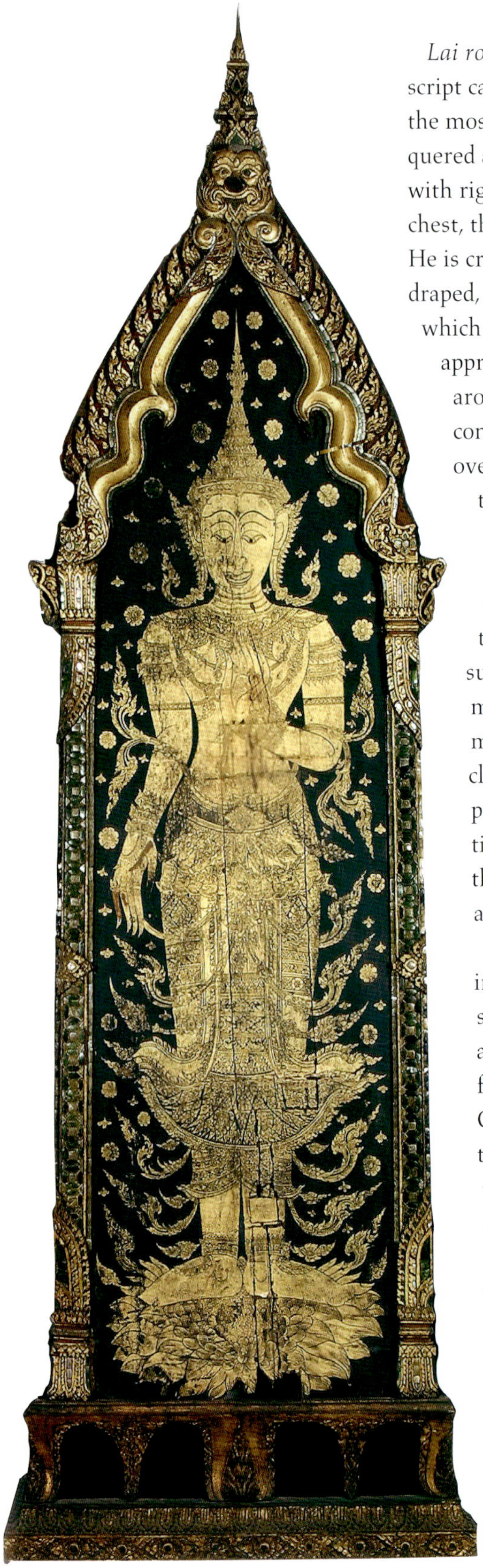

Lai rot nam decoration is not confined to manuscript cabinets, and in the Duke Collection, one of the most dramatic and unusual pieces is a large lacquered and gilt panel (Plate 51). A Buddha stands with right hand at his side and left hand raised to his chest, the gesture of reassurance *(abhaya mudra)*.[20] He is crowned and bejeweled, his clothing elaborately draped, with the lower hem flying. The lotus upon which he stands is finely detailed in an effect that approximates a sunflower. Flowers float airily around him; no close-packed background pattern confines the figure, as would be expected in the overall patterning of a manuscript cabinet. Rather, the manner in which the figure is painted is more in keeping with the style of a cloth banner. (See Plate 32, p. 57; the treatment of the headdress, the background, the drapery, the lotus beneath the Buddha's feet, and the surrounding frame are remarkably similar.) It may be that this large panel functioned in a manner similar to the banners and was placed close to an altar. A tradition of large lacquer panels occurs in central Thailand,[21] yet similarities in the figure's proportions, the treatment of the crown, as well as the carving of the frame also relate to imagery from the north.[22]

A set of three small screens is also decorated in *lai rot nam*. The stories depicted include a scene from the *Ramakian* of battling monkeys and two other unidentifiable stories, possibly folk tales or *jataka* (Plate 52). The presence of Chinese motifs, such as the flying dragon on the upper part of this screen, signifies a departure from more commonly depicted *jataka* or other textually based or apocryphal Buddhist stories. Orbs of the sun and moon contain the peacock and the hare respectively, both Chinese symbols that had become popular in Burma by the eighteenth century (the peacock was the symbol of the Kon-baung kings, 1752–1885) but which are less frequently encountered in Thailand.[23]

One might suppose that had Doris Duke completed the Thai Village Project, she would have had the replica of Wat Phra Kaeo adorned with mural paintings, the one important form of Thai painting not represented here. As the collection stands, the paintings include works in various media and from a broad cross section of Thai society, ranging from the horizontal banners of the villages of the northeast to the highly refined manuscript cabinets created in the Bangkok area. Their primary purpose may have been to serve a didactic function, yet their attractive textures and bright colors add further dimension to the vitality of the religious establishments that they adorned. The extensive holdings in the Duke Collection represent one of the most important collections of Thai paintings in the world.

Plate 51 Large panels (h. 348.5 cm) decorated in gold leaf are rare. This figure with left hand raised in *abhaya mudra* suggests he mirrored another of a pair, as the right is the hand commonly raised. Thailand. AAM

NOTES

1. She would have seen the temple banners at Jim Thompson's home after it was completed in 1958. Since they had met in New York in the 1930s (William Warren, personal communication, 10/02), it seems likely she visited him during that trip.

2. Jim Thompson also acquired a fine group of paintings on cloth of various sizes, a number of which are on display in his house.

3. There is a grand gallery around Wat Phra Kaeo, where the *Ramakian* is depicted and where Hanuman is particularly extolled; his escapades as a rake are given particular import.

4. For a lengthy description of the *Thotsachat*, see Elizabeth Wray, Clare Rosenfield, and Dorothy Bailey, *Ten Lives of the Buddha: Siamese Temple Paintings and Jataka Tales* (New York and Tokyo: Weatherhill, 1972).

5. Henry Ginsburg dates this painting to 1800–1820; personal communication, 10/02.

6. See Forrest McGill, "Painting the 'Great Life,'" in Juliane Schober, ed., *Sacred Biography in the Buddhist Traditions of South and Southeast Asia* (Honolulu: University of Hawai'i Press, 1997), 194–217, for a discussion of a partial set of paintings. Also see Phya Anuman Rajadhon, *Thet Maha Chat* (in English; Bangkok: Fine Arts Department, 1969), and Bonnie Pacala Brereton, *Thai Tellings of Phra Malai: Texts and Rituals Concerning a Popular Buddhist Saint* (Tempe: Arizona State University, 1995).

7. Mattiebelle Gittinger and H. Leedom Lefferts, Jr., *Textiles and the Tai Experience in Southeast Asia* (Washington, D.C.: The Textile Museum, 1992), 124.

8. E.B. Cowell, ed., *Jatakas: Stories of Buddha's Former Births* (Delhi: Cosmo Publications, 1978), vol. 6, 260.

9. Cowell, *Jatakas*, 261.

10. Naengnoi Punjabhan and Somchai Na Nakhonphanom, *The Art of Thai Wood Carving: Sukhothai, Ayutthaya, Ratanakosin* (Bangkok: Rerngrom Publishing Co., Ltd., 2535 B.E. [1992]), 107.

11. For the most detailed discussion of manuscripts in English, see Henry Ginsburg, *Thai Manuscript Painting* (London: The British Library, 1989), and *Thai Art and Culture: Historic Manuscripts from Western Collections* (London: The British Library, 2000).

12. Ginsburg, *Thai Manuscript Painting*, 11.

13. Ibid., 11.

14. Ibid., 45.

15. Brereton, *Thai Tellings of Phra Malai*, 183.

16. Ibid., 185.

17. Pratapaditya Pal, "Fragmentary Cloth Paintings from Early Pagan and Their Relations with Indo-Tibetan Traditions," Donald M. Stadtner, ed., "The Art of Burma: New Studies," *Marg* 50:4 (June 1999): 79–88.

18. Sylvia Fraser-Lu, personal communication, 10/02. The tale of Byat-wi, the outlaw and the single soldier defending the city against Kyanzittha, suggests itself, as the relief portrays a single soldier brandishing his sword on the steps to the palace. Mrs. Fraser-Lu does not know of any instance of the story being depicted. (Maung Htin Aung, *Folk Elements in Burmese Buddhism* [Rangoon: U Hla Maung, 1959], 71.)

19. Hiram W. Woodward, Jr., and Henry Ginsburg suggest this cabinet dates to the second or third reign, the second quarter of the nineteenth century.

20. The fact that his left hand, rather than the characteristic right hand, is raised suggests this figure was one of a pair standing to either side of a central Buddha. The artist would have painted the left hand raised for the sake of symmetry.

21. Forrest McGill, personal communication, 10/02.

22. For northern examples, see the painted standing adorned Buddhas on the rear wall of the Tai Lue temple of Wat Nong Bua in Tha Wang Phu district, Nan Province, with a similar crown (Amranand and Warren, *Lanna Style*, 83 and 110). These figures are also elaborately garbed in patterned textiles, like the Duke figure, and stand in outlined frames. This treatment, with a Buddha outlined in gold, is also found at Wat Prasat in Chiang Mai; that Buddha stands on an elaborately detailed lotus.

23. Pat Chirapravati reminded me of a Si Thep plaque (ninth century) that shows the hare in the moon.

Plate 52 One of a set of three small screens (h. 104 cm) with gold-leaf decoration. Thailand.

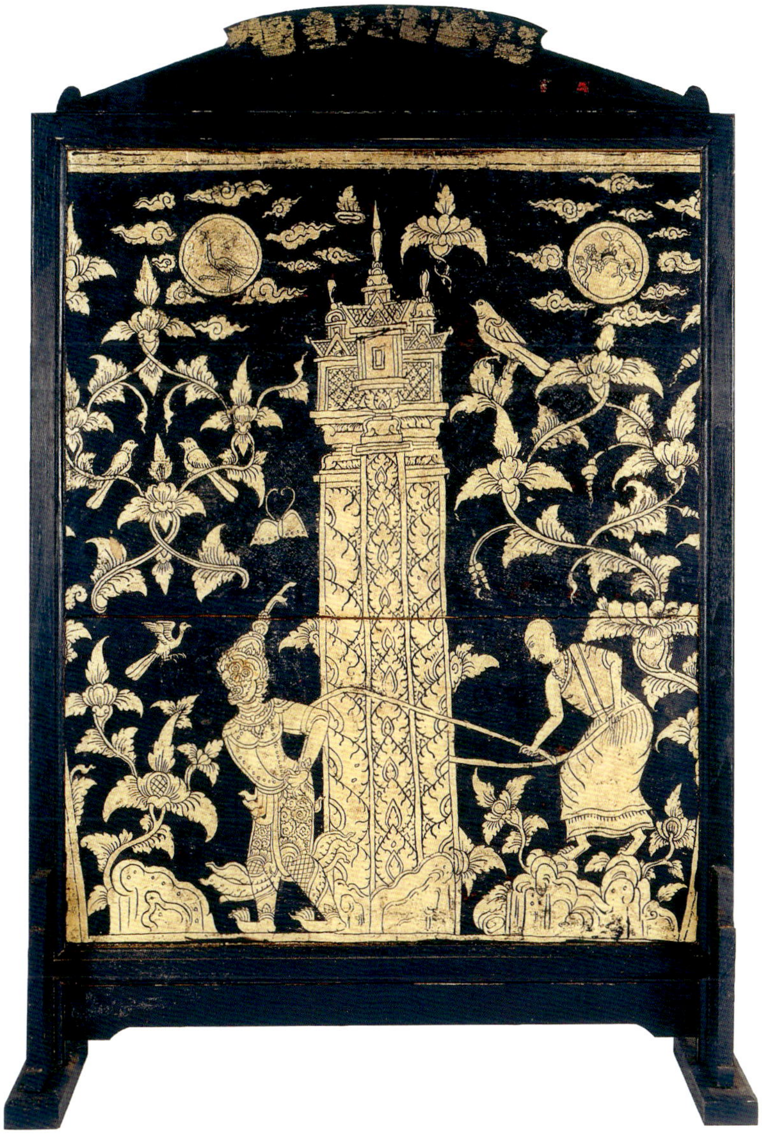

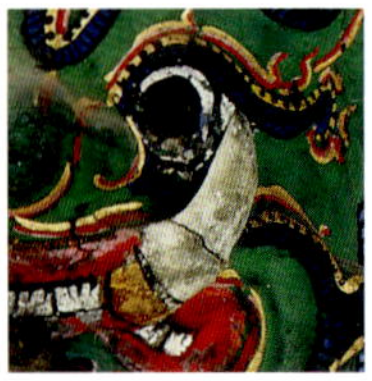

Decorative and Performing Arts

WE KNOW DORIS DUKE HAD GRAND DREAMS REGARDING THE Thai Village Project, but we know little of the day-to-day decisions that shaped her collecting. The reality of furnishing a village dictated that she collect certain types of objects—religious for the *ubosot* and *sala,* and secular for the home. While most of the sculpture and painting—a large portion of the collection—is religious, many of the temple offertory pieces and objects intended for display in the houses could be described as decorative art. In fact, according to Bérenx,[1] her intention was to gather a collection of decorative arts, a designation that probably reflects a perception of the decorative quality of Thai and Burmese art more than it does a conscious decision to indulge in the lesser arts.

Nineteenth-century missionaries and visitors were taken aback by the colorful ostentation they saw in the temples of Thailand and Burma, and in the twentieth century, this same effect conflicted with an aesthetic that valued the perceived subtlety of 'Oriental art.' The gilding, glossy lacquer, and inlaid glass so profusely applied to Thai and Burmese art, and the replication of image types, the result of a conservative artistic tradition, also colored a Western view that prizes the unique work of an individual.

Southeast Asia is renowned for the variety and quality of its artistic productions, including wood carving, bronze casting, painting, mother-of-pearl inlay, textiles, ivory carving, ceramics, and metalwork. When visiting private homes in Thailand, Miss Duke would have seen objects like those she purchased—inlaid boxes and trays, carved ivory implements, weapons, Chinese-made enameled porcelain with Thai designs *(bencharong)*—an eclectic selection, to say the least. She embraced it all, much as she had with her Islamic collection, which she arranged in a very personal manner at Shangri La. If Shangri La informs what the Thai Village Project would have been, then we can imagine the richness that experience would have afforded.

CERAMICS

Ceramics comprise a quarter of the Southeast Asian collection, just over 500 pieces, and attest Miss Duke's abiding interest in them. She assembled other extensive ceramics collections, most notably Islamic wares at Shangri La, where a quarter of that collection falls into this category. This interest coincides with her taste at Rough Point, her home in Newport, where Chinese ceramics are dispersed throughout the house. At Duke Farms, Miss Duke brought together a group of Chinese ceramics, mostly of later-period material, but including a wall case of tomb furnishings in the Palm Room. She displayed the later works

above **detail, Plate 74, page 91**
opposite **detail, Plate 57, page 80**

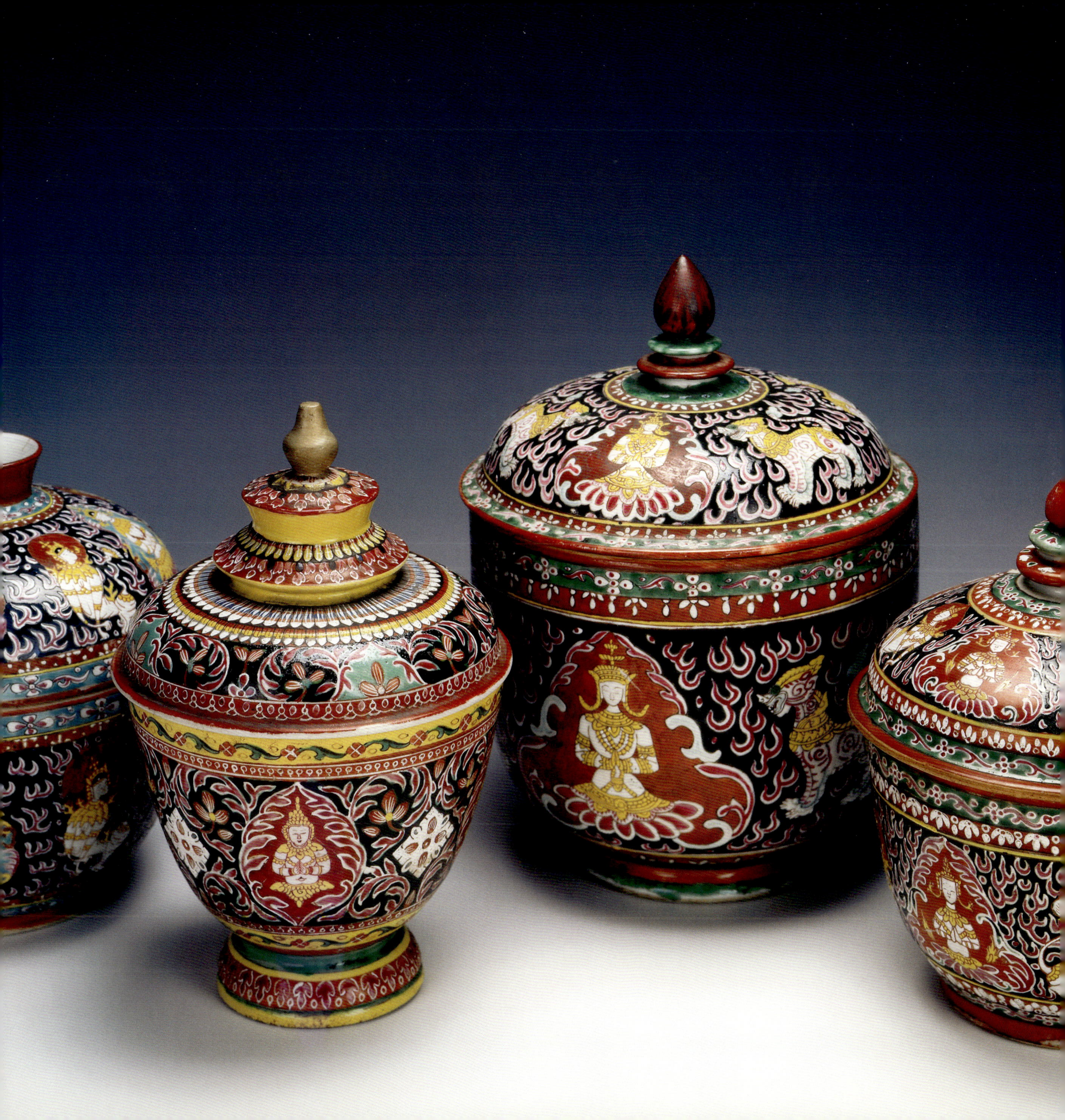

Plate 53 Khmer storage jar (h. 66 cm) of the 12th century.

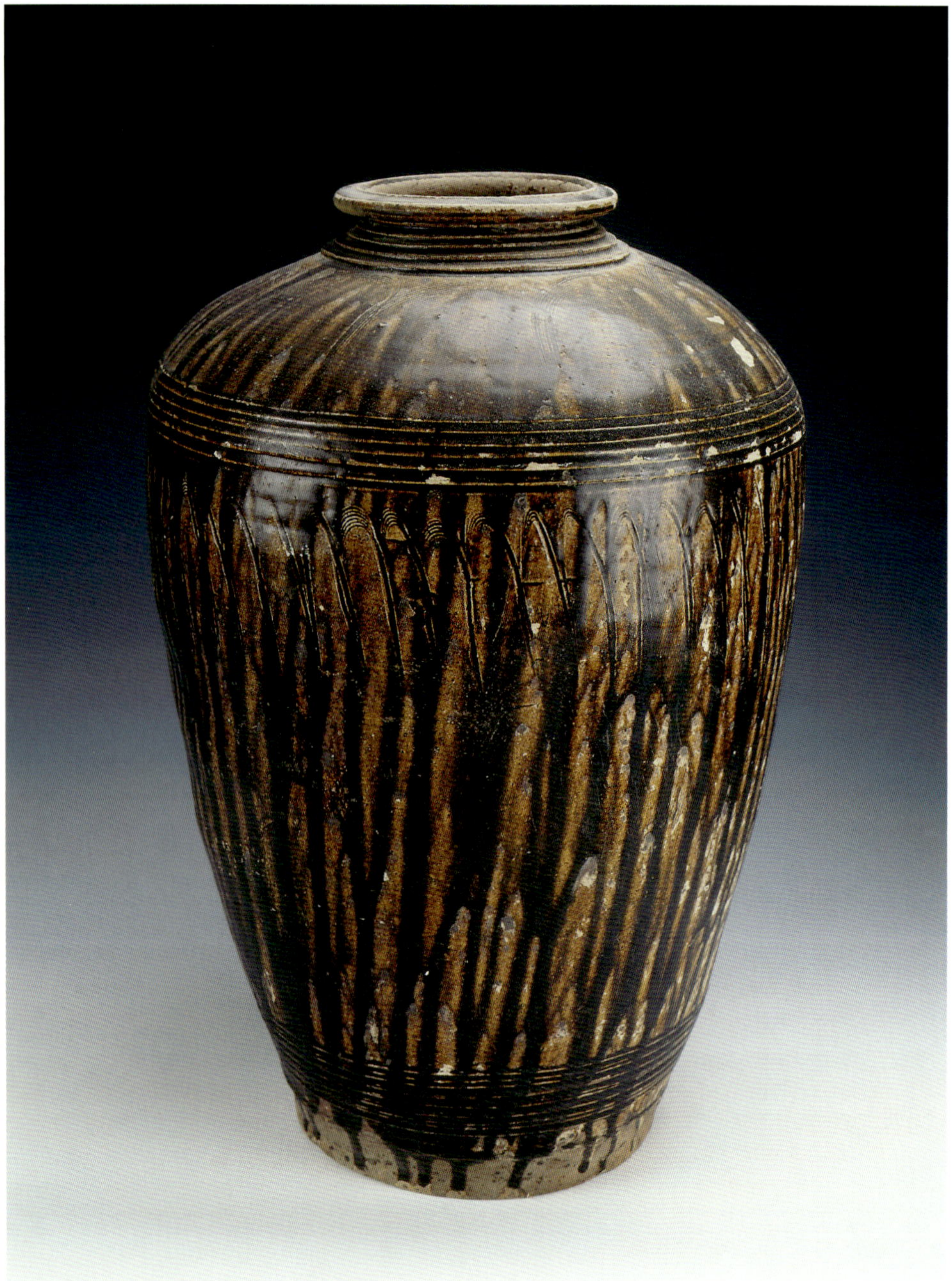

in cases in the entry to her bedroom, which was decorated with Asian furnishings and sculpture.

The Southeast Asian ceramics in the Duke Collection date to the twelfth through nineteenth centuries. The production of unglazed wares may have begun in the region as early as the sixth millennium BCE,[2] and certainly by the third millennium, the making of coiled pots, smoothed with anvil and paddle, was widespread. That same technique of manufacture is still used in many areas of rural Thailand, where lowfire, unglazed wares are made for local use. One large Khmer (Cambodian) twelfth-century storage jar in the collection (Plate 53) illustrates a vessel type that was to become critical for the export market. These glazed jars of varying sizes were used to hold honey, fermented fish, and other products shipped from mainland Southeast Asia to the islands and beyond. The jars served a secondary function after they had been emptied of their cargo, as they continued to be used for storage of water or of local products in the destination areas. Glazed ceramics were particularly coveted and were sometimes kept as prized heirlooms in island Southeast Asia, since they were not produced in that region.

By the fourteenth through sixteenth centuries, large quantities of glazed wares, for both export and local use, were being produced in the kilns of central Thailand. A small number of these pieces are in the holdings of the Doris Duke Collection, though most date to the eighteenth and nineteenth centuries. During the fourteenth through sixteenth centuries, the kiln sites of Sukhothai and Sawankhalok in Thailand produced large numbers of export wares. From the earliest evidence of international trade, ceramics and textiles have constituted a large portion of the cargoes of Chinese, Arab, Indian, and Southeast Asian ships. The Chinese had been exporting ceramics from the Han period (second century BCE–second century CE), with a marked increase in exports in the twelfth and thirteenth centuries. When Emperor Hongwu (1368–1398) prohibited private trade, Southeast Asian merchants took the opportunity to increase their own production and sales. From this period until the end

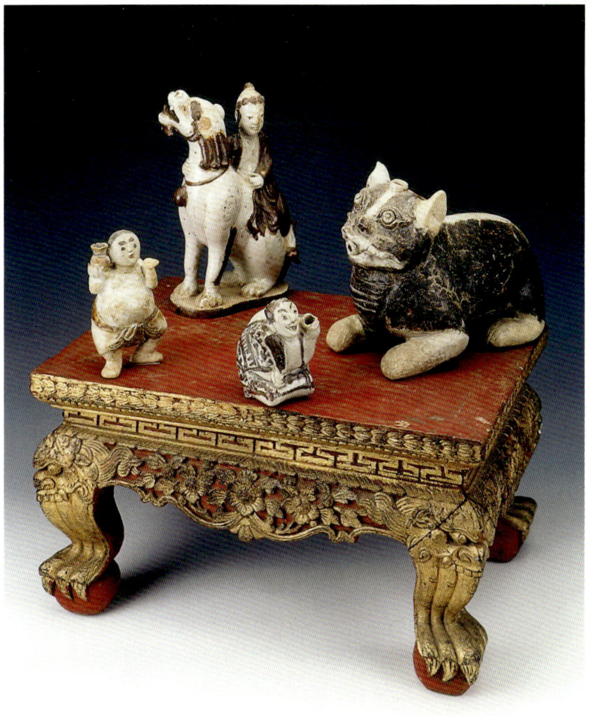

Chinese influence and may be included in a group of ceramics of a slightly later period, possibly the seventeenth century, and quite probably made for local use.[3]

Brahma, the Hindu god of creation, illustrates the presence of Brahmanical deities in the Buddhist pantheon (Plate 55); in Thailand and Burma, Brahma and Indra (the chief god) are often depicted as attendants of the Buddha. But in Buddhist cosmology, the 'Brahma' gods are divinities, who float above the various heavens, and this work undoubtedly served as a finial suggesting the sacred cosmology.[4] Most large-scale pieces of the fifteenth and sixteenth centuries were affixed to buildings, often along the eaves. Anthropomorphic ceramic figures of this period are most often demonic guardians, who stand with club in hand. This figure, with its brown and white glazes, is particularly rare.

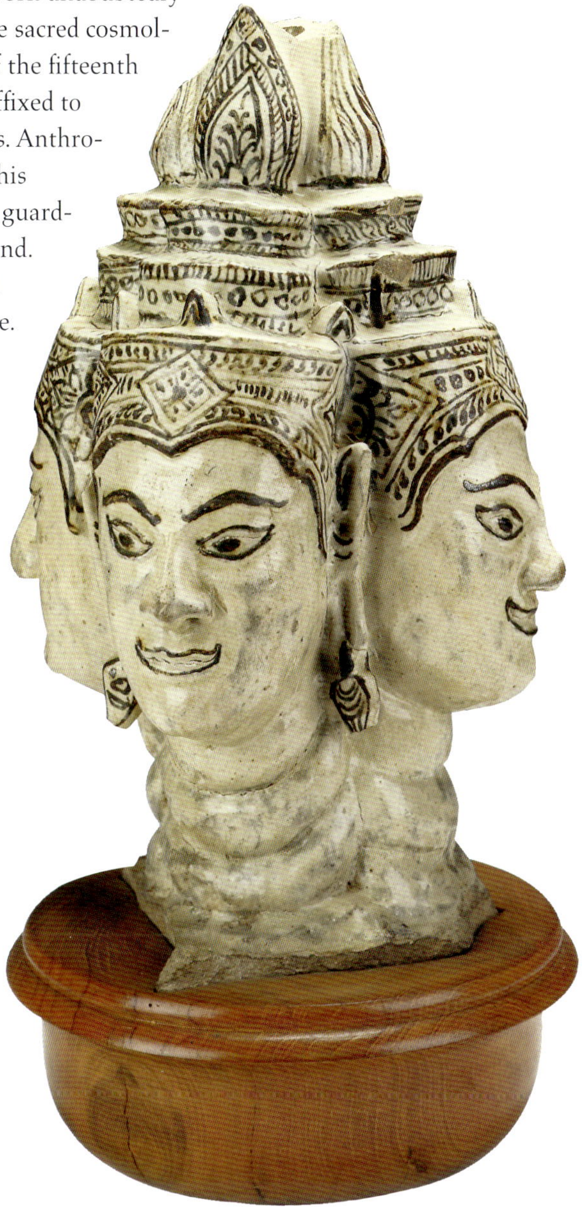

of the sixteenth century, when another Chinese emperor formally revoked the prohibition against trade, Vietnamese and Thai traders filled the gap, contending only with illegally smuggled Chinese goods.

Ceramics from this period consist largely of bowls, covered boxes and jars, miniature boxes, jarlets, and figurines, and to a lesser degree, locally used architectural fixtures. The Duke Collection includes anthropomorphic incense holders, waterdroppers, and a few large architectural fixtures. The smaller pieces (Plate 54) are all glazed with either brown and white glazes or brown underglaze, common choices for Sawankhalok wares. Their uses vary: the hunched man in the foreground is a common type of waterdropper found both in Thailand and throughout insular Southeast Asia, where most of the export wares were shipped; the standing figure functioned as an incense burner, while the cat was used for lustration. The lustration of religious images plays an important role in both Buddhist and Hindu ceremonies. The figure seated on a *fu* dog, a Chinese mythical creature rarely depicted in Thailand, indicates

above **Plate 54 Thai wares (h. 7–18 cm) of the Sawankhalok kilns dating to the 14th through 16th centuries. WAM**

right **Plate 55 Brahma (h. 39 cm), the Hindu god of creation, was adopted into Buddhism. Thailand. WAM**

right **Plate 56** Brocades were produced in Thailand during the 19th century; printed cotton textiles had been imported from India starting at a much earlier period.

below **Plate 57** *Bencharong* enameled porcelain ceramics were produced in China for the Thai market. The *tho* jars (h. 21–26 cm) are characteristic Thai shapes, in contrast to the covered rice bowl (far left), a Chinese shape. AAM

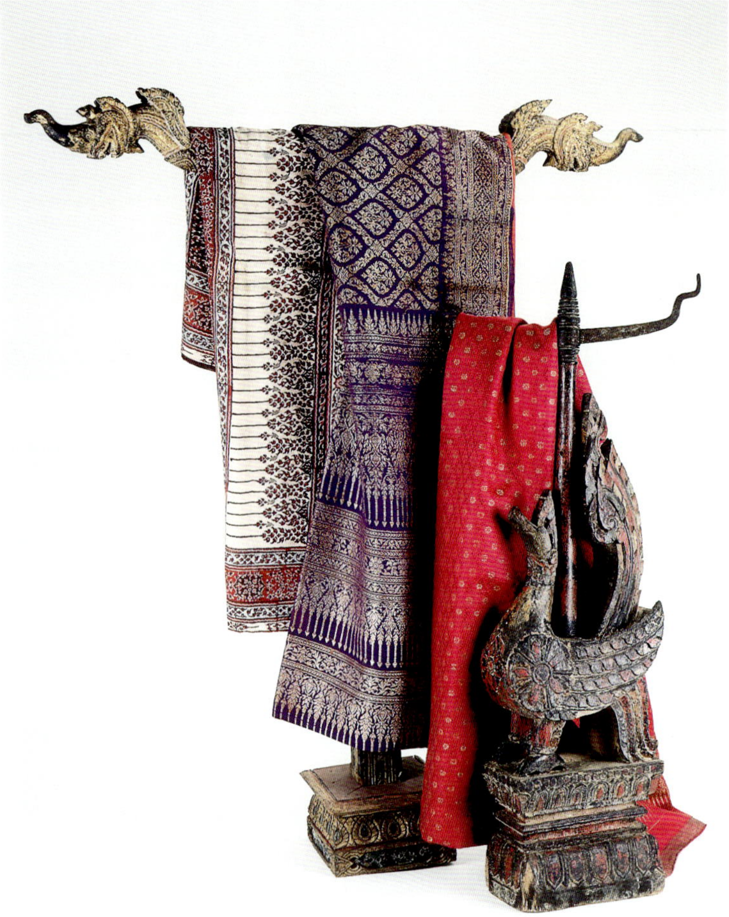

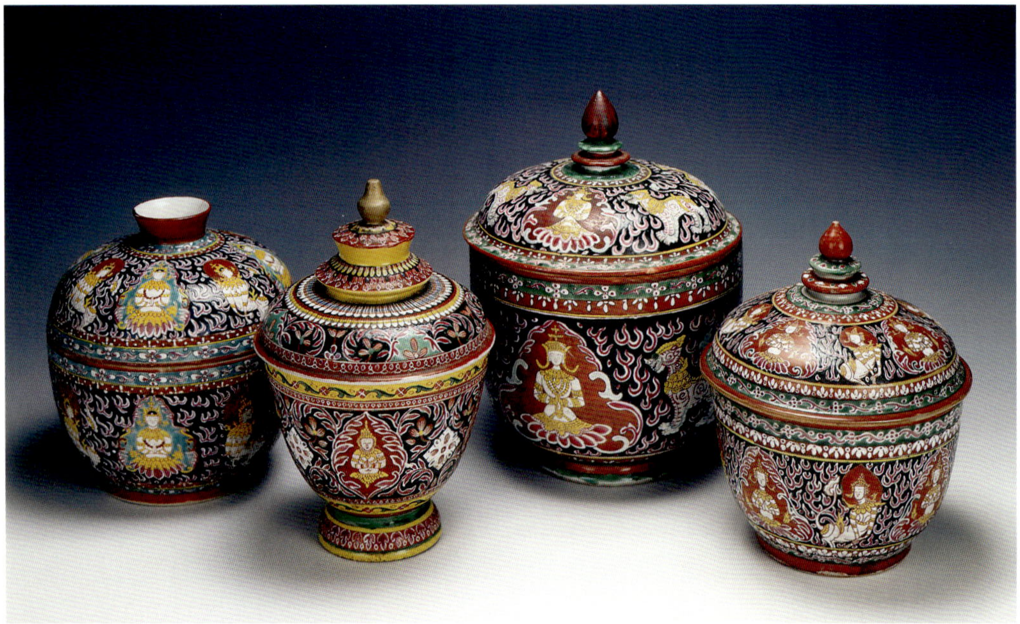

A much larger group of ceramics in the Duke Collection consists of the holdings of five-color *(bencharong)* and gold-washed wares *(lai nam thong)*, produced in China for the Thai market beginning in the sixteenth or seventeenth century, but in greater quantities in the eighteenth and nineteenth centuries.[5] Using model books supplied by the Thai, the potters of the kilns of Jingdezhen produced overglaze enamel porcelains (and occasionally stonewares) in Thai shapes and using Thai motifs. These same motifs are identical to the designs of the printed cottons *(sarasa)* produced in India for the Thai market (textile on far left of Plate 56) and indicate the use in India of pattern books for textiles similar to those used in China for ceramics.[6] In some instances, the glazed pots were produced in Jingdezhen, then shipped to Canton for painting, as were most export wares of the Qing dynasty (1644–1910). Primarily tableware, the most common shapes are the rice bowl, the covered rice bowl, stem plate, and the *tho* jar, a covered bowl in an urn shape.

The form of the *tho* jar is often compared to that of a reliquary, both the large architectural *chedi* and smaller reliquary urns of bronze or (earlier examples) of clay, though there is great variety in the overall form (Plate 57). The knob on the lid mimics the umbrellas that mount the traditional *chedi* and contrasts with a more typical Chinese shape, such as the covered rice bowl on the far left, the lid of which can be turned upside down to create another bowl. The overglaze decoration of these containers is typical of *bencharong* from the end of the eighteenth through the first half of the nineteenth century with alternating heavenly beings from one of the six lower heavens *(theppanom)* and half-man and half-lion *(norasingh)* figures set amid a background of the flamelike *kanok* that fills all remaining space. The largest example has the more unusual combination of lions alternating with the *theppanom* (reverential figure).

Few *bencharong* ceramics survive from the Ayutthaya period, but imports increased with King Rama I's rebuilding of the new capital at Bangkok, as re-creating

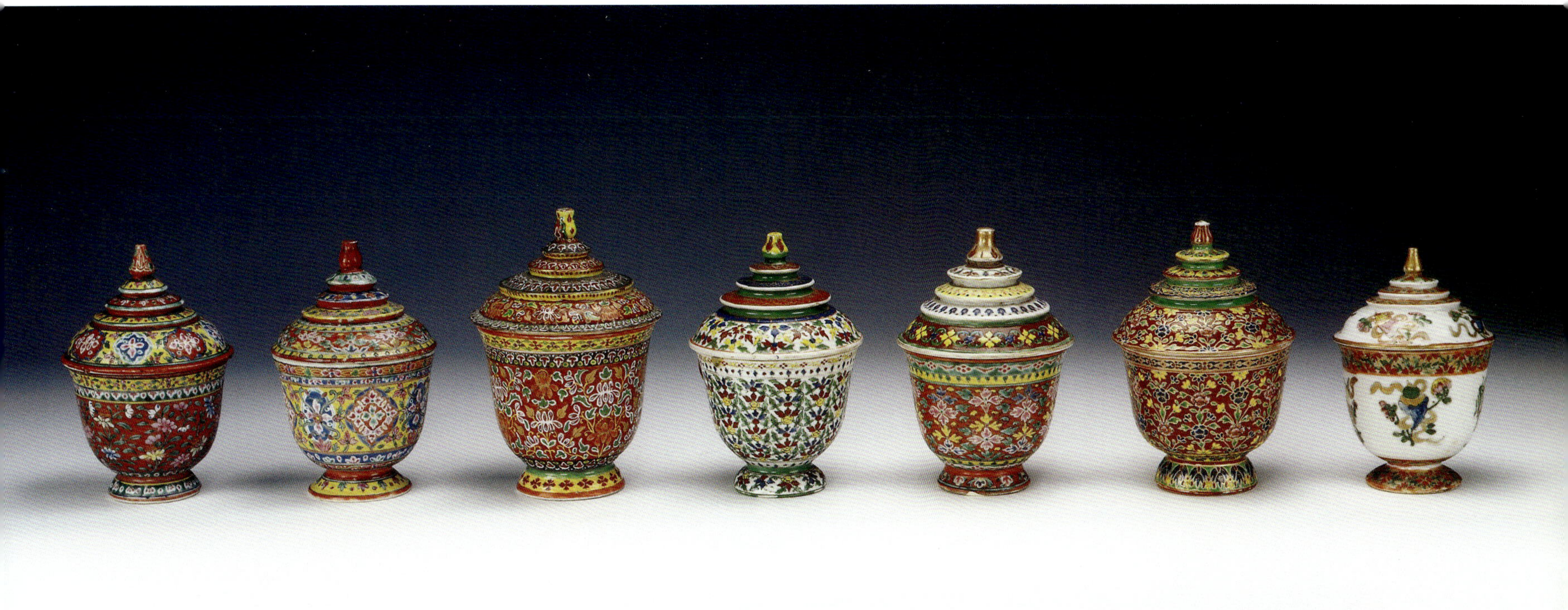

the glories of Ayutthaya probably resulted in new orders for wares based on earlier models from the Chinese kilns. Gold-washed *lai nam thong* wares likely developed during the period of his reign. Many of the *tho* jars in this collection are classified *lai nam thong* (Plate 58).[7] Overglaze enamels require separate firings, probably one or two for *bencharong,* with an additional firing for the *lai nam thong,* as gold is fired at a lower temperature.

The shapes, many of which have no relation to the Chinese repertoire of shapes, and the tightly packed overall designs are characteristic of the *bencharong* and *lai nam thong* wares. Even the decoration on ceramic spoons incorporates the all-over pattern, while in some, a *theppanom* is placed in the bowl of the spoon. Occasionally the motifs are not so tightly packed. A covered serving bowl, one of a set of graduated containers (Plate 59), is sparsely decorated with a gold pattern on a cobalt blue ground that relates it to wares dating to the period of Rama II (1809–1824).[8]

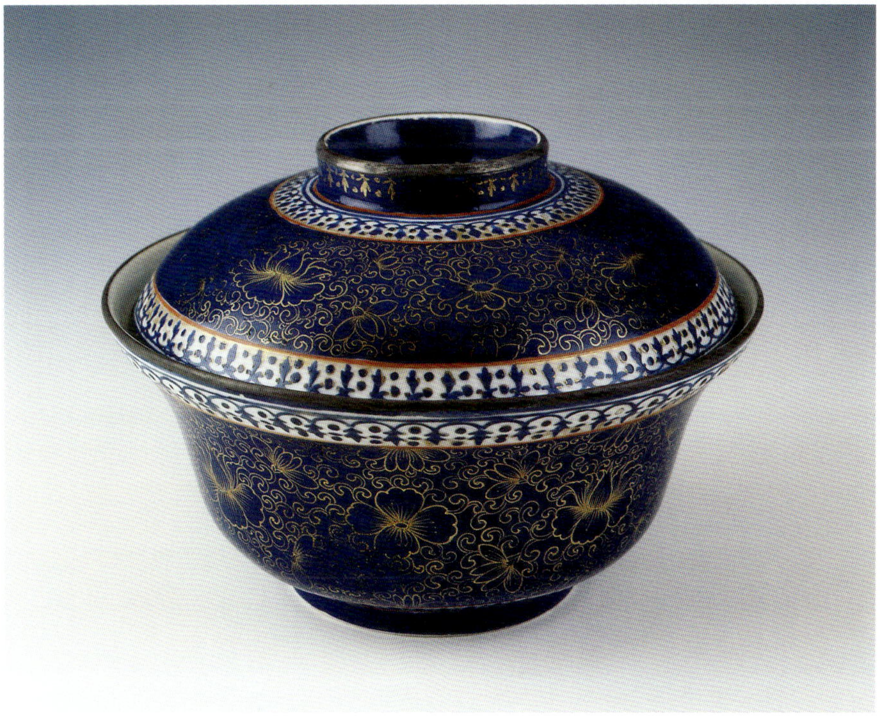

top **Plate 58 The shape of the *tho* jar (average h. 16 cm) resembles a reliquary. China. AAM**

bottom **Plate 59 The gold overglaze on this *lai nam thong* covered serving bowl (diam. 13.5 cm) required an additional firing. China.**

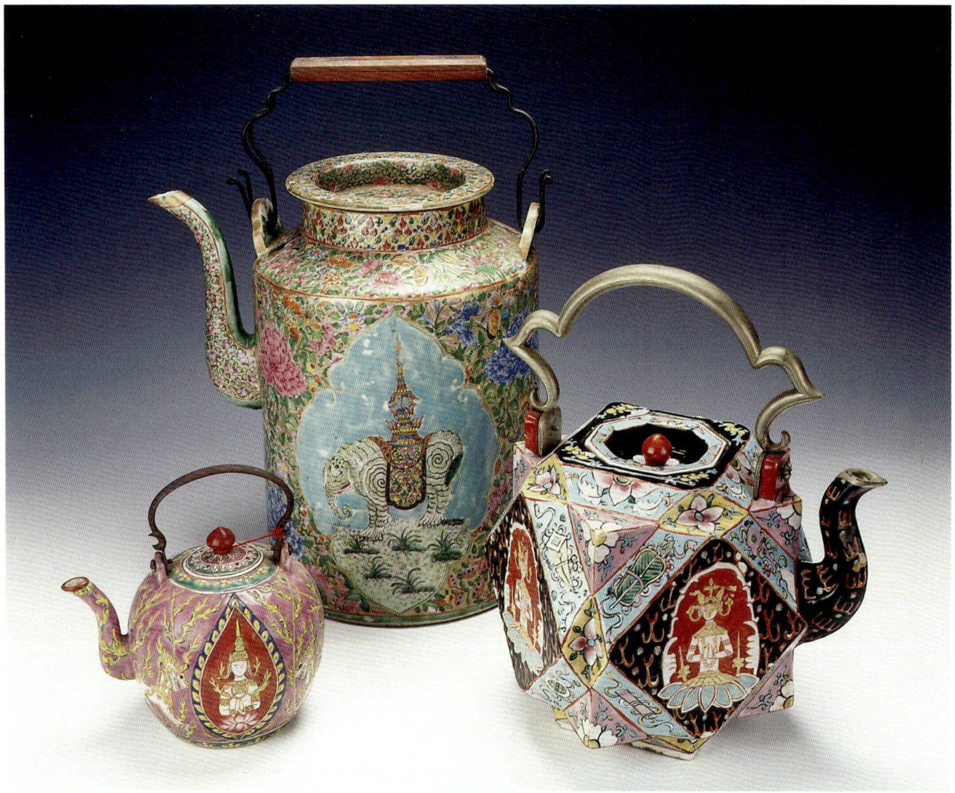

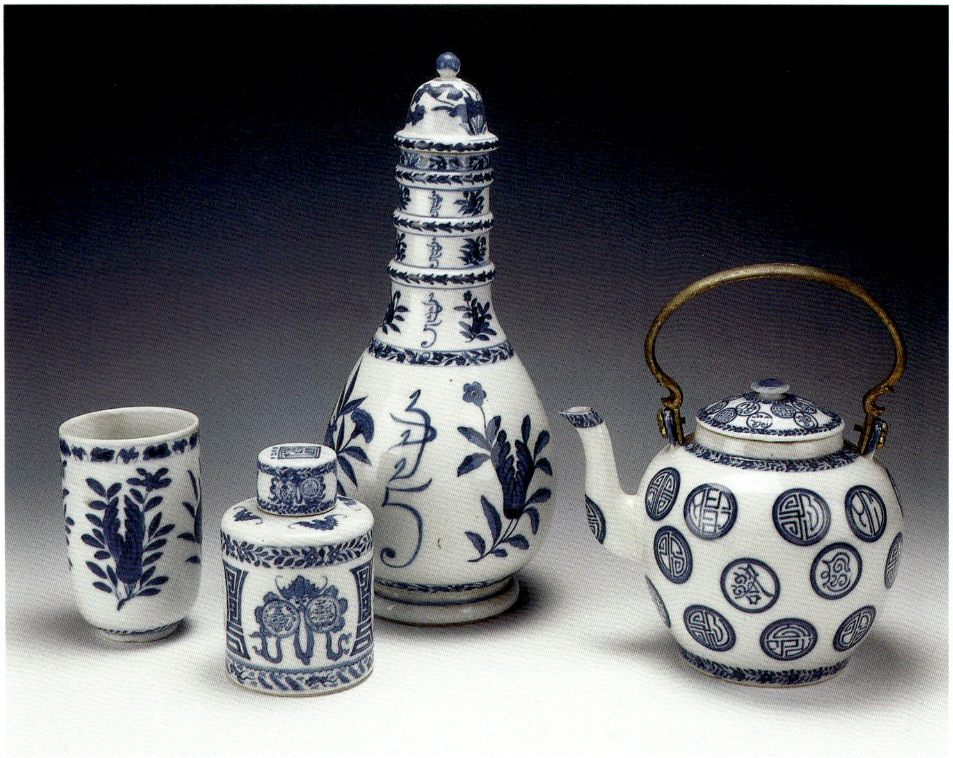

It was with the teapots that the artisans seem to have experimented. Both the shapes and the decor are varied (Plate 60). The largest of the pots illustrated here (one of a pair in the collection) may be a rice wine vessel rather than a teapot; it shows the rare combination of Chinese rose medallion pattern and *lai nam thong*. Yet the elephant, drawn by someone who has clearly never seen an elephant, wears a blanket and carries an offering stand adorned in typical Thai motifs. The multifaceted teapot also combines Chinese and Thai motifs, with the characteristic *theppanom* in cartouches and various Chinese symbols set against a pale blue ground. The small, rose-colored teapot, of a more typical size and shape, also includes the *theppanom* in a cartouche, this time with lions *(singha)* placed at either side against the rose background and with no defining outline; it dates to the period of Rama V (1868–1910).[9]

A group of blue-and-white ceramics created during the reign of King Rama V (1868–1910) and used by members of the royal family (Plate 61), is decorated in a variety of patterns and sometimes includes inscriptions along with motifs, or repetitive patterns of the highly stylized initials of Rama V. Sets of these patterns in the Duke Collection include a cup, teapot, tea caddy (in the foreground), carafe, and spittoon. The ceramics with an auspicious Chinese coin motif (like that on the teapot) are particularly coveted by collectors today.[10]

LACQUER

Lacquer—resilient, waterproof, and lending itself to artistic expression—has been used throughout Asia from a very early period. Sophisticated lacquer bowls have been found in China's Hemudu tomb sites of the fourth to third millennium BCE,[11] but the earliest reference to lacquer use in Burma is in a Chinese text

top **Plate 60** Teapots (h. 16–37 cm) were created in a variety of shapes. China. WAM, AAM

bottom **Plate 61** Blue-and-white ceramics (h. 11.5–32 cm) from the time of Rama V. China.

referring to the Pyu peoples (second century BCE–tenth century CE).[12] No Burmese examples are known from that early period; a plain cylindrical box, datable to approximately 1284, is the earliest example yet found in Burma.[13] This is far earlier than finds in Thailand, where the earliest objects date to the Ayutthaya period (1350–1767), though the use of lacquer certainly predates this period.

The Burmese elaborately decorate the containers in which they carry alms to the monastery.[14] Generally fashioned in fantastic shapes with *thayo*, a putty of lacquer sap mixed with clay, sawdust, or ash applied over a bamboo form, the vessels are further enhanced with colored glass (Plate 62). Today, most of these pieces are produced in Mandalay. One popular bird-shaped form for ceremonial use holds betel paraphernalia. The habit of chewing a quid of a betel leaf containing areca nut and slaked lime (of burned limestone or mollusk shells), with other spices or tobacco added, was prevalent in Southeast Asia into the twentieth century as an important part of social interchange. The *hintha*, an auspicious mythical bird probably deriving from the goose, is seen frequently in Burmese art. The spiky container next to it holds betel leaves.

The third container was used to offer food at the monastery. Since this and the other offering receptacles are of thin strips of bamboo, coiled and stacked, they give the appearance of having been turned on a lathe. Special stands of fantastic design were made to display some offering containers, and one Burmese example is visible before the *thammat* in the Sculpture section (Figure 12, p. 44).

The prevalence of lacquer in the arts of Southeast Asia cannot be overemphasized, for its myriad uses include dry lacquer for freestanding sculpture; lacquer as a surface for wood, stone, and bronze sculpture; and in inlaying techniques, to mention a few. In northern Thailand, dishes are made of red and black lacquer, and a set in the Duke Collection exemplifies the everyday objects collected for use in the Thai houses of Doris Duke's planned village (Plate 63).

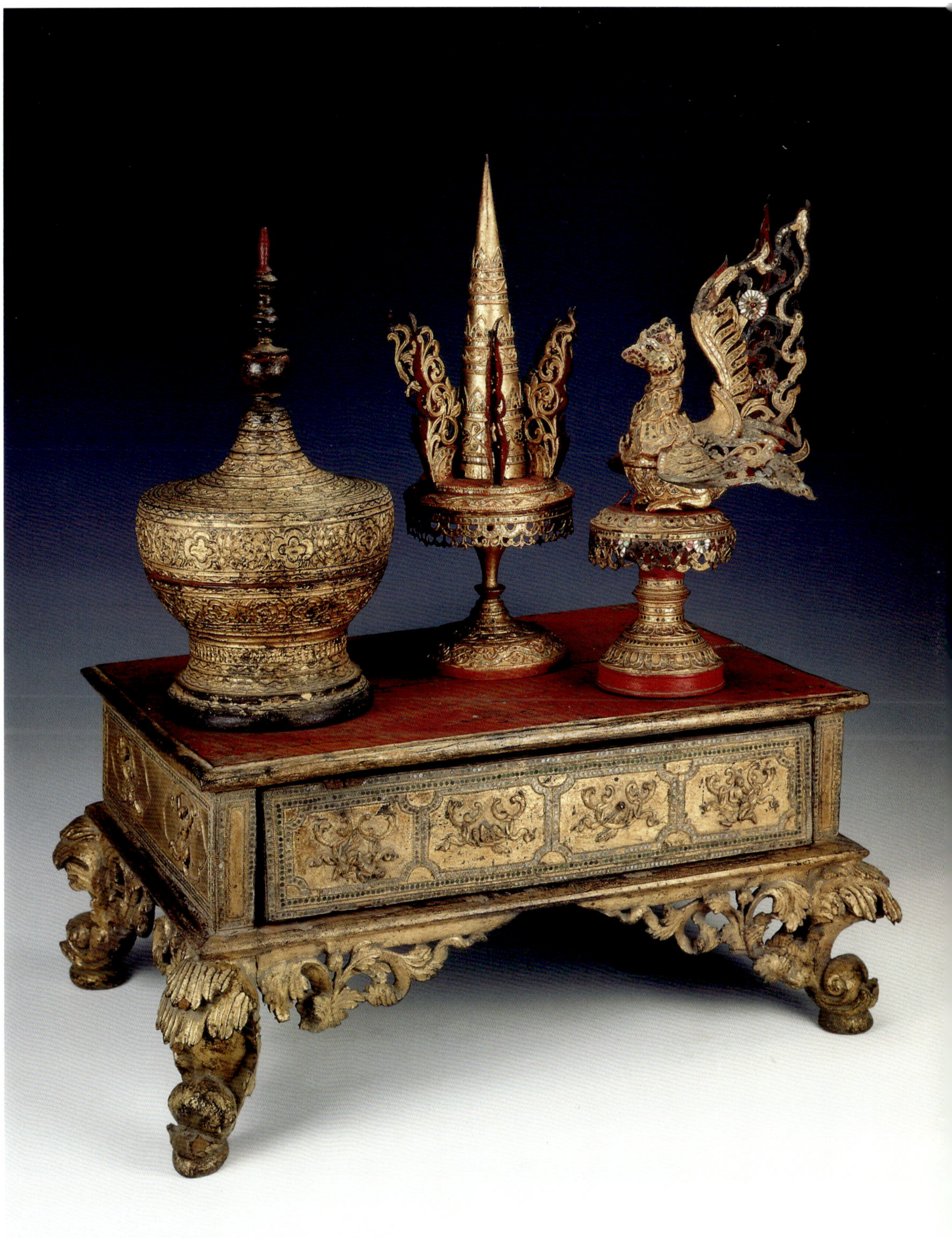

Plate 62 The Burmese vessel on the left was used for carrying food offerings to a monastery; the center container holds betel leaf; and the bird-shaped box is a betel box (h. average 51 cm); displayed on a Burmese table (l. 78.5 cm). WAM, AAM

Plate 63 A set of Thai red and black lacquer dishes.

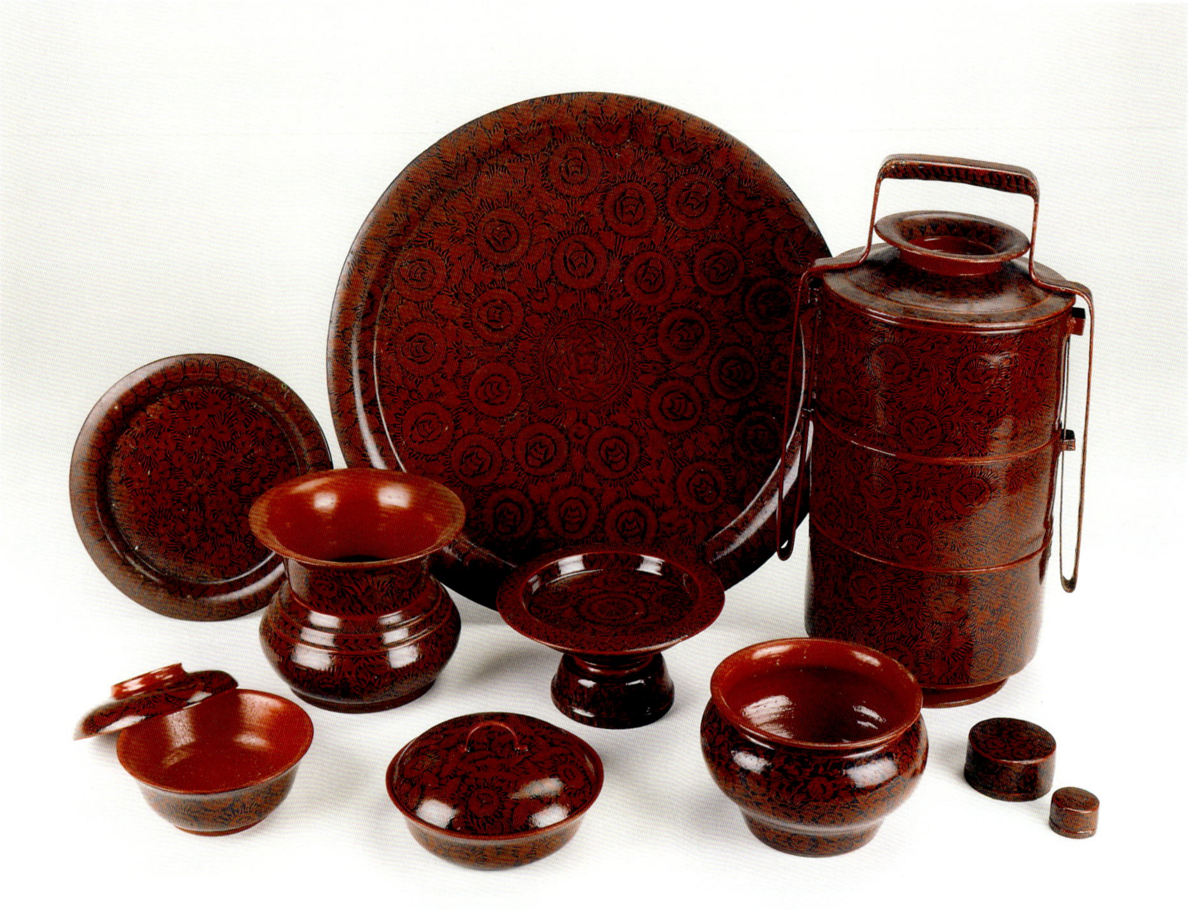

Plate 64 Thai inlaid mother-of-pearl tray (diam. 46.5 cm) used for offerings. WAM

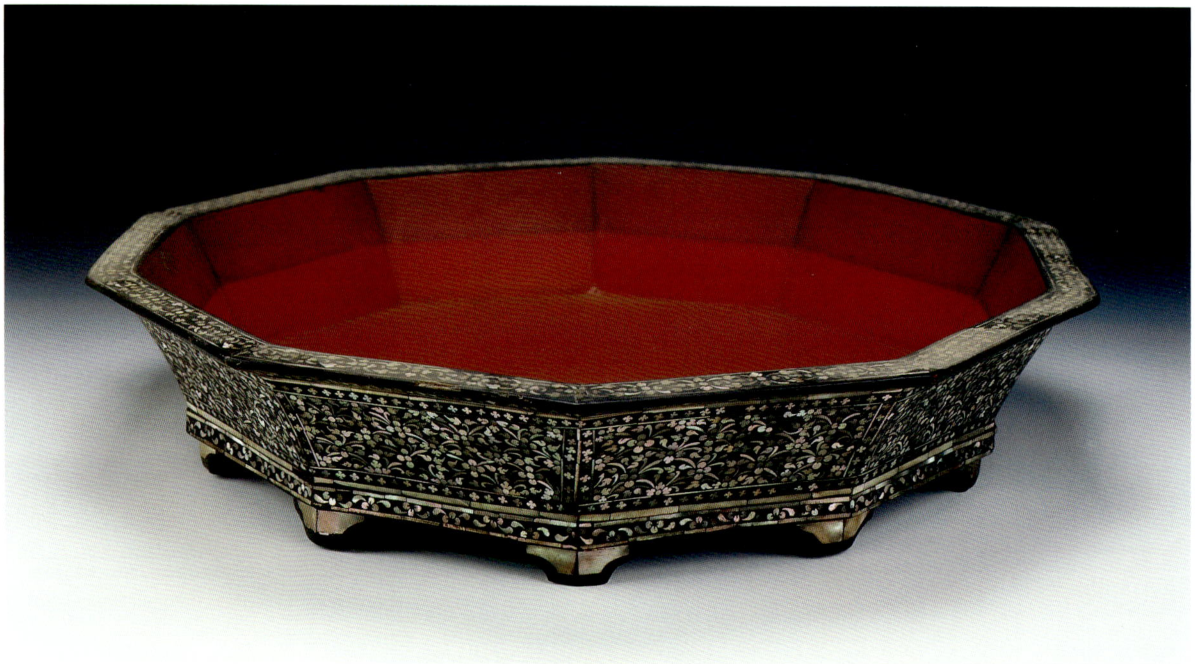

Shell inlay is an ancient art in Asia and is widespread in Southeast Asia. Although objects with mother-of-pearl inlay earlier than the Ayutthaya period no longer exist in Thailand, we do have examples of shell inlaid in the stucco relief of monuments as early as the Dvaravati period (sixth–eleventh century). In subsequent centuries, shell placed in the eyes of a bronze or wooden Buddha image brought the Buddha to life, for this is the final dedicatory step in the creation of Buddha images. By the seventeenth century, all types of objects—furniture, doors, covered boxes, food containers, alms bowls, and manuscript boxes and cabinets—provided surfaces for this delicate art. Many of these items were used by royalty or monks, though the use of mother-of-pearl had become more widespread by the nineteenth century.

Inlaying shell is tedious work. In applying the shell, the artist first draws a sketch of the design to be applied, then transfers it (in reverse) to tracing paper. He then cuts the shells *(turbo* and *trochus)* into small flat pieces that he adheres to the tracing paper. Numerous layers of lacquer are then applied to the object (each is allowed to dry before the next coat is applied), finishing with a layer of quick-drying lacquer against which the shell is pressed. Once the lacquer completely dries, water is used to remove the paper, and a sticky mixture of charcoal and the sap of the *yang* tree is applied to fill the spaces between each of the tiny pieces.

One often-decorated Thai ritual object, the offering receptacle *(phan),* may be round, octagonal, or take the form of a lotus. The Buddhist devotee carries alms and offerings to the monastery in the *phan* (Plate 65). The overall form of this example is particularly lovely, and the surface is elaborate, for not only is it enlivened with tiny squares of shell, but red lacquer complements the black and exaggerates the *phan*'s complex shape. A Thai tray in the collection has particularly fine mother-of-pearl inlay cut minutely and delicately organized in a floral design (Plate 64).

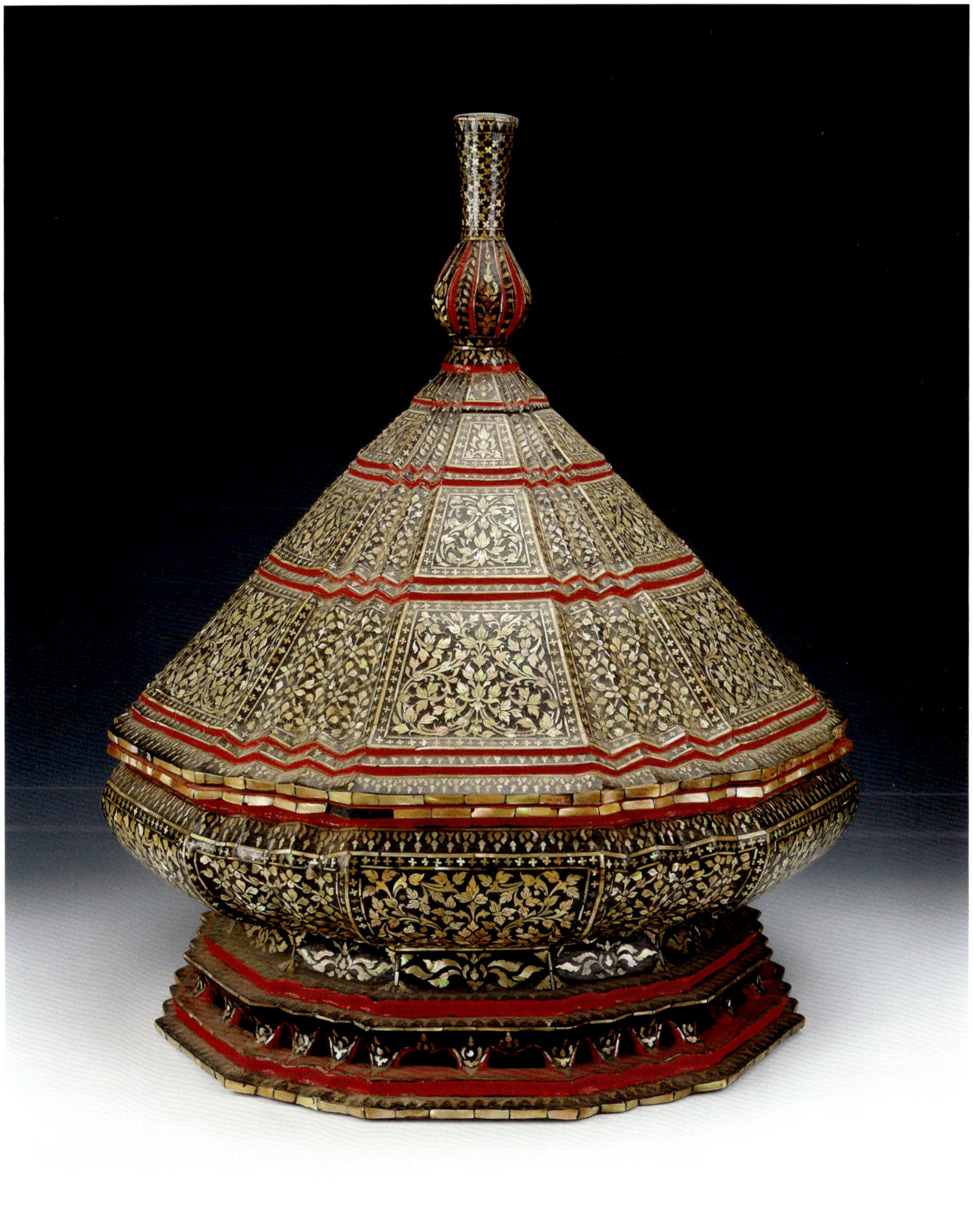

Plate 65 Thai inlaid mother-of-pearl offering receptacle (*phan;* h. 53.5 cm) used for food offerings.

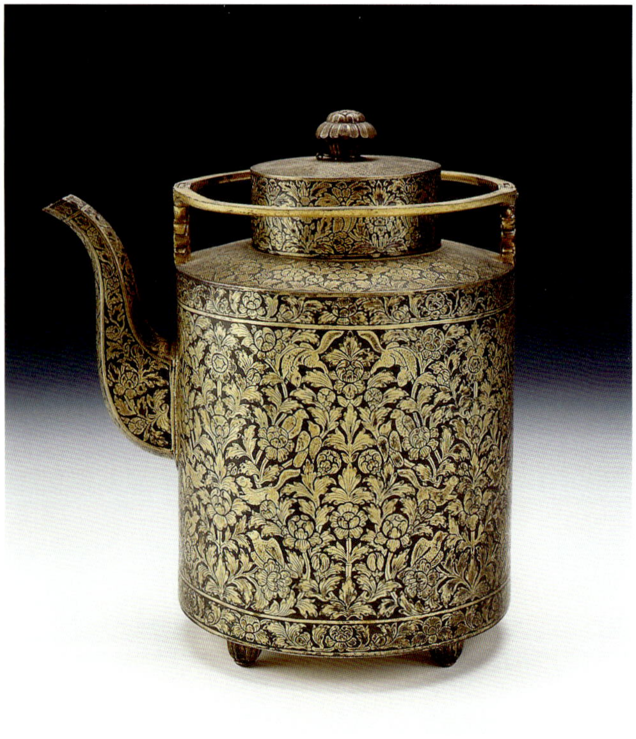

NIELLOWARE

Textual evidence attests to the use of nielloware in the early Ayutthaya period, though in the Bangkok period, it was more widely produced in Bangkok and Nakhon Si Thammarat, where the artisans were most adept.[15] Both silver and gold nielloware have a deeply engraved design filled with black enamel that adheres through heating.[16] Once the enamel fills the crevices created by the engraving, it is smoothed, and the overall surface polished. In some instances, gold takes the place of enamel on silver utensils, forming a contrasting silver and gold surface.

The designs on nielloware are a tight, compact, overall decoration, often floral in motif, or with the characteristic flame-pattern *kanok* motif, though occasionally scenes or depictions of individual figures find their way into cartouches in the design. The technique is used to adorn boxes, betel paraphernalia, food containers and teapots (Plate 66), sword hilts, and jewelry—even thrones are also proper surfaces

above **Plate 66 Nielloware teapot (h. 20 cm). Thailand. WAM**

right **Plate 67 The peoples of Southeast Asia once traditionally chewed betel quid, consisting of lime, areca nut, and betel leaf, though the habit has now died out. Elaborate paraphernalia (h. 4–13.9 cm on table w. 28.5 cm) hold the ingredients. Thailand.**

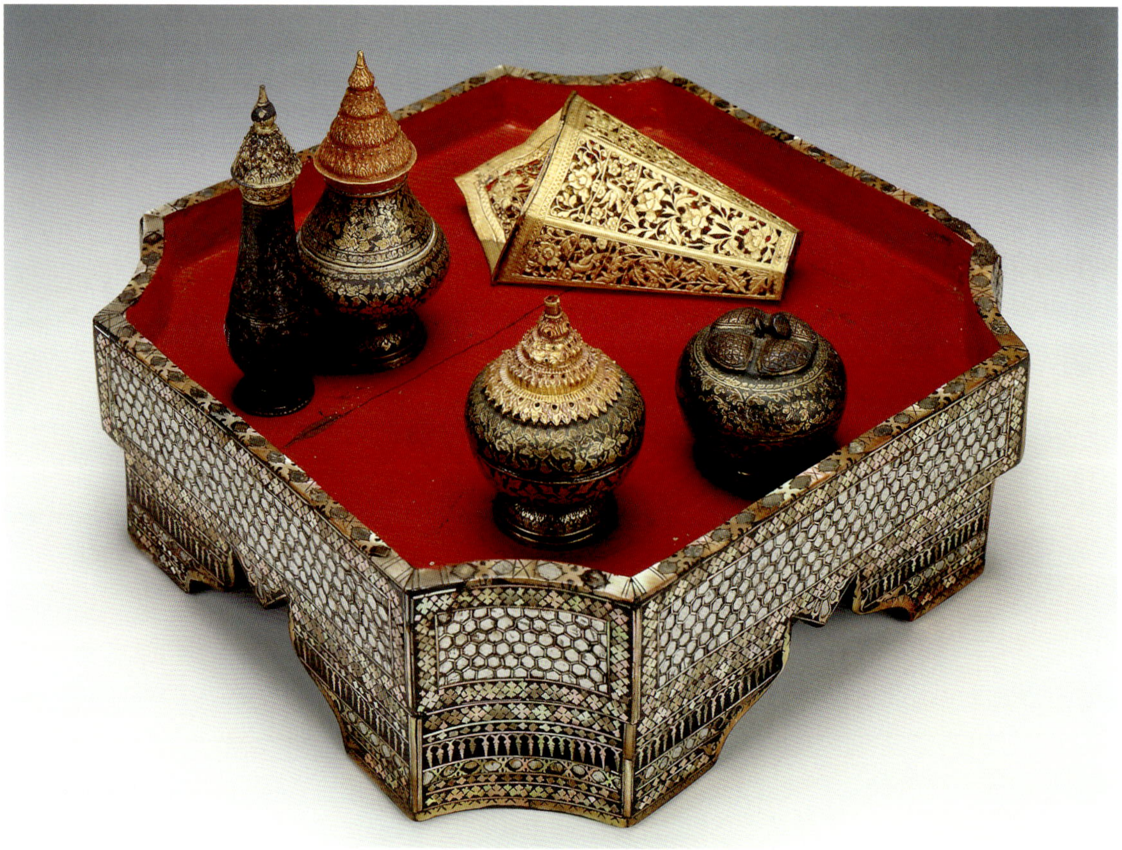

for this characteristically Thai art. The shape of the silver niello teapot derives from Chinese ceramics, which produced this shape as early as the fifteenth century. Sprouting flowers fit into the pattern of leaves that adorn the entire surface. This example compares well with a teapot given to the United States government by Rama IV in 1856.[17]

One common surface for the technique is the paraphernalia associated with betel chewing. In Burma a tightly fitted lacquer box held the ingredients for betel chewing (Plate 62, p. 83), but in Thailand, the small containers often sat on a tray such as this one (Plate 67). The gilt-filigreed triangular piece held the leaves, the taller container the lime, and the other boxes the areca nut and any additional ingredients desired. This grouping is not a set, as can be seen by the differing *kanok* motifs. Sometimes nielloware was enhanced with gold fittings, while other pieces had more elaborate shapes, such as the right foreground box in the shape of a mangosteen.

Copper enamelware, in designs intended to imitate the more costly nielloware, was considered suitable for monks, who had forsaken worldly wealth. These wares, produced in China to Thai specifications, are often brightly colored with a yellow background, like this covered and footed water vessel (Plate 68). First produced during the reign of King Rama III to be given as royal donations, these vessels suited the higher ranks of the monks. The donor purchased the enamelware in sets; the number of pieces in the set varied according to the rank of the monk.

IVORY

For millennia, Asian and Western cultures have coveted the ivory of the elephant's tusk for its rarity, fine grain, color, patina, and durability. Ivory does not burn, nor is it affected by water (though it can crack over time in too much humidity), and it is possible to carve ivory with woodworking tools. In Asian cultures, the additional symbolic significance of the elephant further enhances objects made of ivory. In South and Southeast Asia, where the elephant is an indigenous species, it plays a particularly potent role in Hindu and Buddhist mythology.

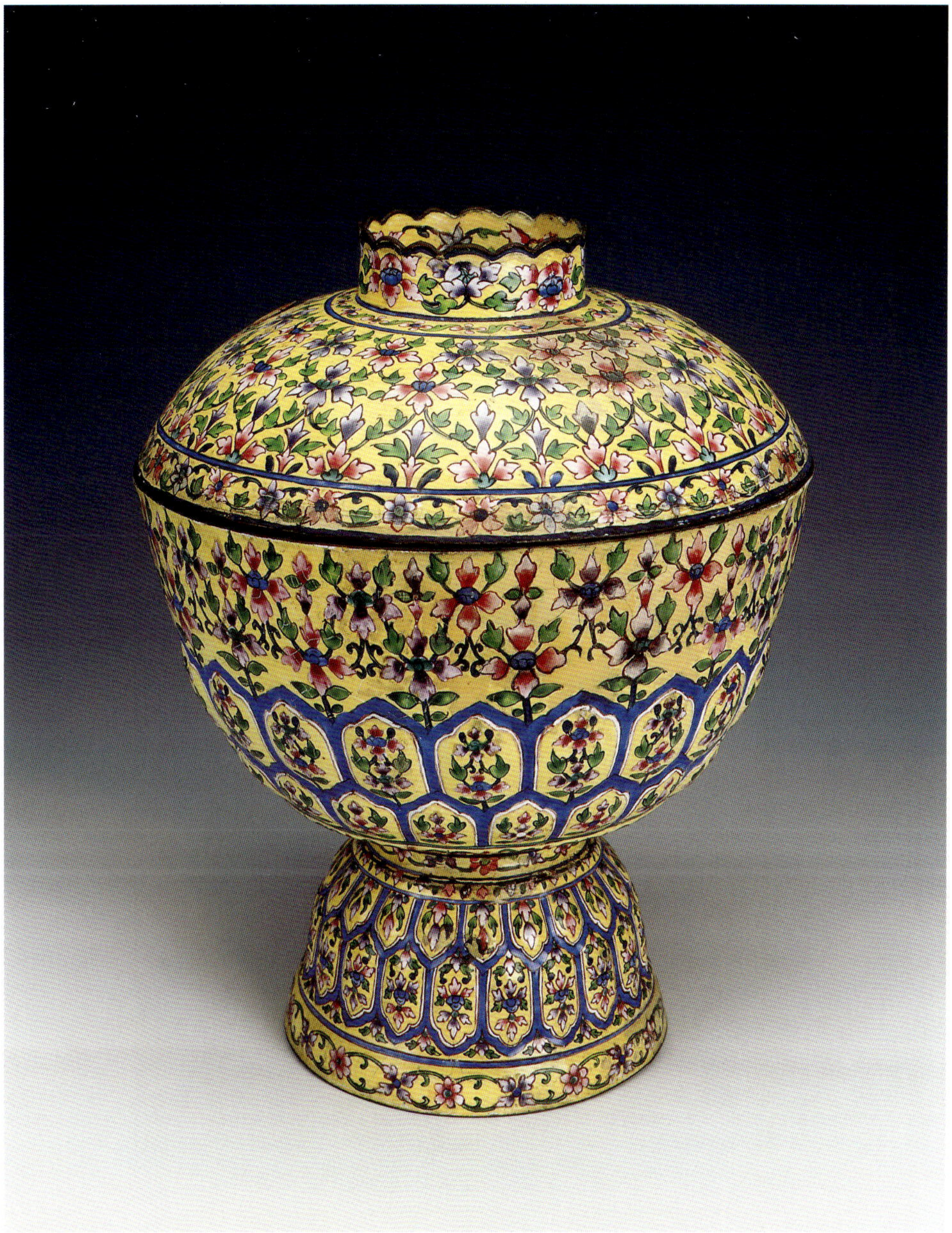

Plate 68 Copper enamelware water vessel (h. 27.5 cm) for a high-ranking monk. Thailand. WAM

Hinduism teaches that Shiva's son Ganesha, the god who removes all obstacles, has an elephant's head, and the king of the gods, Indra, rides the three-headed elephant Erawan (Skt Airavata). In Buddhism, an elephant entered the Buddha's mother's side to impregnate her, and an elephant is one of the seven royal possessions of a *cakkavattin* (a universal monarch; one who turns the wheel of the law).[18] The taming of a wild elephant is a metaphor for disciplining

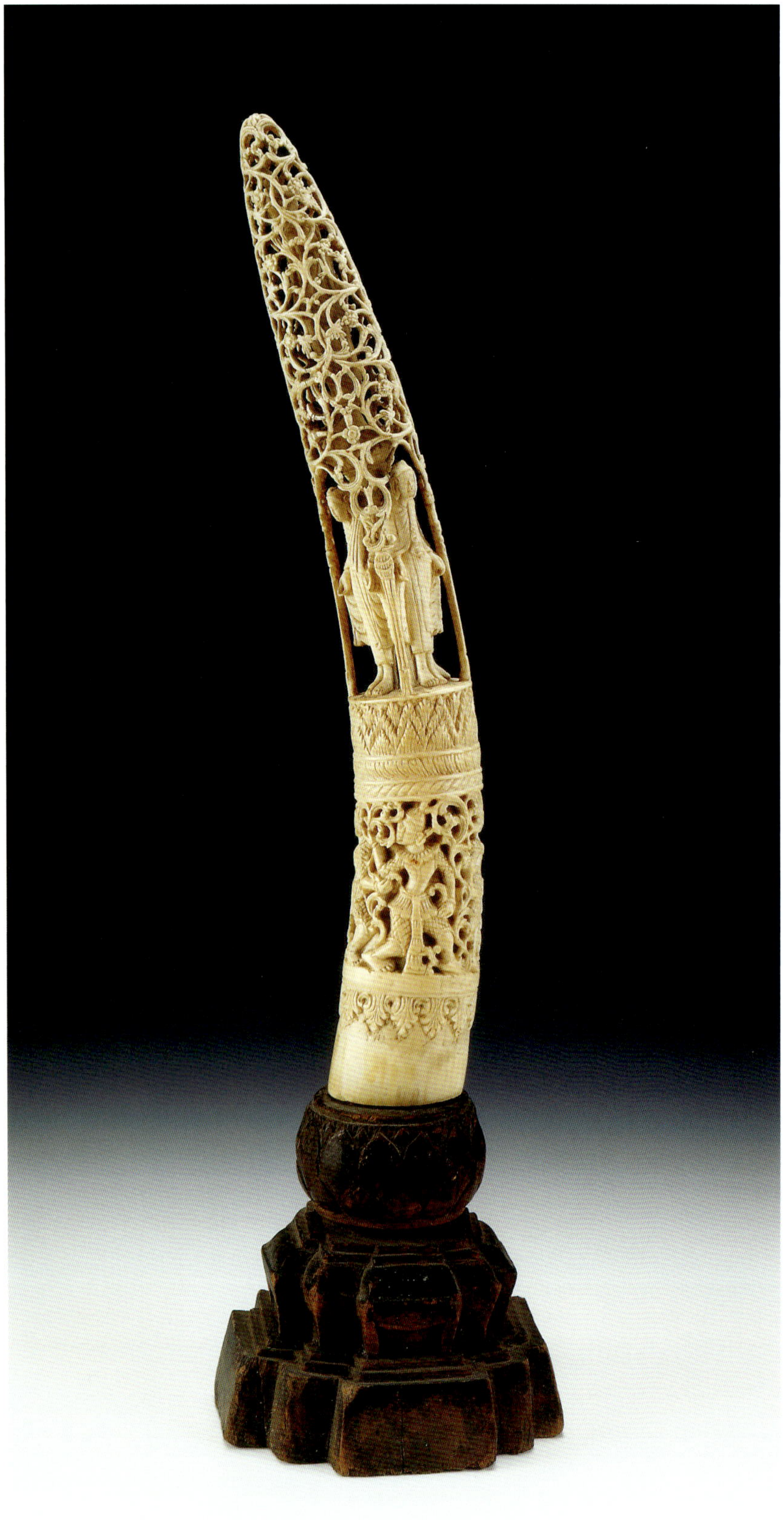

the mind in Buddhism, a metaphor aptly depicted in the story of Nalagiri (Plate 39, p. 63). In Southeast Asia, the elephant served as a royal symbol; a white elephant (which in fact is mottled pink and gray) is considered a potent and magical beast, able to benefit any kingdom owning one. One type of illustrated manuscript consists of treatises extolling their virtue and includes both mythical and natural elephants (Plate 42, pp. 66, 97).

To carve ivory, it must first be boiled in a solution to make it soft. The design is first outlined in charcoal, then chiseled with the grain, and finally filed and polished.[19] In Thailand and Burma, the gift of a carved ivory tusk is a particularly auspicious donation for a temple (Plate 69), and in a royal context, it is a gift demonstrating mutual respect.[20] The style of the standing Buddha midway down this tusk, with robes held out from his sides, is consistent with a nineteenth-century date from Burma (for a large wooden example of a similar Buddha, see Plate 15, p. 36). The artist has carved away the inner portion of the tusk, leaving a matrix to strengthen the piece, but allowing a space between the outer decorated area and the core, so that the delicate vine motif on the thin upper portion of the tusk and the figures entwined in the same motif on the lower portion stand out in the openwork.

A similar technique has been used for the handle of a sword, also from Burma, of a class of weapon called *dha-lwe* (Plate 70). Swords, important regalia for ceremonial use, were graded according to the level of the official to whom they belonged.[21] The fineness of Burmese swords is apparent in the workmanship of this example, with its openwork ivory handle and repoussé scabbard with inset, filigreed panels of gilded metal. The overall effect of ivory, gilding, repoussé silver, and the silver fittings of the handle is sumptuous and indicates the weapon belonged to a man of high rank.

A gunpowder flask carved of ivory and with silver fittings was produced in either Thailand or Burma (Plate 71), and like the Burmese saber, provides an example of the use of luxury items for weaponry. The technique of undercutting the ivory on the sword has

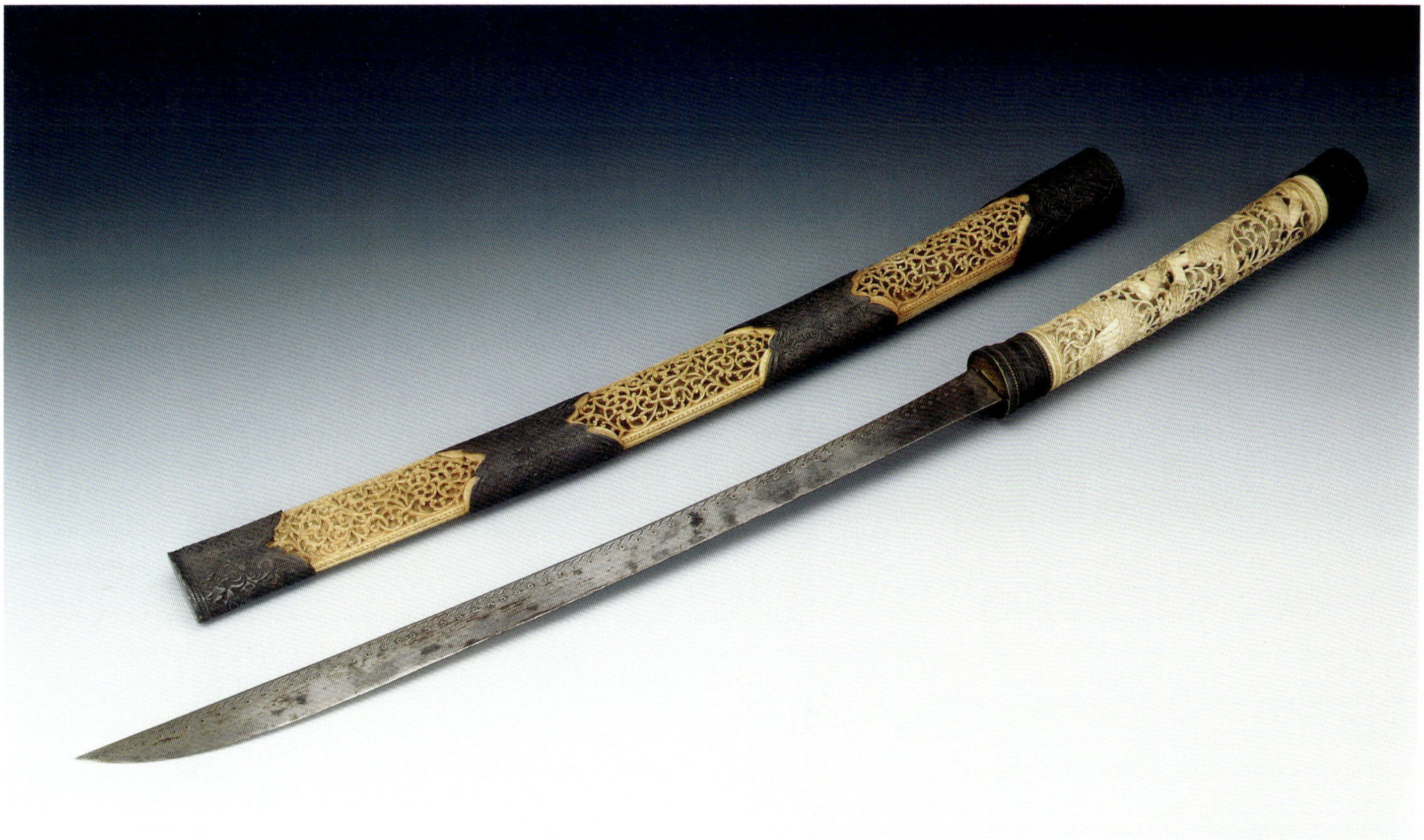

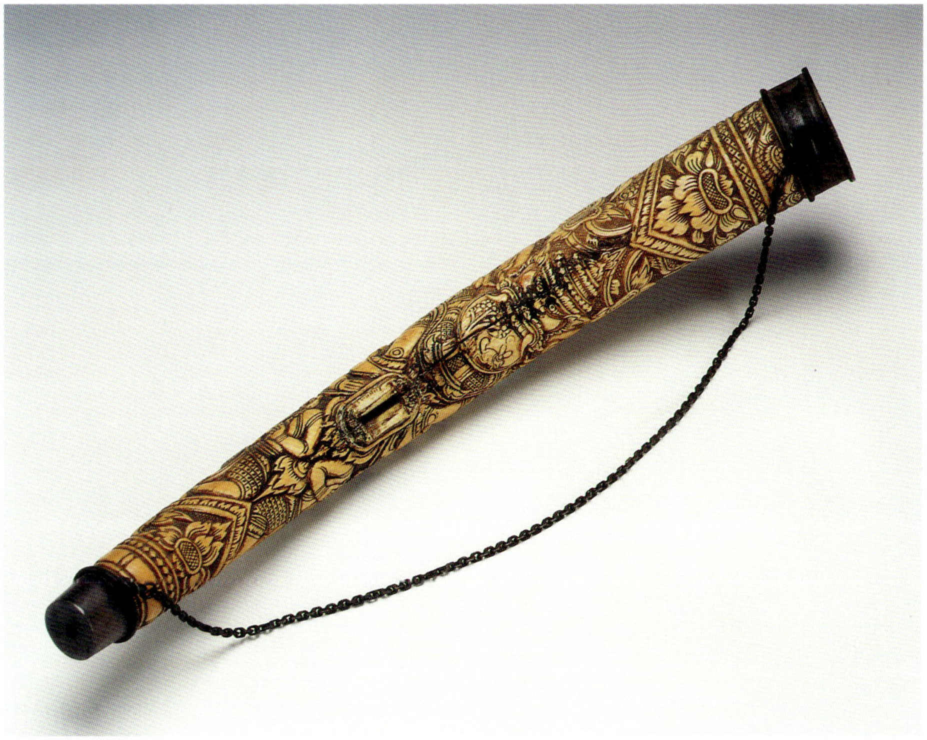

opposite **Plate 69** Carved ivory tusk from Burma (h. 43 cm), depicting the image of the Buddha.

above **Plate 70** Burmese sword (l. 79.5 cm) with a carved ivory handle. AAM

right **Plate 71** Thai ivory gunpowder flask (l. 39.5 cm). WAM

not been used, as the tusk has been hollowed out to hold gunpowder. Still, the carving is quite fine and detailed; the demonic figure centered on the curve of the tusk opens his mouth wide as he swallows the moon, clearly identified by the rabbit that inhabits it—a symbol adopted in Burma and Thailand from Chinese mythology. The artist has combined that symbolism with the myth of Rahu, the embodiment of the ascending node of the moon, usually shown as only a head and arms, who devours the moon, thus causing an eclipse.[22]

As an important luxury material, ivory is used for other secular objects, such as this finely carved Burmese box (Plate 72). Slices of ivory are carved in an openwork pattern, backed with an additional sheet of ivory, then attached with tiny nails to a wooden box. The decoration on this box, of demons and heavenly beings, relates to that on the sword handle described above. The style of clothing worn by the figures relates to that found on carvings of all types, for instance, the large dancing figures and gong-bearers also in the collection (Figure 20). This box is quite large, and its use is unclear; smaller, similar boxes were made in the nineteenth century to hold cigarettes.

In nineteenth-century Thailand, government officials and monks used ivory seals (Plate 73), the monks to identify *sutta* (sacred texts) and other temple belongings and to mark temple receipts. Officials used the seals for receipts in similar ways; one of these seals names a district office, suggesting it was applied to official papers.

below left **Plate 72** A Burmese wooden box with ivory panels carved with figures. WAM

below right **Plate 73** Thai ivory seals (h. 6.5–10 cm) used by both secular and religious officials in Thailand. WAM

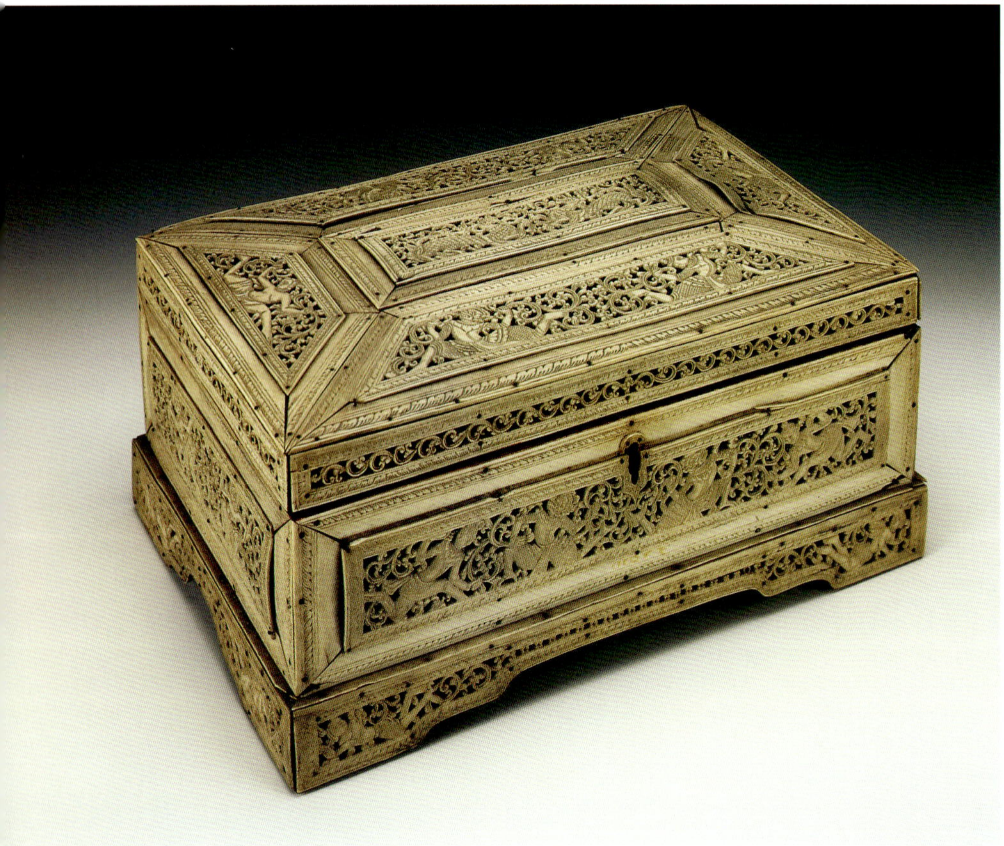

PERFORMING ARTS

Rama I and his courtiers wrote a version of the *Ramakian* (Skt *Ramayana*) in 1798, based on their recollection of texts that had been destroyed by the Burmese when they sacked the Thai capital of Ayutthaya in 1767. The tale follows the Indian original, with the main plot the exile of Phra Ram (Rama, an incarnation of Vishnu), his wife Nang Sida (Sita), and his brother Phra Lak and the subsequent kidnapping of Nang Sida by the demon king Thotsakan (Ravana) of Longka (Sri Lanka). With the assistance of the monkey army led by General Hanuman, Phra Ram succeeds in retrieving his wife. Hanuman plays a particularly large role in the Thai version of the story, with his notorious philandering given special attention.

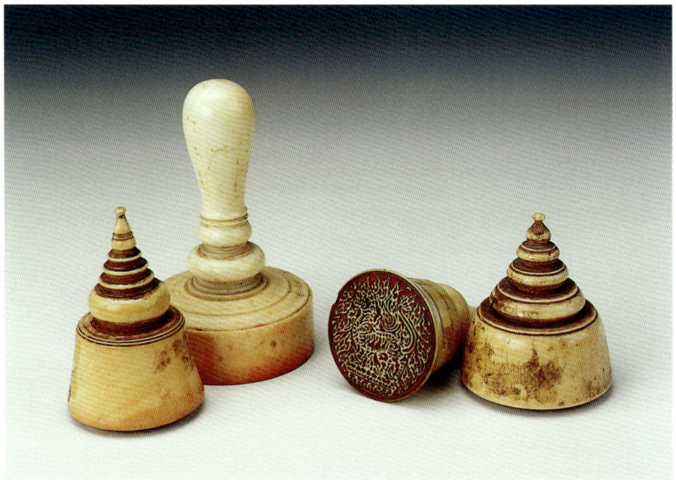

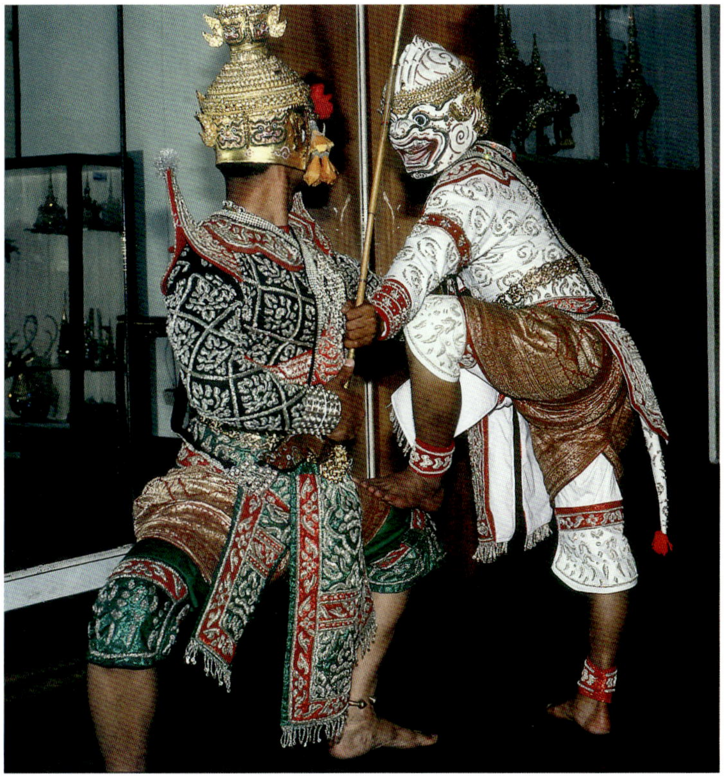

left **Figure 19** *Ramakian* masked dance practice with Thotsakan and Hanuman. Bangkok, National Performing Arts School, February 13, 1990. © Leedom Lefferts

right **Plate 74** Thai dance drama, both *khon* and *lakhon*, use masks in their performances. This Thotsakan (Ravana) mask (h. 65 cm) can be identified by the multiple heads and green color.

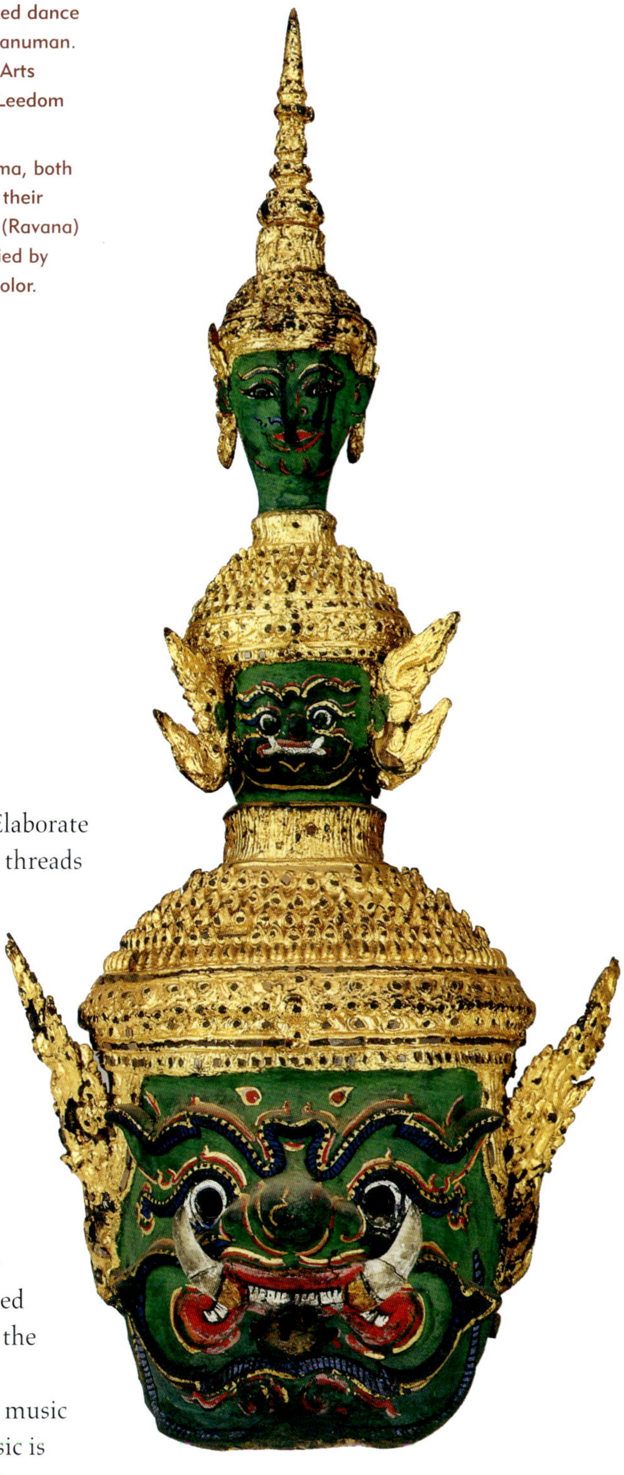

The *Ramakian,* an important source for all the arts of Thailand, provides the story danced in the *khon,* the classical dance drama performed by an all-male troupe and originally restricted to royal palaces (Figure 19). Both *khon* and *lakhon nai* (the latter performed by an all-female troupe in lesser palaces) are two of the six dramatic dance forms traditionally performed in Thailand, and both use masks for the demons and animals.[23] The dancers begin training in childhood, learning the stylized gestures that reveal the *Ramakian,* which in its complete form would take over a month to perform and include 311 actors. Like Indian dance from which it derives, each gesture represents a specific emotion.

The dancers wear painted, gilded, and jeweled papier-mâché masks formed on terracotta molds constructed with as many as twenty layers of *khoi* paper. Custom dictates the color of each mask; for instance, the mask representing Hanuman is always white. Specific traits identify certain of the characters, such as Thotsakan's fierce snarl and his multiple heads piled above his primary face (Plate 74); demons generally have bulging eyes and broad mouths. Elaborate costumes of rich brocade with metallic threads and sparkling bejeweled accessories add further glamour to the figures on the stage.

Some of the textiles in the collection are brocades of the type used in the dance dramas (Plate 56, p. 80). For centuries, the Thai had imported textiles from India, both silks and cottons. By the nineteenth century, they produced their own brocades, like the two shown here. The gold metallic thread would have sparkled in the lamplight and further enhanced the performance.

In Southeast Asia, dance, drama, and music are inseparable. Thai and Burmese music is based on an eight-note scale arranged in seven full intervals without the semitones we are accustomed to hearing in Western music. All Southeast Asian music relies heavily on percussive instruments,

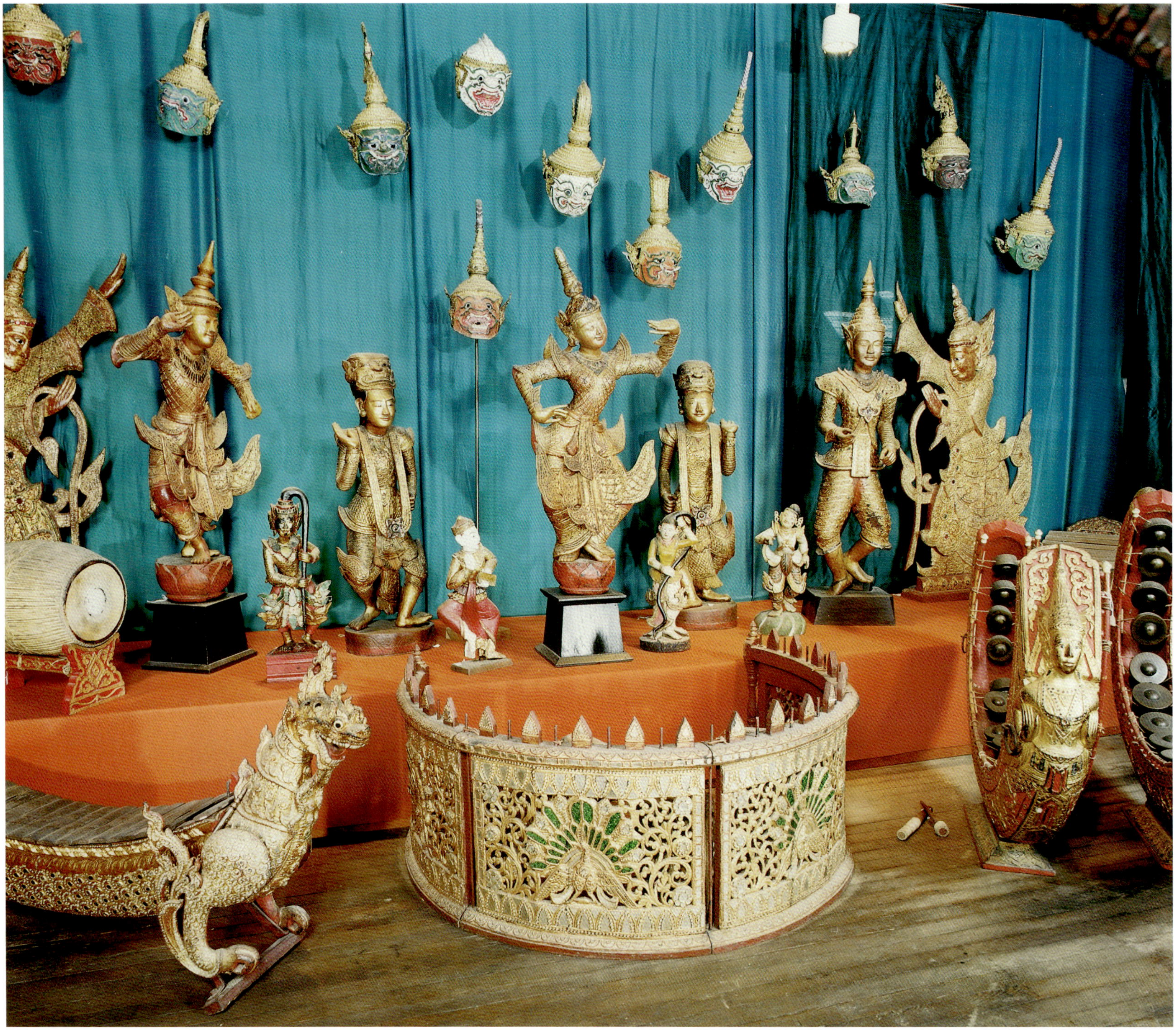

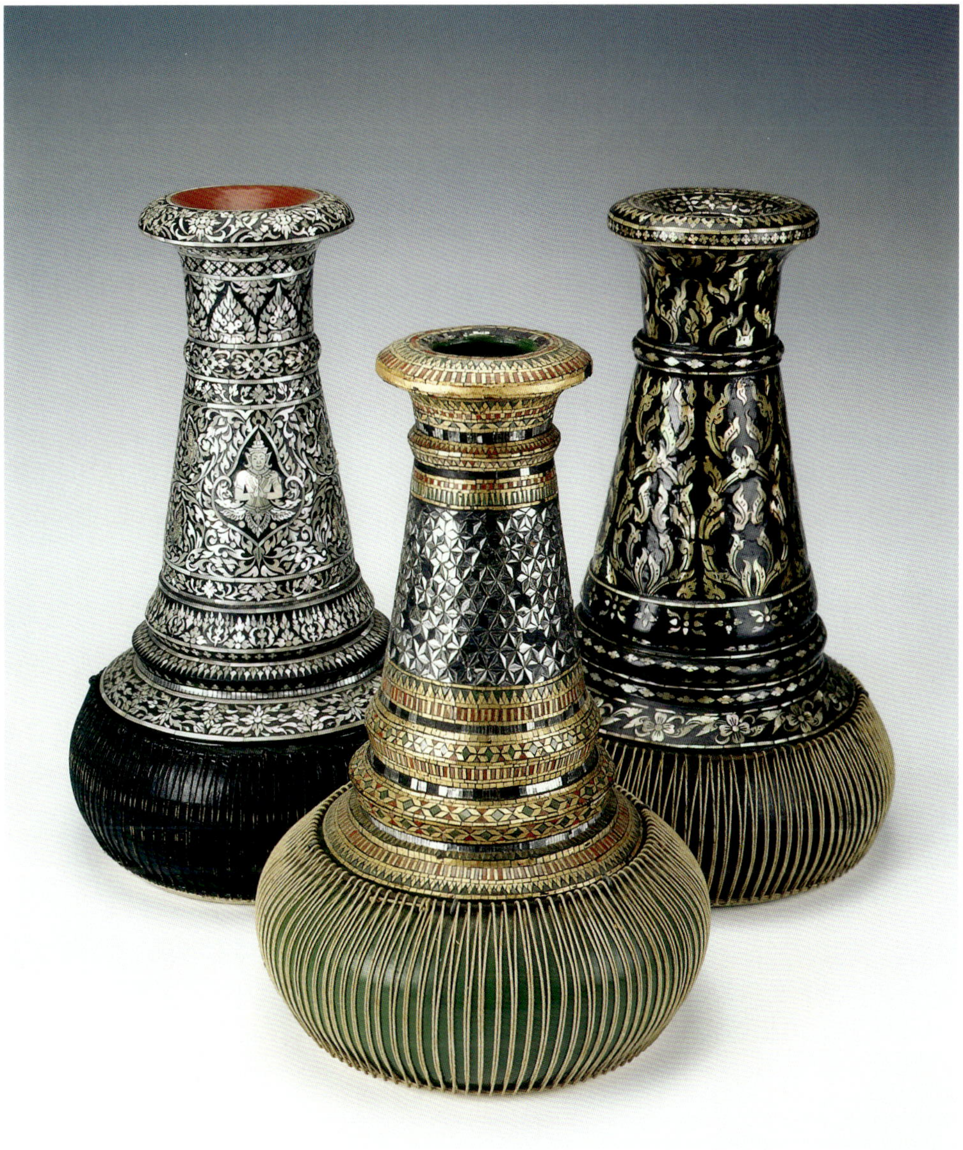

opposite **Figure 20** View of instruments, masks, and sculpture in dance poses in the Coach Barn of the Duke Farms, Hillsborough, New Jersey, 2002.

left **Plate 75** Thai drums (h. 35 and 38.5 cm) of wood (center) and of clay.

including drums, gongs, and xylophones (Figure 20). Small hand drums made of clay *(thon mahori)* or wood *(thon chatri)*, always slightly smaller in size than the clay drums, are often elaborately decorated. The wood drum (center, Plate 75) is adorned with colored glass. The clay drums are inlaid with mother-of-pearl and the familiar flamelike *kanok* covers both, with *theppanom* featured only on one. The drummer uses a single hand to play both types of drum and may cover the bottom to dampen the sound. They are intended for specific ensembles, the ceramic version with a string ensemble, and the wooden drum with an ensemble that accompanies shadow play.[24]

There are more than thirty instruments in the Duke Collection, both Thai and Burmese, many of which were installed in the Coach Barn during the thirty years that Southeast Asian art was displayed in that building (Figure 20). With his conquest of Ayutthaya in 1767, the Burmese King Hsinbyushin returned to Burma with Thai court dancers and musicians, who revitalized a dying musical tradition. This accounts for the similarities between the music and instrumentation in the two countries. Various Thai xylophones, gong stands, and drums are arrayed in the Coach Barn, but another instrument shaped as a composite animal (Plate 76), one of the most beautiful in the collection, is a Burmese *pattala*, a type of xylophone with metal keys. (Many of the Southeast Asian tuned percussion instruments have wooden keys.) The artist has achieved the form of the animal with the built-up lacquer *(thayo)* used to great effect on so much of Burmese art.

The installation of instruments in the Coach Barn causes one to wonder where they would have been displayed in the Thai Village, had it been completed. The open-air *sala*, with its heavy timber pillars, would have been a good place to create and to listen to music. Both musicians and audience could have seated themselves on the teak floors, polished from years of use. Or perhaps Miss Duke imagined music wafting from the 'Golden Pavilion,' which she always thought of as being situated in the middle of a lake; sound carries so beautifully across water. While the dispersal of the collection puts an end to those dreams, it also affords an opportunity for thousands of people to enjoy these beautiful objects in the museums to which the Doris Duke Charitable Foundation has donated them.

Plate 76 Southeast Asian performance integrates music with dance drama. This fine Burmese, tuned percussion instrument (*pattala*; l. 88.5 cm) is shaped like a dragon.

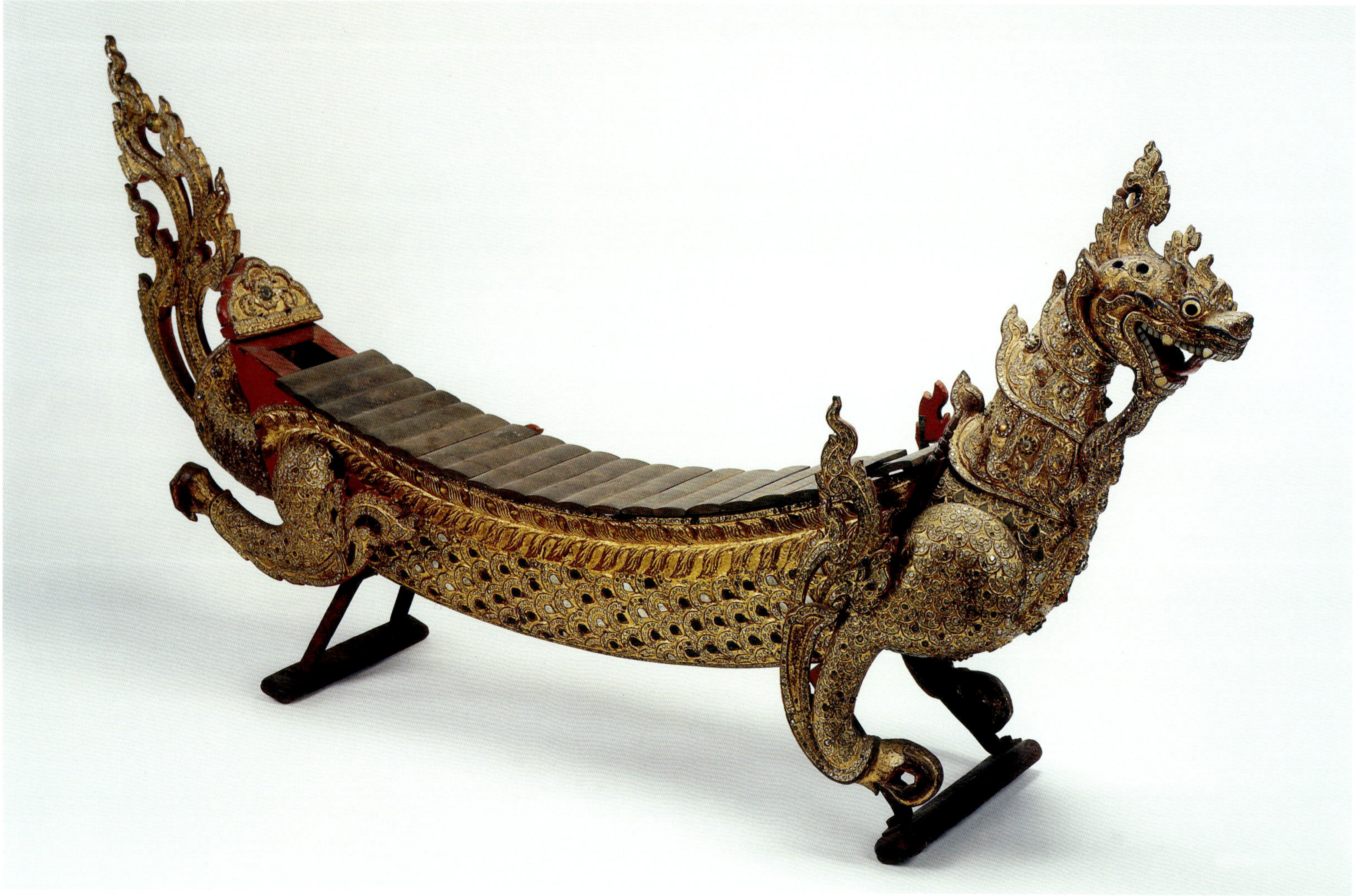

NOTES

1. François Duhau de Bérenx, personal communication, 8/28/02; see memo from Bérenx, p. 13.

2. Charles Higham and Rachanie Thosarat, *Prehistoric Thailand: From Early Settlement to Sukhothai* (Bangkok: River Books, 1998), 30.

3. Nancy Tingley, "A Brief Note on the Terminal Date of the Si Satchanalai Kilns," in *Living a Life in Accord with Dhamma: Papers in Honor of Professor Jean Boisselier on His Eightieth Birthday* (Bangkok: Silpakorn University, 1997), 483–87.

4. I would like to thank Hiram W. Woodward, Jr., for clarifying its use.

5. For a discussion of *bencharong* and *lai nam thong* ceramics, see Natalie V. Robinson, *Sino-Thai Ceramics in the National Museum, Bangkok, Thailand, and in Private Collections* (Bangkok: Department of Fine Arts, 1982), and idem, "Bencharong and Lai Nam Thong Ceramics," in *The Artistic Heritage of Thailand: A Collection of Essays* (Bangkok: Sawaddi Magazine, 1979), 139–50.

6. For a discussion of these textiles, see John Guy, *Woven Cargoes: Indian Textiles in the East* (New York: Thames and Hudson, 1998), 121–51. For an illustration of folios from a pattern book, see page 151.

7. The ribbon motif on the jar on the far right dates this piece to approx. 1890–1900.

8. Robinson, *Sino-Thai Ceramics*, fig. 175.

9. Ibid., plate XVIII.

10. Wes Kirkham, personal communication, 5/02.

11. Michael Knight, personal communication, 10/02.

12. Ralph Isaacs and T. Richard Blurton, *Visions from the Golden Land: Burma and the Art of Lacquer* (London: British Museum Press, 2000), 21.

13. Fraser-Lu, *Burmese Crafts*, 221.

14. For a discussion of Burmese lacquer, see ibid., 221–31, or Issacs and Blurton, *Visions from the Golden Land*. For a survey of Thai decorative arts and crafts, see William Warren and Luca Invernizzi Tettoni, *Arts and Crafts of Thailand* (San Francisco: Chronicle Books, 1996).

15. Songsri Prapatthong, ed., *Thai Minor Arts* (Bangkok: Department of Fine Arts, 1993), 83–84.

16. The black enamel is a compound of silver and sulphur. When both the silver and the enamel are polished, they form an attractive, contrasting surface.

17. Lisa McQuail, *Treasures of Two Nations: Royal Gifts to the United States of America* (Washington, D.C.: Smithsonian Institution, 1997), 57.

18. The other symbols of a *cakkavattin* are a horse, wife, minister, general, the *dhamma* as represented by the wheel, and riches, represented by a gem.

19. *Treasures from the National Museum, Bangkok* (Bangkok: Thar Watna Panich Press Co., Ltd., 1987), 82.

20. McQuail, *Treasures of Two Nations*.

21. Fraser-Lu, *Burmese Crafts*, 148–49.

22. The flask probably dates to the seventeenth or eighteenth century.

23. *Lakhon* is the generic word for theater and includes four main categories, the first of which is *lakhon nai*, or indoor theater, commonly called *khon*. The term *lakhon* is generally applied to outdoor theater, or street theater.

24. Dhanit Yupho, *Thai Musical Instruments* (Bangkok: Department of Fine Arts, 1987), 43–45.

Acknowledgments

THE ENTIRE STAFF OF DUKE FARMS IN HILLSBOROUGH, NEW Jersey, was most helpful and supportive during my work with the Doris Duke Southeast Asian Collection; I thank them all. It was as great a pleasure to work with Zibby and Richard Walker as they photographed these works of art as it was to see the results of their efforts. I owe special thanks to Liz Steinberg, Cupie Singh, Digi Singh, Marianne Bowles, and Patrick Lerch for their assistance, and to Chris Carden in particular, for his many hours in the original cataloguing of the collection—a task I would have found impossible without his help. Sharon Littlefield and Deborah Pope at Shangri La, Bruce MacLeish at Rough Point, and Sarah Bekker gave me additional perspectives on Doris Duke, as did Violet Mimaki and François Duhau de Bérenx, who knew her at the time she collected this material. Their insights helped me appreciate Miss Duke's independent spirit and passionate interest in her many projects.

Olga Garay at the Doris Duke Charitable Foundation has consistently supported me in working with the collection, and I thank her for her consideration. A number of specialists in the field of Thai and Burmese art and culture have given their advice, suggestions, and time in answering my questions and in reading the text drafts. I am most indebted to their insights and patience, and cannot adequately thank Dr. Hiram W. Woodward, Jr. of the Walters Art Museum, Baltimore; Dr. Forrest McGill and Dr. Pat Chirapravati of the Asian Art Museum of San Francisco; Dr. Henry Ginsburg of the British Library, all of whom read the text; Dr. Susan Conway; Sylvia Fraser-Lu, and William Warren, independent scholars; and Dr. Peter Skilling, Research Fellow, Lumbini International Institute, Nonthaburi, Thailand.

Nancy Tingley
Independent scholar

opposite **detail, Plate 42, page 64**

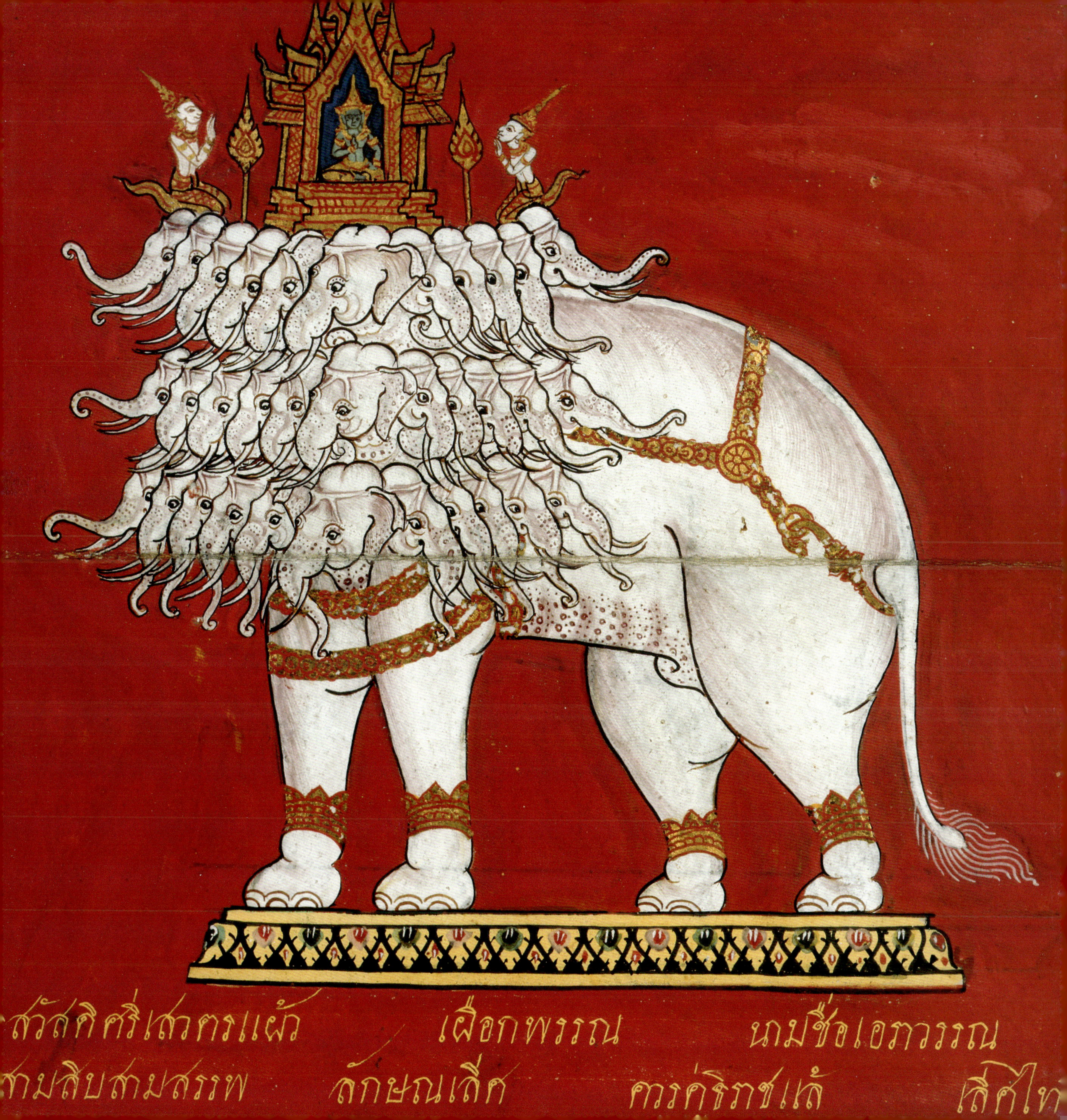

สวัสดิศรีเสาวรแผ้ว
เผือกพรรณ
นามชื่อเอราวรรณ
สามสิบสามสรรพ
ลักษณเลิศ
ควรค่ธิราชแล้
เลิศไท

Glossary

abhaya mudra (Skt): Gesture with hand raised, palm out; with two hands raised, 'calming the ocean' (Thai *ham samut*).

abhidhamma (Pali): Pali-language treatises on various philosophical issues.

anjali mudra (Skt): Gesture of respect and salutation.

attachan (Thai): A covered freestanding altar with stepped shelves.

bencharong (Thai): Five-color, enamel-glazed porcelain produced in China for the Thai market.

bhumisparsha mudra (Skt): Earth-touching gesture; refers to the Buddha's enlightenment at Bodh Gaya.

bodhisatta (Pali): In the Theravada tradition, refers to the Buddha during his lives before final enlightenment.

cakkavattin (Pali): One who turns the wheel of the law; a universal monarch in either a religious or a secular sense.

chedi (Thai *stupa;* Skt *caitya;* Burmese *cetiya*): A reliquary mound with relics of the historical Buddha or a great monk or teacher.

dana (Pali, Skt): Charity.

dhamma (Pali): The Buddhist law.

Erawan (Skt Airavata): Three-headed elephant, mount of Indra, king of the gods; it gained independent status and great popularity in Thailand.

garuda (Skt): Mythical bird, the name derived from that of Vishnu's vehicle.

Himaphan (Thai; Skt, Himavanta): Forest at the base of Mount Meru, the cosmic mountain, abode of various, fantastic creatures.

hintha (Burmese): Auspicious mythical bird probably derived from the goose (Skt *hamsa*).

hip phra thet (Thai): Chests to hold texts.

hsun ok (Burmese): Food container for offerings to monks.

Jambupati: Heretic king to whom the adorned Buddha displays himself.

jataka (Skt): The 547 stories of the Buddha's lives.

Kammavaca (Pali; Burmese, *kamawasa*): Text of the rules of the monastic order.

kanok (Thai): Vegetal motif, often flamelike.

khoi (Thai): *Streblus aster,* plant from which paper is made.

khon (Thai): Classical masked drama derived from Indian temple dance with stories based on the *Ramakian* (Skt, *Ramayana*).

kinnara (Skt, fem. *kinnari*): Fantastic creature, half human, half bird.

kyaungtaik (Burmese): Monastery.

lai nam thong (Thai): Gold-washed, enamel-glazed porcelain produced in China for the Thai market.

lai rot nam (Thai): 'Ornaments washed with water'; the technique of applying black lacquer and gold.

lakhon (Thai): Popular dance drama.

makara (Skt): Crocodile.

mandala (Skt): Political unit describing a periphery with commercial ties to a powerful center.

Moggallana (Pali): One of the Buddha's two most dedicated disciples, who was converted to Buddhism when he heard the Buddhist creed 'Whatever proceeds from causes, their causes have been stated, as also [the means of] their cessation.'

Mount Meru: The cosmic mountain, *axis mundi,* in Hindu and Buddhist cosmology.

naga (Skt; Thai *nak*): Mythical serpent.

Nang Sida (Thai; Skt Sita): The wife of Phra Ram; she is kidnaped by the demon king Thotsakan, in the *Ramakian,* the Thai version of the great Indian epic, the *Ramayana.*

nat (Burmese): Indigenous spirit.

nibbana (Pali; Skt *nirvana*): Final extinction.

nielloware: A method of decoration involving engraving a gold or silver object with a design that is then filled with black enamel.

parabaik (Burmese): Manuscript.

pattala (Burmese): Tuned percussion instrument similar to a xylophone.

phan (Thai): Offering container.

phra bot (Thai): Hanging cloth painting.

Phra Lak (Thai; Skt Lakshman): Brother of Phra Ram, hero of the *Ramakian.*

Phra Malai (Thai): Monk who acquired enough merit to visit heaven and hell.

phra phim (Thai): Votive tablets.

Phra Ram (Thai; Skt Rama): Hero of the *Ramakian,* the Thai version of the great Indian epic, and an incarnation of Vishnu.

Rahu (Skt): Embodiment of the ascending node of the moon who devours the sun and moon to cause eclipses.

Ramakian (Thai; Skt Ramayana): Thai version of the Indian epic the *Ramayana* tells of the exile of Phra Ram (Rama), his wife Nang Sida, and his brother Phra Lak. The demon king Thotsakan of Longka (Sri Lanka) kidnaps Nang Sida, but with the assistance of the monkey army led by the monkey General Hanuman, Phra Ram succeeds in retrieving her. Hanuman plays a particularly large role in the Thai version of the story.

sadaik (Burmese): Manuscript chest.

samsara (Skt): Endless cycle of rebirth.

sangha (Skt): Monastic community.

Sariputta (Pali): One of the Buddha's two most dedicated disciples; see Moggallana.

thammat (Thai; Pali *dhammasana*): Pulpit.

thayo (Burmese): A putty of lacquer sap mixed with clay, sawdust, or ash, which can be molded or sculpted.

theppanom (Thai; Skt *devapranama*): Worshipful figure.

Thet Mahachat (Thai; Pali *desa mahajati*): Recitation of the Vessantara *jataka.*

Thotsakan (Thai; Skt Ravana): The ten-headed demon king of the *Ramakian.*

tho (Thai): A covered bowl of an urn shape.

Thotsachat (Thai; Pali, *dasajati*): Last ten lives, or births, of the Buddha; in Thai, also called *phra chao sip chat* (Ten Lives of Our Lord).

tu phra thom (Thai; Pali *dhamma*): Furniture for holding the scriptures; manuscript cabinet.

ubosot (Thai): Ordination hall used as an assembly hall; in smaller *wat* laymen will assemble here for instruction or to pay homage to the main image of the *wat.*

vitarka mudra (Skt): Teaching gesture.

wat (Thai): Temple compound, monastery.

wihan (Thai; Skt *vihara*): Assembly hall in a monastery.

Selected Bibliography

Aung-thwin, Michael. *Pagan: The Origins of Modern Burma.* Honolulu: University of Hawai'i Press, 1985.

Bird, Betty, and Associates. "Coach Barn (Building 12), Duke Farms, Somerville [Hillsborough], New Jersey." Unpublished manuscript, July 2002.

Bowie, Theodore, ed. *The Arts of Thailand: A Handbook of the Architecture, Sculpture and Painting of Thailand (Siam), and a Catalogue of the Exhibition in the United States in 1960–61–62.* Bloomington: Indiana University, 1960.

Brereton, Bonnie Pacala. *Thai Tellings of Phra Malai: Texts and Rituals Concerning a Popular Buddhist Saint.* Tempe: Arizona State University, 1995.

Chandler, David. *A History of Cambodia.* Boulder, Colorado: Westview Press, 1983.

Chirapravati, M.L. Pattaratorn. *Votive Tablets in Thailand: Origins, Styles, and Uses.* Kuala Lumpur: Oxford University Press, 1997.

Conway, Susan. *Silken Threads Lacquer Thrones: Lan Na Court Textiles.* Chicago: Art Media Resources, 2002.

Cowell, E.B., ed. *Jatakas: Stories of Buddha's Former Births.* Delhi: Cosmo Publications, 1978.

Dhanit Yupho. *Thai Musical Instruments.* Bangkok: Department of Fine Arts, 1987.

Diskul, M.C. Subhadradis. *Art in Thailand: A Brief History.* Bangkok: Amarin Press, 1986.

Diskul, M.C. Subhadradis, William Warren, Oragoon Pokakornvijan, and Viroon Baidikul. *The Suan Pakkad Palace Collection.* Bangkok: Princess Chumbhot of Nagara Svarga, 1982.

Fraser-Lu, Sylvia. *Burmese Crafts, Past and Present.* Kuala Lumpur: Oxford University Press, 1994; reprint 2002.

Gear, Donald, and Joan Gear. *Earth to Heaven: The Royal Animal-Shaped Weights of Burma.* Chiang Mai: Silkworm Books, 1992.

Ginsburg, Henry. *Thai Manuscript Painting.* London: The British Library, 1989.

———. *Thai Art and Culture: Historic Manuscripts from Western Collections.* London: The British Library, 2000.

Gittinger, Mattiebelle, and H. Leedom Lefferts, Jr. *Textiles and the Tai Experience in Southeast Asia.* Washington, D.C.: The Textile Museum, 1992.

Guy, John. *Woven Cargoes: Indian Textiles in the East.* New York: Thames and Hudson, 1998.

Hibbard, Don J. "Shangri-La: Doris Duke's Home in Hawai'i." Nov. 2001 (unpublished manuscript; not fully paginated).

Higham, Charles, and Rachanie Thosarat. *Prehistoric Thailand: From Early Settlement to Sukhothai.* Bangkok: River Books, 1998.

Isaacs, Ralph, and T. Richard Blurton. *Visions from the Golden Land: Burma and the Art of Lacquer.* London: British Museum Press, 2000.

Littlefield, Sharon, with an Introduction by Carol Bier. *Doris Duke: Shangri La.* Honolulu: Doris Duke Foundation for Islamic Art, 2002.

Lowry, John. *Burmese Art.* London: Her Majesty's Stationery Office, 1974.

Maung Htin Aung. *Folk Elements in Burmese Buddhism.* Yangon: U Hla Maung, 1959.

McGill, Forrest. "Painting the 'Great Life.'" In Juliane Schober, ed., *Sacred Biography in the Buddhist Traditions of South and Southeast Asia.* Honolulu: University of Hawai'i Press, 1997, 194–217.

McQuail, Lisa. *Treasures of Two Nations: Royal Gifts to the United States of America.* Washington, D.C.: Smithsonian Institution, 1997.

Naengnoi, Punjabhan and Somchai Na Nakhonphanom. *The Art of Thai Wood Carving: Sukhothai, Ayutthaya, Ratanakosin.* Bangkok: Rerngrom Publishing Co., Ltd., 2535 B.E. (1992).

Neijenrode, Cornelis van. *Vertoog van de gelegenheid des koninkrijks Siam, 1621* (Account of the situation in the kingdom of Siam, 1621). In *Kroniek van het Historisch Genootschap gevestigd te Utrecht* (Chronicles of the Historical Society of Utrecht) 27 (1871): 279–318.

Olbrich Botanical Garden. http://www.olbrich.org.

Pal, Pratapaditya. "Fragmentary Cloth Paintings from Early Pagan and Their Relations with Indo-Tibetan Traditions." In Donald M. Stadtner, ed., *The Art of Burma: New Studies, Marg* 50.4 (June 1999): 79–88.

Penth, Hans. *Kham charuk thi than phra phuttharup nai Nakhon Chiang Mai* (Inscriptions on the bases of Buddha images in the city of Chiang Mai). Bangkok: Samnak Nayok Ratmontri (Office of the Prime Minister), 1976.

Phya Anuman Rajadhon. *Thet Maha Chat* (in English). Bangkok: Fine Arts Department, 1969.

Ping Amranand and William Warren. *Lanna Style, Art and Design of Northern Thailand.* Bangkok: Asia Books Co., Ltd., 2000.

Robinson, Natalie V. "Bencharong and Lai Nam Thong Ceramics." In *The Artistic Heritage of Thailand: A Collection of Essays.* Bangkok: Sawaddi Magazine, 1979, 139–50.

———. *Sino-Thai Ceramics in the National Museum, Bangkok, Thailand, and in Private Collections.* Bangkok: Department of Fine Arts, 1982.

Sanguan Chotisukharat. "Phra Kaen Chan Legend." *Conference on Lanna Thai Legends,* 2514 B.E. (1971), 66–68; as cited in Naengnoi Punjabhan, Aroonrut Wichienkeeo, and Somchai Na Nakhonphanom. *The Charm of Lanna Wood Carving.* Bangkok: Rerngrom Publishing Co., Ltd., 2537 B.E. (1994).

Songsri Prapatthong, ed. *Thai Minor Arts.* Bangkok: Department of Fine Arts, 1993, 83–84.

Swearer, Donald. *The Buddhist World of Southeast Asia.* New York: State University of New York, 1995.

Tingley, Nancy. "A Brief Note on the Terminal Date of the Si Satchanalai Kilns." In *Living a Life in Accord with Dhamma: Papers in Honor of Professor Jean Boisselier on his Eightieth Birthday.* Bangkok: Silpakorn University, 1997, 483–87.

Treasures from the National Museum, Bangkok. Bangkok: Thai Watna Panich Press Co., Ltd., 1987.

Van Der Cruysse, Dirk (trans. Michael Smithies). *Siam and the West 1500–1700.* Chiang Mai: Silkworm Books, 1991.

Warren, William, and Luca Invernizzi Tettoni. *Arts and Crafts of Thailand.* San Francisco: Chronicle Books, 1996.

Woodward, Hiram W. Jr., et al. *The Sacred Sculpture of Thailand: The Alexander B. Griswold Collection, The Walters Art Museum.* Bangkok. The Trustees of the Walters Art Museum, 1997.

Wray, Elizabeth, Clare Rosenfield, and Dorothy Bailey. *Ten Lives of the Buddha: Siamese Temple Paintings and Jataka Tales.* New York and Tokyo: Weatherhill, 1972.

Index

Note: Page numbers in *italics* indicate illustrations.